THE PRACTICE OF EMPIRE

THE PRACTICE OF EMPIRE

H. G. Koenigsberger

EMENDED EDITION OF
The Government of Sicily under
Philip II of Spain

CORNELL UNIVERSITY PRESS
ITHACA, NEW YORK

First published 1951 by Staples Press Limited, London,
and Staples Press Incorporated, New York
Copyright reserved

Emended Edition
copyright © 1969 by Cornell University
All rights reserved. Except for brief quotations in a review, this book, or parts thereof, must not be reproduced in any form without permission in writing from the publisher. For information address Cornell University Press, 124 Roberts Place, Ithaca, New York 14850.

To
MARY, KENNETH *and* JOHN

Library of Congress Catalog Card Number 69-18213

PRINTED IN THE UNITED STATES OF AMERICA
BY VALLEY OFFSET, INC.
BOUND BY VAIL-BALLOU PRESS, INC.

CONTENTS

	FOREWORD TO EMENDED EDITION	page 5
	FOREWORD	9
	PREFACE	37
Chapter I	INTRODUCTION	43
II	THE SPANISH THEORY OF EMPIRE IN SICILY	47
III	IMPERIAL ADMINISTRATION AT THE CENTRE	59
IV	IMPERIAL ADMINISTRATION IN THE PROVINCES: THE DEVELOPMENT OF CONCILIAR GOVERNMENT IN SICILY	
	(1) Introduction: The Economic Background	73
	(2) The Organization of the Central Government	82
	(3) The Central Control of Local Government	105
	(4) The Administration of Law	116
V	TAXATION AND THE EFFECTS OF EMPIRE FINANCE ON SICILY	124
VI	THE SICILIAN GOVERNMENT AND THE INDEPENDENT POLITICAL ORGANIZATIONS	
	(1) The Government and the 'Monarchia Sicula'	144
	(2) The Government and Parliament	149
	(3) The Government and the Inquisition	161
VII	THE VICEROYS AND MADRID	171
VIII	CONCLUSION	196
Appendix I	Viceroys and Presidents of Sicily in the Sixteenth Century	199
II	Some Sicilian Coins and Measurements	200
III	Notes on the Political Thought of Scipio di Castro	201
IV	Popular Song, 1591	206
	BIBLIOGRAPHY	209
	INDEX	223
	REPRODUCTION OF MAP OF SICILY BY GERARDUS MERCATOR	End papers

FOREWORD TO EMENDED EDITION

SINCE the publication of the first edition, a great deal of work has been done on different topics treated in this book. It is certainly no longer true that Sicilian scholars are virtually ignorant of the sources of their country's history in Spanish archives. In Simancas they now have the invaluable help of Don Ricardo Magdaleno's *Catálogo XIX del Archivo de Simancas, Papeles de Estado, Sicilia, Virreinato español* (Madrid, Patronato Nacional de Archivos Históricos; Valladolid 1951). Unfortunately, there is as yet no catalogue of the almost equally important Sección Secreterías Provinciales.

Most of the detailed work done, for example A. Petino's study of prices in Catania,[1] supplements the evidence presented in this book but does not affect my conclusions. Nor are my conclusions affected by new views on two of my literary sources. It is now generally thought that the attribution of the *Viaje de Turquía* to Cristóbal de Villalón is wrong, and that this famous dialogue represents an imaginary tale rather than actual events.[2] My use of one of its episodes as an illustration of the attitude of Spaniards towards their empire is, however, not affected (p. 47). An even more important literary source, Scipio di Castro's *Avvertimenti*, has now received a definitive edition.[3] The editor argues, plausibly, that this treatise was not written specifically for Colonna, and he thinks that it should really be called *Discorso sopra il governo di Sicilia*.[4] However that may be, the significance of Castro's treatise as a historical source is hardly affected by this argument. My own re-evaluation of this significance proceeds along different lines.[5]

More important than such corrections of points of detail has been the work done on larger topics, work which has greatly increased our understanding of the whole period and which has provided this book with a much better historiographical framework than it had twenty years ago. Such work has been done in four

---

[1] A. Petino, I prezzi del grano . . . a Catania dal 1512 al 1630, in *Studi in onore di Gino Luzzatto*, vol. II (Milan 1950), pp. 189–226.
[2] M. Bataillon, *Érasme et l'Espagne* (Paris, 1937), pp. 712 ff.; V. Titone, *La Sicilia dalla Dominazione Spagnola all'Unità d'Italia* (Bologna 1955), pp. 357 ff.
[3] A. Saitta, ed., *Avvertimenti di Don Scipio di Castro a Marco Antonio Colonna quando andò Vicerè di Sicilia* (Rome 1950).
[4] Ibid. pp. 25–27.
[5] The Parliament of Sicily and the Spanish Empire, in *Mélanges Antonio Marongiu* (Palermo 1967), pp. 81–96. Cf. below, p. 7.

main fields. Firstly, there is Fernand Braudel's *La Méditerranée et le Monde méditerranéen à l'époque de Philippe II* (Paris 1949; 2nd edition, in two volumes, Paris 1966). It is especially the economic and social history of Sicily, and the island's strategic position in the great political and naval struggle for the control of the Mediterranean, that can now be seen much more clearly in the light of Braudel's magisterial volumes.

Secondly, there is the series of books by Virgilio Titone on the history of Sicily during the period of Spanish rule.[1] These books have thrown new light on the structure and traditions of Sicilian society and on the nature of government and politics in Sicily in general. I do not think, however, that any of my conclusions about Sicilian history in the second half of the sixteenth century are contradicted by Titone's major points about the wider aspects of Sicilian history.

Thirdly, there is the considerable amount of work published on the development of monarchy and governmental institutions in the sixteenth and seventeenth centuries, and of the Spanish monarchy in particular. Much of this work, together with extensive bibliographies, is summarised in two reports to the International Congresses of Historical Sciences: R. Mousnier and F. Hartung, *Quelques problèmes concernant la Monarchie absolue*, X^o *Congresso Internazionale di Scienze Storiche, Relazioni, Storia Moderna*, IV (Rome 1957), pp. 1–55, and J. Vicens Vives, *Estructura administrativa estatal en los siglos XVI y XVII*, *XIe Congrès International des Sciences Historiques, Rapports IV, Histoire Moderne* (Stockholm 1960), pp. 1–24. J. H. Elliott, *Imperial Spain 1469–1716* (London 1963), and J. Lynch, *Spain under the Habsburgs*, vol. I (Oxford 1964), incorporate the results of the great amount of research done on Spanish history since the publication of R. B. Merriman's classic *Rise of the Spanish Empire*. The forthcoming book by Kenneth Garrad on the revolt of the Moriscos of Granada is particularly illuminating on an aspect of the Spanish political system that was also characteristic for Spanish rule in Sicily: the paralysing effects of rivalries between different corporations and organs of government, their links with the factions at the court of Madrid, and Philip II's equivocal policy towards these rivalries. L. Villari, *La rivolta antispagnola a Napoli: Le origini (1585–1647)* (Bari 1967), shows the effects of Spanish imperial rule on Naples and the reasons for its collapse in the mid-seventeenth century, as does

[1] See list in Additional Bibliography.

J. H. Elliott, *The Revolt of the Catalans* (Cambridge 1963), in the case of Catalonia. Fairly soon, it should become possible to write "the book" on the Hapsburg Monarchy, of which J. M. Batista i Roca spoke in the foreword to the first edition of this book.[1]

The last major area in which important new work has been published is that of parliaments and representative institutions. This is also the only topic on which there have been significant differences of opinion. Antonio Marongiu, in his *L'Istituto Parlamentare in Italia* (Rome 1949), and, latterly, in his comprehensive *Il Parlamento in Italia nel Medio Evo e nell'Età Moderna* (Milan 1962), has consistently ascribed greater political importance to the Sicilian Parliament in the sixteenth century than I have been prepared to do. The difference is rooted in different evaluations and interpretations of the existing evidence. Unless far more evidence should come to light (perhaps in the form of private diaries of parliamentary proceedings and negotiations which might conceivably be found in provincial or private archives) it does not look as if either position can be proved beyond a shadow of doubt. I have formulated my present views, partly on the basis of new evidence found in the British Museum, in my article "The Parliament of Sicily and the Spanish Empire."[2] Briefly, I believe that the Sicilian Parliament was reasonably effective in keeping the rate of taxation from rising as fast in Sicily as it did in Naples, although, even then, it is difficult to prove conclusively that it was really the Sicilian Parliament which was mainly responsible for the difference between these two Spanish dominions. The viceroys themselves tried to limit Madrid's financial demands, and they motivated this policy by the poverty of the kingdom and not by any unwillingness of the Sicilian Parliament to grant such demands—a very different pattern from that revealed for the Netherlands by the contemporary correspondence of Margaret of Parma. The Sicilian Parliament participated in legislation, but it had no exclusive right to such activity, and it was never able to insist on any proposal against the will of the king. Giuseppe Schichilone has shown that the Deputation played a much greater rôle in the administration of Sicilian finances than used to be thought; but its members were appointed and controlled by the viceroy.[3] Lastly, Scipio di Castro's view that every session of Parliament represented a major crisis for the viceroy, a view

---

[1] Cf. below, p. 9.   [2] Cf. above, p. 5, n. 5.
[3] G. Scichilone, *Origine e Ordinamento della Deputazione del Regno di Sicilia*, *Archivio Storico per la Sicilia Orientale*, 4th ser., an. III, 1950.

which I followed (p. 153), I would now regard as exaggerated and due to Castro's habit of overdramatization. There is nothing in the many other memoranda written by or for the viceroys, nor in the viceregal correspondence with Madrid, which would support Castro's view. Most recently, Gordon Griffiths has suggested that a systematic study of the legislative activities of the Sicilian Parliament, compared with the legislative activities of the crown, would throw much-needed light on the institution.[1] Such a study might indeed go some, though probably not the whole, way towards resolving the controversy over the political importance of the Sicilian Parliament.

In this edition I have attempted to correct the spelling and printing errors of the first edition but have otherwise left the text as it stood. I have added an Additional Bibliography and changed the title of the book.

H. G. KOENIGSBERGER

Ithaca, New York
May 1968

[1] G. Griffiths, *Representative Government in Western Europe in the Sixteenth Century. Commentary and Documents for the Study of Comparative Constitutional History* (Oxford 1968), pp. 83–84.

FOREWORD

'THE BOOK' on the Hapsburg Monarchy, or Spanish Empire, has still to be written. Before any complete work on this association of states and countries as a whole is practicable much spade work must be done. Fortunately a number of valuable monographs are appearing which provide the elements for the final synthesis. These consist of special studies of various parts of the empire, such as the most valuable contributions of Prof. Haring of Harvard and his school of historians of Spanish America who are following the high standards set by Prof. Merriman; studies of special institutions, such as the recent volumes of Prof. Schäfer on the Council of the Indies, or studies of certain periods, such as the work of Prof. Karl Brandi on Charles V, or even more general works on human geography or history of ideas, such as the first class books of Fernand Braudel on the Mediterranean in the days of Philip II and of Prof. Bataillon on the influence of Erasmus' ideas in Spain.

Dr. Koenigsberger's book on the administration of Sicily in the time of Philip II falls into this group of monographic studies. This is valuable material and, when a complete collection of such books for the other member states of the Hapsburg Monarchy is available, we shall have gained an accurate picture of its real structure and functioning.

Dr. Koenigsberger who studied under the guidance of Previté Orton, one of those British scholars who had a better understanding of the history of the Mediterranean countries, was a scholar and research student at Gonville and Caius College, Cambridge, and is now lecturing on economic history at Queen's University, Belfast. For his researches on Sicily he has worked in the Sicilian archives, at Simancas and in other Spanish archives, and he has been one of the comparatively few to delve into the practically untapped wealth of Spanish documents kept in the MSS. Department of the British Museum.

Since the days of the Roman Empire men had not seen anything equivalent to the world-wide Hapsburg Monarchy. It consisted of completely different parts, brought together by an unique and unrepeatable coincidence of dynastic and other factors in which chance played its part.

The union of the dynasties of Castile and Aragon, by the marriage of Isabella and Ferdinand, conferred their still separate crowns on one single head, that of Charles of Hapsburg. The Crown of Aragon included the possessions which had gradually been acquired in the Mediterranean by the Catalans from the close of the thirteenth century (Sicily, Sardinia and Naples). The Crown of Castile extended over the Atlantic to the recently discovered America.

Charles brought the Hapsburg inheritance (the county of Burgundy and the states of the Low Countries). His election to the Imperial Crown of Germany, and the acquisition of Milan, extended his influence over most of Europe.

If the Imperial Crown did not pass to Philip II, he yet obtained Portugal and her colonies in America and Asia.

The Monarch

The common link that kept together the states of the Hapsburg Monarchy was the person of the monarch.

The states that were united under it were old countries, had enjoyed a full, independent and separate life for centuries, and had, as a consequence, each developed political institutions and traditions of their own. When the Hapsburgs came to rule over them, the monarch remained the sovereign of each rather than of the whole. Each state retained its own institutions including the sovereign, who, therefore, had a different title and different powers in each of them.

The Belgian historian, Pirenne, has remarked that the 17 Provinces of the Netherlands all recognized the same Prince, but each by a different title and that he in turn ruled in each with different powers. Great as was his power the Emperor Charles V did not mind becoming Duke of Brabant, Count of Flanders, Count of Hainault, etc., in order to deal with his subjects in each of these provinces. He was equally proud of retaining his title of Count of Burgundy. He had followed the request of his aunt Margaret '*pour non abolir le nom de la maison de Bourgogne . . . de garder et retenir en ses mains le dit Comté*', and recommended it affectionately to his son Philip as '*el mas antiguo patrimonio de la Casa de Borgoña.*'

The same was true in his Spanish states, where he used the old style of the sovereigns of each of them and adapted his rule to the powers that the constitutions of each realm allowed to him. In obvious flattery, probably inspired by Gattinara, he told the Catalans that he valued more his title of Count of Barcelona than that of King of the Romans and tactfully explained to the Castilians that to use first his title of Emperor in his style was no disregard for the kingdoms of the Crown of Castile.

There was no single title for the man who ruled over such a diversity of countries, as there was no common name for them all. The Low Countries were still known by the old Burgundian denomination of *'les pays d'Embas'* or *'les pays de par dela'*. The Peninsular possessions of the Hapsburgs were called *las coronas de España* (i.e. the Crown of Castile and the Crown of Aragon) or *los reinos de España*, while *estos nuestros reinos* usually meant only those of the Crown of Castile.

The successive abdications of the various states of his monarchy by Charles V was in keeping with this constitutional structure. He had given the kingdom of Naples and the duchy of Milan to Philip on his marriage to Mary of England (1554). The Netherlands were handed over to him in the famous assembly at Brussels (October 25, 1555), when Charles announced his intention to retire to a monastery. Not until January 16th, 1556 did he abdicate his crowns of Spain and overseas dominions.

On that day he made three successive abdications in three separate documents and before different witnesses. By the first deed, written in Castilian, he abdicated the kingdoms of Castile, León, Granada, Navarre and the Indies, as well as the Grand Mastership of the Military Orders of Santiago, Alcántara and Calatrava. The other two documents were in Latin; by one he handed over to Philip the states of the Crown of Aragon (Aragon, Catalonia, Valencia and Majorca) together with Sardinia; and by the other, the kingdom of Sicily.

Charles V still retained the Franche-Comté until April 1556. As for the Empire, he resigned the imperial crown to his brother Ferdinand, but not until February 1558 did the Electors accept his resignation and agree to the elevation of Ferdinand.

The sovereign had a double constitutional personality. Over and above these multiple local sovereignties the monarch stood as the head and common link of this vast confederacy of states. This, it is true, was no constitutional office, but a personal one arising from the coincidence in one single man of a variety of constitutional titles as sovereign of each of those states. But, as the monarch, he was the representative of his world-wide monarchy, kept it welded together, conducted the internal policy of each part and the external of the whole, and was thus able to command large resources of men and money from each of them to be used in the foreign policy of the monarchy. In his treatise on the laws of the Indies, Solórzano Pereira, the Castilian jurist, neatly defined the position: 'These kingdoms have to be ruled and governed as if *the king who keeps them together were only the king of each of them.*'

Never before had the world seen a monarchy extending over most of Europe and the New World. In Christendom the monarch could be in the temporal sphere the counterpart of what the Pope was in the spiritual. The Crown had its quarrels with the Tiara until, finally, it became the best protector of Rome, as well as the strongest influence upon it. People in the middle of the 16th century could dream of a *Monarquia Universal*, of *un rey, una ley, y una espada*, as Acuña said in his well-known sonnet to Philip II. 'Sire, God has been very merciful to you,' the Grand Chancellor Gattinara wrote to Charles on his election as German Emperor. 'He has raised you above all the kings and princes of Christendom to a power such as no sovereign has enjoyed since your ancestor Charles the Great. He has set you on the path towards a world monarchy, towards the uniting of all Christendom under a single shepherd.'

The King's Secretaries

Next to the king came his secretaries, the links in the constitutional machinery connecting him with his councils and, in a wider sense, with his various states. The value of the secretaries was a function of the value of the person of the monarch. A great man, such as Charles V, took no exception to having a chancellor at his side. Charles retained the old Burgundian institution of the Grand Chancellor, entrusted with the management of the monarchy and, especially during Charles' youth, with framing its general and foreign policy.

When the young sovereign arrived in Castile, Jean le Sauvage, Grand Chancellor of Burgundy, was with him. His functions were now extended to cover the lands Charles had just inherited. A timely death (1518) saved him from the increasing hatred of the Castilians and opened the way for the most remarkable of Charles' political advisers, Mercurino Arborio, marquis of Gattinara.

Gattinara was a man of his time, scholar and humanist, idealist and statesman of wide vision, he accepted the new classical theory of state and prince, and came to be one of its outstanding practical exponents. He took Charles away from the narrow path of Burgundian dynastic interests and made him the modern Caesar, destined to rule over a universal monarchy.

When Gattinara died (1530) no successor worthy of him was in view. Meanwhile Charles had grown into maturity, and power had gradually become concentrated in his own hands. Then his former confessor, cardinal García de Loaysa, a Castilian who had been president of the Council of the Indies, advised 'that your Majesty become your own chancellor', and that Francisco de los Cobos and Nicolas Perrenot, lord of Granvelle, might be used to help in the despatch of affairs of state. Charles followed this advice.

Philip II, with his shy, distrustful nature, could hardly tolerate a chancellor or minister near him. He personally attended to all matters of government, studied all incoming despatches and outgoing orders, and directed the work of all his secretaries. While Charles was his own chancellor, Philip was his own clerk. He had, of course, advisers and, following his father's counsel, always more than one. A Castilian, the duke of Alva, two Portuguese, Ruy Gómez de Silva and Christóvão de Moura, Requesens, almost a Catalan, a Burgundian, cardinal Granvelle, and a Basque, Juan de Idiáquez: these were among the most prominent. Only when, later in his life, the heavy toil was beginning to tell on his health, did Philip employ a secretary, an obscure man of Corsican origin, Mateo Vázquez de Lecca. Far from being a chancellor or principal minister, he was no more than Philip's private secretary. They worked together for eighteen years (1573–1591).

After the recall of cardinal Granvelle from Rome and of Idiáquez from Venice (1579), a kind of *consulta*, or inner committee, was organized: Juan de Idiáquez (state affairs), count of Chinchon (Aragon and Italy), and Christóvão de Moura (Portugal), together with Vázquez de Lecca. Granvelle reserved for himself the supreme direction of foreign affairs and wisely refused to deal with internal problems. They met together at the royal palace, usually by night, and studied important despatches; notes were made of the views expressed by each of them and Vázquez de Lecca, acting as secretary, submitted their work to the king.

With the lesser Philips of the seventeenth century the situation changed again. While the importance of the monarch declined, the figure of the principal minister, or *privado*, came into prominence. The good intentions of some of them, including the count-duke of Olivares, cannot be denied but, on the whole, they were inefficient and self-seeking servants of incompetent masters. The chancellor had been a Burgundian institution; the seventeenth century *privado* was a revival of a medieval Castilian institution. For, by that time, the monarchy had changed from the universal enterprise it was in the days of the emperor to a primarily Castilian affair.

Under the chancellor, or the principal secretaries, there were a number of other secretaries, each at the head of a *secretaría*, or office, to deal with a branch of the administration or with one of the states of the monarchy or a group of these. Only a short sketch of the functions of these officers can here be given. They were often chosen from among junior secretaries or clerks. Sometimes they were the sons of former secretaries, as was Antonio Pérez, son of Gonzalo Pérez, or the Idiáquez who served Charles V and Philip II for generations. In other cases a secretary would recommend a successor in his will, as when Mateo Vázquez recommended Jerónimo Gassol, his brother-in-law, as his successor. It seems that, in many respects, these bureaucrats tended to form a distinct class.

On appointment by the monarch the secretary received a set of written instructions about his duties, and a senior secretary took his oath. He received a lump sum as an annual salary for himself and for the clerks who worked under him. Surprising as it seems, there were no rooms in the royal palace, or in any official building, for the *secretarías*. Each secretary took the official papers to his home and worked there with his clerks.

Incoming despatches were sorted out by the secretaries and sent to the king or to the president of the council that had to deal with the particular matter. The king's secretaries attended the meetings of the councils but could neither vote nor take part in the discussions. They could also take papers from the council to the king, though this was often done by the president of the council.

If the secretaries tended to form a class, it was a heterogeneous class. Some of them, in the sixteenth century, were highly cultured men with a humanist education. They were deeply influenced by Erasmus' ideas, and this was obviously due to their contacts with the Netherlands. Alfonso de Valdés is probably the earliest, and outstanding case. But others followed him: Diego Gracián de Alderete, translator of Xenophon, Thucydides, Plutarch and other classical authors; or his son, Antonio Gracián Dantisco, to whom Philip II entrusted the first organization of the Escurial Library; there was Gonzalo Pérez whose collection of Greek and Latin manuscripts (mainly from Sicily) was one of the first that went to that Library; and, finally, the Aragonese Gerónimo de Zurita, secretary of the Council of the Inquisition, who, with his scholarly work *Anales de la Corona de Aragón* (1562–1579), won for himself the reputation of a first class historian.

Unfortunately, not all the secretaries were of this high quality. It is true they were all hard-working, reliable and efficient civil servants, although without far-reaching ambitions, yet most of them were self-seeking and ready to accept gifts from foreign ambassadors, merchants and bankers. Corruption was deeply rooted in the administration and played its part in the decadence of the Hapsburg Monarchy and of Spain. The sovereigns knew it, and often turned a blind eye to it, as is evident from the remarks of Charles V about Cobos, contained in his *Secret Instructions* to his son Philip. In some cases legal proceedings undertaken against corrupt secretaries were stopped, probably in consideration of services rendered to the crown. An outstanding example is the case of Francisco de Eraso. As financial secretary to Charles and Philip he was known to have accepted bribes from German bankers with whom he had negotiated loans. But the inquiry (*visita*) ordered by Philip II led to no substantial charge (1564–1566).[1]

Apart from Cobos, the duke of Lerma and the count-duke of Olivares offer the outstanding examples of greed. Lerma, the powerful and rapacious *privado* of Philip III was finally overthrown by a court intrigue (1618) in which his own son was one of the leaders, and he saved his life only because he managed to have himself appointed a cardinal by the Pope. Of his associates, secretary Franquesa ended his days in prison, following an inquiry that revealed the incredible amount of jewels and other valuables he had amassed; Rodrigo Calderón, after years of imprisonment, confiscation of all his goods and trials on such charges as murder and witchcraft was finally sent to the scaffold.

The Councils

The system of councils was the organization of the central administration characteristic of the Hapsburg Monarchy. This group of unconnected councils round the monarch were the product and the clearest manifestation of the heterogeneous character of the monarchy and its states. The older institutions of each state were preserved, though sometimes modified, while they often offered a pattern to set up similar institutions in other states when annexed to the monarchy or when reforms were introduced in the government. In some cases the central councils were adaptations of older councils

[1] But note the effect of this on the career of the viceroy Toledo; below, p. 181.

of the states as, for instance, the Councils of Aragon and Castile.

The councils round the monarch neither had all the same status nor extended their jurisdiction over the same territory. It is useful, therefore, to attempt a classification of them in order to gain a clear idea of this system of government.

A first group may be formed of those councils (State and War) which helped the monarch in his foreign policy and with that of the Inquisition which gave to him a most powerful politico-religious instrument. They extended their authority over all or most of the monarchy.

A second and much larger group was that of the councils for the government, from the centre of the monarchy, of its various states. These councils acted also as High Courts of Justice for the State concerned and they, together with those of the first group, were *Supremos* in the sense that they were in no way dependent on any other council above them. This group comprised the Councils of Castile, Aragon, Indies and Italy, as well as those of Portugal and Flanders during later and shorter periods. Obviously, the monarch in his relations with each of these councils acted only as sovereign of the state in question.

The last group included councils dealing with particular aspects of the internal administration of the Crown of Castile. They were the Councils of the Military Orders, of the *Cruzada* and, for a time, of the *Hermandad*. The Council of Finances technically belongs to this group, as its original purpose was the management of the finances of Castile, but since it provided the resources for the foreign wars it can be considered to be in an intermediate position between this and the first group.

The *Honorable Consejo de la Mesta de los Pastores de estos Reinos* (Honourable Council of the Mesta of the Shepherds of these Kingdoms), though not a Royal Council as the above, may be included in this group of Castilian Councils, taking into account its close association with the Council of Castile, its powerful influence in shaping the economic and social life of that nation and the financial help it tendered to the crown in days of difficulty, which were very frequent.

Let us see now each Council in turn with some more detail.

I. ADVISORY COUNCILS TO THE MONARCH.

1). *Council of State.* – It advised the monarch on foreign policy and important matters of State. Spanish historians tend to attribute much importance to it as the central organ of the government of the monarchy. Gounon-Loubens on the other hand, while agreeing that its importance increased somewhat under Philip II, thought that it was no more than a private council to which the monarch could refer for advice. His views are mainly based on the reports of such experienced political observers as the Venetian ambassadors who all agree in not attaching too much importance to it and believing that the will of the monarch was the real force. Gounon-Loubens further remarks that the legal compilations contain no law about it and do not even mention its name, that in the court protocol no reference is made to the precedence of its members, that it had no president, and that the king himself presided over its meetings.

While the two strong sovereigns, Charles V and Philip II kept the Council of State well in hand, its importance grew with the weak kings in the seventeenth century, and the grandees who sat in it really managed, and often mismanaged, the foreign affairs of the monarchy.

The *Council of War* was the same Council of State reinforced with some generals or experts on military matters.

2). *Council of the Holy and Supreme Inquisition.* – The Inquisition under the authority of the Pope or of bishops had existed in many countries in the Middle Ages. We are not concerned with it here, but only with the Royal Inquisition first organized in Castile by Ferdinand and Isabella by a decree issued at Seville in 1477 and recognized by the Pope Sixtus IV by successive bulls of 1478, 1482 and 1483.

The Inquisition in the countries of the Crown of Castile was first entrusted (September 17th, 1480) to two friars, as Inquisitors, and two priests, one Queen Isabella's chaplain as Prosecutor, and the other, as Adviser, one of the members of the Royal Council of Castile, Dr. Juan Ruiz de Medina, who was later bishop of Astorga, Badajoz, Cartagena and Segovia in succession, and finally ambassador to Rome.

Following the Papal bull of August 2nd, 1483, Fray Tomás de Torquemada was appointed Inquisitor-General for Castile. Later, on October 17th, he was also appointed Inquisitor-General for the states of the Crown of Aragon where, after a long and bitter opposition, the Inquisition was finally established. At his death (1498) Diego de Deza, archbishop of Seville, was his successor. He was first nominated by the queen and king (November 24th) for Castile. The papal confirmation of the commission was issued on December 1st. Not until September 1st, 1499, was he appointed Inquisitor-General for Aragon.

When, on the death of Isabella, the two crowns were separated again, each had its own Inquisition and Inquisitor-General. Cardinal Francisco Ximénez de Cisneros, Archbishop of Toledo, who was the governor of Castile, was also Inquisitor-General for this kingdom (1507). Joan Enguera, Bishop of Vic, was appointed by Ferdinand for the Crown of Aragon. It was not until 1518 that one person, Cardinal Adrian of Utrecht, the future Pope Adrian VI, re-united in himself again the posts of Inquisitor-General of the two crowns.

Round the Inquisitor-General a council grew. It has already been said above that the two Inquisitors first appointed in 1480 for Castile had one adviser and a public prosecutor adjoined to them.

This body grew into one of the Royal Councils. This was set up in 1483 for Castile by Isabella and Ferdinand. Its president was *ex officio* the Inquisitor-General Torquemada, the other members being Alfonso Carrillo, bishop elect of Mazzara (Sicily), Sancho Velázquez de Cuéllar and Ponce de Valencia, the last two doctors in Law. In purely religious matters the Inquisitor-General decided by himself, hearing his advisers and the two members of the council, if necessary. In temporal affairs, also under royal jurisdiction, the two members of the council had a vote. Later on, the posts of president and of Inquisitor-General fell to different persons.

A separate council was set up for the states of the Crown of Aragon. The two councils continued for some time to be two separate bodies. But their president was often the same person. Thus Martin Zurbano was president of both councils in 1516, and García de Loaysa in 1522. Even as late as 1540, payments to Inquisition officials in Aragon required a special order from the crown, probably because it came from a different treasury. To the end of the existence of the Inquisition there were two different offices (*secretarías*) in the council under two different secretaries for the Crowns of Castile and of Aragon.

Throughout the reign of Philip II two different men were Inquisitor-General and president of the council. The former had a salary of 200,000 maravedis, the latter had 150,000. This was one of the many causes of envies and rivalries between them. Finally, in 1598, the two offices were unified, leaving the presidency to lapse.

The Inquisitor-General was appointed by the crown. This power had been acquired by Ferdinand, was reasserted by Charles V, and remained undisputed thereafter. In theory Rome did not recognize this right, and confirmed appointments as if they had been done *motu proprio* by the Holy See.

The council usually had five members, plus the Inquisitor-General when he was a different person from the president. Philip II ordered two members of the Council of Castile to be members of the Council of the Inquisition, thus reinforcing the political power of both institutions. Philip III ordered (1614) his confessor to be a member, and the same was done by Philip IV. A petition of the Holy See to let the Papal Nuncio be a member of the council was refused by Philip II.

Originally the crown appointed and removed members of the council, as already seen. Later, however, when a vacancy occurred the council submitted to the crown the names of three suitable candidates.

Under Charles V other officials were also appointed by the crown, though the council countersigned the commissions. This method continued under Philip II, though he tended to pass the responsibility on to the Inquisitor-General. Then local Inquisitors were appointed by him, after consultation with the council, but a supervisory power on appointments was still recognized to remain with the crown under Philip III.

II. COUNCILS FOR THE GOVERNMENT OF THE STATES.

1). *Council of Castile.* – This was the medieval Royal Council of the Kings of Castile and León, reorganized to meet more modern needs in the days of Ferdinand and Isabella.

At first it was called *Royal Council* or *Council of Justice*, or, in royal documents, *our Council*, but in the later period of their reign after the Council of Aragon had been reorganized (1494) and under the influence of the latter's name, it came to be called *Council of Castile* to avoid confusion between the two Royal Councils.

In older days it had been in the hands of the grandees, but the Catholic kings, following petitions of the Cortes, ordered it to be composed of one prelate, three knights and eight or nine jurists (*letrados*). The grandees who had been members of the older council could attend the sessions of the reorganized one, but without vote.

The importance of the reform, therefore, lay in the fact that it excluded the influence of the grandees and brought the council under that of the jurists. These were men mainly from the urban middle class, though some came from the country gentry (*hidalgos*) and others from the peasantry, educated in the new political ideas of the Renaissance favouring a strong royal power as the central force in setting up the modern state. Through the Royal Council, with its double power on government and administration of justice, the crown asserted its firm rule over Castile.

2). *Council of Aragon.* – Ferdinand, when he reorganized it, called it simply *our Royal Council*, but Charles in the reshuffle of 1522 called it *Sacro y Real Consejo de los Reinos de la Corona de Aragon*. Sometimes the qualification of *supremo* was also added, but it was usually referred to as *Consejo de Aragon*.

As in the case of the Council of Castile, its remote origin was the Royal Council of the Kings of Aragon which, together with the Chancery and Treasury, had reached a mature development in the later part of the fourteenth century in the reign of Peter IV.

After Ferdinand inherited the crown of Aragon at the death of his father John II, he allotted some rooms of the royal palace at Valladolid (1480) to some barons and jurists, natives of Aragon, Catalonia, Valencia and Sicily, and well instructed in the laws and practices of those countries, to deal with their affairs.

The arrangement was probably not satisfactory and led to the setting up of a reorganized Royal Council. The reorganization was done by a decree of Ferdinand (November 19th, 1494). Its purpose was 'to deal, provide and concede on our Royal Council.' A vice-chancellor, a prothonotary and a treasurer-general were appointed, together with some councillors, the king reserving his right to make further appointments. Their main duties were connected with the administration of justice.

The main feature of Ferdinand's reform was to exclude the nobility from the council and leave it entirely in the hands of the jurists. The royal policy in this respect was the same in Castile and in Aragon.

The Chancery and the Treasury, which were two separate branches of the medieval Aragonese royal administration, were now brought together into a Royal Council of just a few jurists. It was a highly centralized institution in the number of its members, in the social class from which they came, in its concentration of functions, and in its subordination to the crown.

After various later reforms, the council had a vice-chancellor as its head, five regents or councillors, usually doctors in law, a treasurer-general of the Crown of Aragon, appointed by the king, a prothonotary, head of the Chancery, and his lieutenant, and an Advocate of the Fisc to represent public interest which, usually, was the interest of the Crown. The treasurer had no vote in matters of justice. The advocate fiscal and the prothonotary could attend the sessions, but had no vote. There were four secretaries, one for Italy and the others for the three Peninsular states of the Crown of Aragon.

The treasurer might be a native of the countries of the Crown of Aragon or not. The royal policy, based on centralization and the patrimonial conception of the monarchy, was to appoint some Castilian nobleman. On the other hand the vice-chancellor and the regents had to be natives, two from each of the three countries, Aragon, Catalonia, Valencia. They were not, however, representatives of these countries, only experts in their laws and customs whose duty it was to advise, as royal officials, on the best policy to be followed by the crown in their affairs.

Charles V brought his Grand Chancellor Gattinara into the council (1522), with the right of sitting as its chairman. Nicolas Perrenot de Granvelle held the same position.

The council studied reports, petitions, enquiries, claims coming from the authorities of the countries with whose governments it was concerned, submitted resolutions to the king, issued in the king's name orders for their government and acted as the link between the crown and its representatives in each country. Most important was also its work as a high court to hear appeals from the local courts of justice. Its status was the same as that of the Council of Castile and of the highest authorities in the monarchy. In public functions and processions, while the other councils preceded the king, (that of the Inquisition being the last, as the most important), the Councils of Castile and Aragon walked right and left of the king.

3). *Council of Italy.* – The most important change in the Council of Aragon was the separation of the Italian states from it (1558).

Sicily was closely connected with Catalonia since the end of the thirteenth century; Sardinia was conquered during the fourteenth, and in the sixteenth century Catalan influence was still very strong; Naples was acquired by Alfonso V in the fifteenth, separated at his death and recovered by Ferdinand. These states formed a close unit with the Peninsular countries of the Crown of Aragon connected not only by maritime trade but by the similarities and traditions which link together all Mediterranean countries.

Nevertheless, Ferdinand brought more Castilians than Catalans into the administration of Naples after recovering it. Charles V added

Milan to his Italian possessions and this, together with the kingdom of Naples, was given to Philip on his marriage to Mary Tudor (1554). Thus, at least in theory, these states were separated from the monarchy, and in practice from the Crown of Aragon. This breaking up of the unity of the Crown of Aragon caused protests and petitions of the Corts of Catalonia.

From the Italian point of view there were some gains. Italians had in the past sat in the Council of Aragon. Now, however, of the six regents, three had to be natives of each of the three states, Sicily, Naples and Milan, the other three might not be, and they usually were Castilians.

So the net gain was for the Castilians, who resented not being able to enter the Council of Aragon and entered now into that of Italy. The setting up of the Council of Italy, breaking up the Crown of Aragon, removing from the Italian states Catalan and Aragonese connections and bringing the Castilians into their government, was therefore an important step in the process of establishing Castilian hegemony in the Hapsburg Monarchy.

As an institution the Council of Italy was a double of the Council of Aragon. This latter was the model taken to organize it, and both had the same structure and the same way of functioning.

Originally it had three regents or councillors, but by the reforms of Philip II (1557 and 1559) the number was increased to six.

To fill vacancies among regents, the council submitted to the crown a list of six candidates from which the king selected one. In the seventeenth century this, as well as other councils, was left open to councillors of *capa y espada*, i.e. noblemen as distinct from *letrados* or jurists. They, however, had no vote in matters of justice.

In the seventeenth century the president was usually a Castilian nobleman, with a salary of 2,000 gold escudos. The second high official was the governor of the council who acted as substitute for the president and who, again, was a Castilian. As a survival of the government of the Council of Aragon, the treasurer-general was common to both councils. Thus, at least the financial unity of the states of the Crown of Aragon and of Italy was preserved. Other officials were a Keeper of the Royal Patrimony of Italy (*Conservador General del Patrimonio de Italia*) and an Advocate of the Fisc (*Abogado Fiscal*) appointed as from 1634.

The secretary dealing with Italian affairs in the Council of Aragon, Gabriel de Zayas, became a secretary of state for Italy when the new council was set up. At his death, Francisco de Idiáquez, his assistant, occupied the vacancy. In 1595 Philip II divided the secretaryship (*Secretaría*) in three to deal respectively with affairs of Naples, Sicily and Milan appointing as secretaries for each Idiáquez, Martin de Gante and Juan López de Zárate.

On the same day, June 28th, the King issued Ordinances in 36 chapters for the functioning of the council.

4). *Council of Portugal.* – After Philip II acquired the Crown of Portugal, the basis for the new rule was laid down at the Portuguese Cortes of Tomar (1582). Its main lines coincided with those of the organization for the states of the Crown of Aragon, as far as the Royal Council, Viceroy, Cortes and internal administration were concerned.

One of the decisions of the Cortes dealt with the setting up of a council which was always to follow the king whenever he absented himself from Portugal. It was provided that a prelate or churchman, a supervisor of finance (*védor de fazenda*) a grand-chancellor, a secretary and two judges (*desembargadores do paço*) all natives of the country, would form a body to be called Council of Portugal to deal with all the affairs of the kingdom. There would also be two financial clerks (*escrivães de fazenda*) and two confidential clerks (*escrivães da camara*) to follow the court, all documents having to be written in Portuguese.

When Philip II left Lisbon (February 11th, 1583) to return to Madrid, he took with him four advisers to help him in the dispatch of Portuguese affairs. They were a bishop (his principal chaplain), two doctors in law, (Pedro Barbosa and Rui de Matos de Noronha) and Christóvão de Moura, who had been his agent for the acquisition of Portugal.

Portuguese and Spanish historians are not helpful on this council, and information is lacking about it. It seems that Philip III issued a body of rules for it in 1607, according to which the council should have a president. It has been stated, however, that Philip III suppressed it in 1611, setting up a 'Junta de Gobierno de Portugal', and that it was restored by Philip IV when it was already too late, in 1648.

5). *Council of Flanders.* – The original idea of setting up a council to deal with the affairs of the Netherlands appeared during the period in which that country was governed by Luis de Requesens. He was trying to undo the havoc created by the ruthless policy of the duke of Alva and was therefore inclined to receive more favourably native suggestions.

A petition to this effect was adopted by the Estates General on June 7th, 1574. So that the king should keep fully in touch with the affairs of the Netherlands, they petitioned that a council should be set up, to which they could always appeal, and to be also used as the way to advise His Majesty on the resolution of those affairs, the council to be formed of natives of the country, well versed in the laws, customs and habits of the Netherlands.

On the margin of the petition the governor, Requesens, wrote that he would not fail to bring it before the king, especially this point of setting up a council to inform His Majesty of the affairs of the country.

The favourable attitude of Luis de Requesens is not surprising, remembering that, born and educated in Catalonia, he had to know of the Council of Aragon and, having been in an official capacity in Milan, he had experience of the working of the Council of Italy.

But in Madrid conditions were different and no decision was taken on the petition. Many years passed and meanwhile the Council of Portugal was set up. All parts of the Monarchy now had their Councils, except the Netherlands. It was increasingly difficult not to take any decision on their government. Finally a Council of Flanders was organized in Madrid by a decree of January 7th, 1588. It had, however, a short life. Ten years later, when the Archdukes Albert and Isabel became nominally independent sovereigns of the Netherlands, the council came to an end.

6). *Council of the Indies.* – As the American dependencies belonged to Castile this Council developed from that of Castile.

Soon after the discovery Queen Isabella appointed a Councillor of Castile, Juan Rodríguez de Fonseca, her own chaplain and archdeacon of Seville, to administer America.

From 1508 various other councillors helped him. A poor administrator with a difficult temper, he quarrelled with Columbus and Cortés but retained the royal favour. But at Ferdinand's death, the Regent of Castile, Cardinal Ximénez de Cisneros dismissed him and entrusted America to two Councillors of Castile, Luis Zapata and Galíndez de Carvajal. When Charles arrived, Fonseca came back to preside over some Councillors of Castile dealing with America. In 1520 a *procurador* (solicitor), a *relator* (reporter) and, later, a lawyer were added to this group soon known as Council of the Indies.

Its functions were only administrative, the Council of Castile remaining the supreme judicial authority. Commerce was from 1503 under the *Casa de Contratación*.

At Fonseca's death (1524) Charles gave full administrative and judicial powers to the Council of the Indies. Its first president was Fray García de Loaysa, the Emperor's confessor, general of the Dominican Order, later archbishop of Seville and a cardinal.

Besides its president, the council had four or five councillors, usually *letrados* or clerics, a secretary, a *Fiscal* (crown attorney) and a *Contador* (accountant). Mercurino Gattinara, the Grand Chancellor, brought the council under his authority (1528). When, after his death, Francisco de los Cobos became one of the two principal secretaries, his son took the office and title of Chancellor of the Indies. They were discontinued after him.

Other changes took place during the sixteenth century, the most important being the appointment of a *Receptor* (collector of monies), three more accountants and two solicitors attached to the crown attorney.

After this sketch of the councils the outline of their related origins stands out clearly. There were originally two councils of equal status, the Council of Castile and the Council of Aragon. They were the continuations of the medieval Royal Councils of each of the two crowns, modified by Isabella and Ferdinand to remove them from the influence of the nobility and bring them under that of the *letrados*, the jurists of the urban middle class.

Out of the Council of Castile that of the Indies evolved. In a similar way the office of the secretaryship of the Council of Aragon, dealing with the affairs of Sicily and Naples, developed into the Council of Italy, at the accession of Philip II. Milan was brought under the new council. Sardinia, on the other hand, just as the Balearic Islands, remained under the Council of Aragon.

The independent position enjoyed by the Crown of Aragon in the monarchy offered the model for the position of Portugal when Philip II brought her into his possession. Then a Council of Portugal was set up on the model of the Council of Aragon. The same model, now both of Aragon and of Portugal, was followed in the setting up of the Council of Flanders.

The gradual disintegration of the monarchy brought with it the disappearance of the councils. The separation of Portugal and Flanders was followed by the extinction of their councils.

The constitutional reorganization of Spain, following the accession of the Bourbons, is a landmark. The decrees of Philip V, proclaiming 'the legitimate right of conquest', following on the victory of his armies over the states of the Crown of Aragon, the abolition of their laws, institutions and national freedom, and their reduction to the laws of Castile, brought about the extinction of the Council of Aragon (decrees against Aragon and Valencia, of June 29th, 1707, against Majorca, of November 28th, 1715, and against Catalonia, of January 16th, 1716).

The Council of Castile remained, therefore, the only council for the government of the whole of Spain. It subsisted until the setting up of the constitutional state during the last century. A decree of March 24th, 1834, put an end to the Council of State, the Council of Castile and the Council of the Indies. The Castilian colonies in America had by then become independent republics. A Royal Council and, later, the cabinet were the successors of the Council of Castile.

The Members of the Councils

One of the most surprising aspects of the court, the administration and the councils, in the days of Ferdinand, was the large proportion of converted Jews (*conversos* or *Cristianos nuevos*) they contained. In this Ferdinand continued the policy of his father, John II of Aragon, and it must be admitted that the Saragossa group of wealthy and influential Jews, or *conversos*, always served the dynasty with absolute loyalty. To quote only one outstanding instance, the success of the crafty old king's schemes to secure the hand of Isabella for his son Ferdinand was largely due to the skill and support of this group in the royal courts of Aragon and Castile.

Under Ferdinand, Jews and *conversos* are to be found in the highest offices of the administration of Aragon – as members of the Royal Council, two of the king's secretaries, the treasurer-general, the king's lieutenant, the 'Maestre Racional' (chief accountant) and one accountant, the Keeper of the Royal Patrimony of the kingdom of Aragon, the cup-bearer, the steward, the governor of the kingdom of Aragon, and in other offices.

Some of the *letrados* who were members of the Council of Aragon belonged to New Christian families. Prominent among them was Alfonso de la Cavalleria, its first vice-chancellor, appointed by Ferdinand after the reform. His family had always been loyal to John II, and Ferdinand trusted and supported him in spite of the fact that his relatives had been rigorously persecuted by the Inquisition. Of course, Ferdinand's clemency left the vice-chancellor of Aragon entirely in his hands as a tool of the royal policy.

Even in the days of Charles V the names of some members of the Council of Aragon point to the same origin (Bonavia and Mai, regents in 1523; Celdran, treasurer-general, and Ram, regent in 1538) or were known as those of converted families (such as Luis Sánchez, treasurer-general in 1527).

Conditions were similar in Castile. Apart from Jews who were the physicians of the royal family, there were in the early part of the reign of Isabella members of the Royal Council, such as Pedro de Cartagena and Pedro Arias Dávila, who were Jews. The latter was also the chief accountant, and one of his assistants was Gonzalo Franco, a member of the well-known *converso* family of Franco. Another *converso* was Pedro Díaz de Toledo, who had been *oidor* in the days of John II of Castile. The treasurer, Ruy López, and Fernando de Zafra, one of the king's secretaries, were thought to belong to *converso* families, and three other secretaries, Fernando Alvarez, Alfonso de Avila and Fernando del Pulgar, were New Christians. The men who farmed the royal revenue were two prominent Jews, Abraham Senior, Chief Rabbi of the Kingdom of Castile, and Isaac Abarbanel, and they also obtained the contract for feeding and supplying the Christian army in the last campaign against the Moorish kingdom of Granada.

But it was mainly in the episcopal sees that *conversos* were found: Alonso de Burgos, bishop of Palencia; Juan de Maluenda (of the Santa Maria family, who held so many sees) bishop of Coria; Alfonso de Valladolid and Alonso de Palenzuela, bishops of Valladolid and Ciudad Rodrigo; Pedro de Aranda, bishop of Calahorra; Juan Arias Dávila, of Segovia; Juan de Torquemada, later a cardinal.

The establishment of the Inquisition and the persecution of the Jews and *conversos* altered the situation. The laws of September 4th and 21st, 1501, banned descendants of those burned or sentenced by the Inquisition, down to the second generation in the male line or the first in the female, from the office of member of the Royal Council, *oidor*, secretary, *alcalde* and *alguacil* of a chancery or audiencia, chief-accountant, treasurer and others, except by very special permission of the crown. The Cortes of Castile of 1532 passed a petition to the crown that enquiries into the ancestry of people should not be pursued further back than the fourth generation.

Since the names of the members of the councils have not yet been listed, it is not possible to enquire very far into their social origin. We are, however, indebted to Professor Schäfer for a complete list of presidents, secretaries and members of the Council of the Indies, and from this certain conclusions may be drawn.

The various councils were recruited from various social groups. The Council of State was of course the almost exclusive preserve of the grandees and the high nobility. Most of its members in the active years of their lives had been abroad as viceroys, captains-general, or ambassadors. Appointment to the Council of State was the crowning honour of their career.

Taking as a sample the 40 councillors of state for the later period of Philip II and for that of his son, listed by Sr. Alcocer y Martinez, one finds that 28 were members of the high nobility, 9 were ecclesiastics, and 3 *hidalgos*.

Of the 28 noblemen, 11 had been viceroys (in Catalonia, Valencia and Navarre, but more often in the Italian states and chiefly in Naples). Curiously enough none had been in the Indies, the reason being that since the Council of State was concerned largely with foreign policy and war in Europe, only those who had experience of these matters were chosen.

Three had been ambassadors. One, Antonio Folch de Cardona y Fernández de Córdoba, had been Philip II's envoy to the Holy See. Of the others, Pedro de Toledo y Zúñiga was Philip III's ambassador to the Court of St. James, and Baltasar de Zúñiga had been his representative to the Holy See, Germany, France and Flanders.

Military experience was the contribution of another group of 10 councillors, who had held commissions as generals or captains-general, in the army and the navy.

Royal favour played a part in the appointment of ecclesiastics to the council. Five out of the nine had been either confessors or chaplains to the king, while only three had been archbishops. Seven were also members of the Council of the Inquisition, five of them holding the powerful office of Inquisitor-General; thus the Council of the Inquisition and the Council of State were linked.

Of this group of 40 councillors, two at least, Juan de Idiáquez and Rodrigo Vázquez de Arce, were not titled noblemen but *hidalgos*, and a third, Juan de Acuna, though an illegitimate son of the count of Buendia, and awarded later in life the title of Marquis of Vallecerrato by Philip III, had a career like that of an ordinary *letrado*.

We have analysed in some detail the membership of the Council of State, since it shows whose hands were in control of the foreign affairs of the monarchy when, with the reign of Philip III, it had begun to go downhill.

The Council of Castile remained to a large extent what Ferdinand

and Isabella intended it to be – a body of lawyers (*letrados*). So also were the Council of the Indies and that of Finance, and, though separate from them, the Council of Aragon.

Galíndez de Carvajal, the trusted servant of Charles V, has left us an invaluable document, a confidential report on every member of the Royal Council of Castile, in his days.

Its President was Antonio de Rojas, archbishop of Granada, a member of the powerful families of the Manriques and the Rojas.

Of the 14 members, one, Dr. Oropesa, is stated to have been a priest, but so old and infirm that he no longer attended the meetings. Another, D. Alonso de Castilla, a man of noble spirit, good sense and some experience, had no education. Besides, he was said to come of a *converso* family.

Whether a man had had *converso* ancestors or was *limpio* was deemed an important point and is duly recorded in this report. Dr. Tello and Dr. Cabrero, not born in 'these kingdoms', had some *converso* blood, and Dr. Guevara, also of 'doubtful' origin, had moreover married a *conversa*.

Of the others, 9 were stated to be *limpios*, 3 because they were *hidalgos*, and 3 others because they were of peasant stock (*labradores*).

They were all *letrados* except the president and D. Alonso de Castilla. But 7 of these 13 were considered by Galíndez to have poor or mediocre legal knowledge. Fortunately there was among them one outstanding figure, Dr. Juan López de Palacios Rubios, better known by the last part of his name, that of the village where he was born.

Galíndez thought that two of the members were unworthy to sit on a Royal Council, and that two others were unscrupulous in financial dealing. Dr. Tello, who collected much wealth when he was in the accounts' office (*contaduria*) and Leonardo Vargas, who was *cobdiciosísimo*, 'having amassed and spent so much in a short time that it seems impossible for a single man.'

There were two Fiscals, one, Prado, the grandson of a woman sentenced by the Inquisition, of whom it was said it was 'a shame that such a man should be a Fiscal.'

As for the clerks, there were, for Galíndez, far too many – many young men and others of small learning and *conversos*. He suggests that a selection be made from among them, as Ferdinand and Isabella did when reforming the council. Should any vacancy occur in the council he recommended two *oidores* of the Valladolid *audien-*

cia, who were good *letrados*, honest, and *limpios*, being sprung from peasant families.

He goes on to give the advice that no one should be called into the Royal Council as his first job, but that councillors should be chosen from among members of the chanceries so that, when promoted, they should be tried and tested men. It is worth keeping this in mind because, as we shall see, this was what actually was done thenceforth, whether through his advice or not.

The importance of the *letrados* was such that they merit examination. They came chiefly from the class of the *hidalgos*, the lesser nobility. For even the lower posts of the administration in Castile (judges, *corregidores*, finance officials) to be of noble birth was almost, if not absolutely, essential.

The degree of nobility required was not, of course, as high as for the highest posts of the administration – viceroys, captains-general, state councillors. To be a *hidalgo* was enough.

After the grandees and the titled nobility came the *hidalgos*, the lower, but the most numerous, rank of the nobles. They all claimed, more or less justifiably, a noble ancestry, often derived from remote cadet branches of titled families. Their honour forbade them to work or engage in trade or industry; so their armorial bearings were richer than their purses. The type of the proud, idle, hungry *hidalgo*, pestering his friends at Court for a job or, better, a sinecure, was the target of many gibes in the literature of the period.

Their number was exceedingly large, particularly in Asturias. The Guipúzcoans overshot the mark by proclaiming that there was none among them who was not of noble birth. Thus was aristocracy democratized.

Some, however, trained for a public post by studying law. The large number of students that crowded the universities of Salamanca, Alcalá de Henares and Valladolid was rather an indication of this social trend than of the progress of learning.

Summing up, the *letrados* seem to have come mainly from the *hidalgos* and the middle class, chiefly of León and Old Castile, and had a thorough university training, particularly at Valladolid, in Roman Law.

Some approximate idea of the number of people employed in the administration can be formed from scattered evidence.

In the realms of the Crown of Castile, early in the seventeenth century, 530 judges and magistrates were said to sit on the benches of *audiencias*, law courts under them, and the courts of the Inquisition, their total salaries amounting to some 400,000 ducats. This figure of 530 probably included other members of the courts, like the *relatores* and *fiscales*, but not the large number of secretaries, clerks, collectors of fines and money (*receptores*), executors of the court's decisions, *alguaciles* and other minor officials. These, with the exception of secretaries and perhaps some clerks (*escribanos*), were commoners and not necessarily graduates in law.

The number of the subordinate officials of the Inquisition was exceedingly large. While Lea gives no figures for the number of *familiars* of the Inquisition in Castile, Ambrosio de Salazar says that there were 20,000 in the kingdoms of Spain, each with an annual salary of 30,000 *maravedís*, or a little more than 80 ducats. If the figures are correct, the familiars received the impressive total of 1,600,000 ducats a year.

In Sicily, where the Royal Inquisition had been introduced from Castile, though Ferdinand had limited to 20 the number of familiars in each large city (1510), the Viceroy stated in 1577 that there were 25,000, that the Inquisitors wanted to increase them to 30,000, and that they included 'all the nobles, the rich men and the criminals'.

The Castilian Exchequer employed an even larger number of men, particularly as inspectors and tax-collectors; some seventeenth century authorities put the number as high as 60,000, although this was probably an exaggeration.

The administration of the Indies employed a very large number of people. The meticulous work of Professor Schäfer provides us with a true picture as far as the higher posts of the administration are concerned. The appendices to his first volume include the names of a total of 484 men who worked in the Council of the Indies (249 were councillors), and of 187 in the Casa de Contratación at Seville, up to 1700. The appendices to his second volume list some 3,200 men employed in the Indies, as viceroys, members of *audiencias*, provincial governors, archbishops and bishops. Minor officials are not included, but they must have been legion. The vast majority overseas were from Castilian Spain; only a small number were natives.

A word must now be said on the age of the members of the councils. It has been seen above that grandees and members of the high nobility reached the Council of State only when they were old. Much the same can be said of the members of the other councils. Juan de Salazar gives an outline of the periods of preparation in the life of a letrado. The ordinary university law courses would finish when he was 24 or 25. He might then practise law, and after five or six years win in competitive examination (*oposición*) a fellowship at one of the colleges in Salamanca or Valladolid. Nine or ten years might be spent there, and at about 40 he might be chosen to be a judge (*oidor*) or *fiscal* in one of the *audiencias* or chanceries.

Only after some years in this position could he expect to be appointed to a council.

To take the Council of the Indies as an example, of the 19 councillors appointed in the reign of Charles V whose previous position is known (out of a total of 24), 13 came from chanceries, (10 from Valladolid, and 3 from Granada). Of those appointed by Philip II, we have the previous record of 37 out of a total of 39. Of these, 17 came from chanceries and *audiencias* (7 from Valladolid, 7 from Granada and 2 from Seville), 7 had been *oidores* in the exchequer (*Contaduría Mayor*) 6 *fiscales* in the same Council of the Indies, and 4 members of the Tribunal of the *Alcaldes de Casa y Corte*. For the period 1598–1665, out of the 115 appointed members of the council, 25 had been Fiscals, 20 *alcaldes* of the last-named tribunal, 17 councillors of finance, 6 from the Council of the Orders of Knighthood, 4 from the Council of War, and 10 from the chanceries of Valladolid and Granada, and 3 from the *audiencia* of Seville.

These figures show that the proportion of members from chanceries and *audiencias* tended to decrease. But on the other hand, the organs of the administration had expanded, and employed more men with legal training.

The result was that men reached the council only in mature age, and sometimes were able to serve only for a comparatively short time. Of the 36 members of the Council of the Indies appointed by Philip III, 11 died after short periods ranging from two months to three years.

The highest honour was to be at length promoted to the Council of Castile, but this was achieved only when the *letrado* was approaching or entered upon his sixties.

The placing of the government of the monarchy in the hands of the *letrados* had been a revolutionary step in the days of Ferdinand and Isabella, but by the close of the sixteenth century the system was becoming clogged. An indication of the downward trend appears in the decadence of the universities where the future *letrados* were being trained.

Accompanying this decadence was the evil of a general increase in presumptuous ambition to be of the nobility and to look for a livelihood not in work but in a state job. Arms had been the customary occupation of the nobles, but the period of relative peace in the early years of Philip III forced them to look for civilian jobs, which they tried to obtain as a favour from the king or from friends suitably situated in the administration, or simply by the increasingly popular device of 'buying' them, in other words, not so bluntly, obtaining them in exchange for a donation to the depleted royal treasury. Then a new type of councillor begins to appear – the *consejero de capa y espada* (of cloak and sword), the nobleman or hidalgo, supposed to be an expert in military affairs and matters of government, in contrast to the *consejero togado* (gowned), the traditional *letrado*, expert in matters of law and justice.

The appearance of *capa y espada* nobles in the councils was in fact a symptom of the changes in the highest spheres of government of the Hapsburg Monarchy. It was a breach in the system which had been introduced at the end of the fifteenth century and maintained all through the sixteenth, of keeping the nobility out of the government and entrusting it to commoners and hidalgos with legal training. As long as the monarchs were strong and able, like Ferdinand, Charles and Philip, the system worked well, but when they were weak and incompetent, like the lesser Philips, the nobility took advantage and came back. This they did not only by infiltrating into the councils but by taking into their hands the government of the monarchy at the highest level, grandees like the duke of Lerma, the duke of Osuna, and the count-duke of Olivares acting as incompetent ministers for inefficient kings. This return of the nobility was made possible by the swelling, though not the strengthening, of their ranks.

The Council of the Indies seems to have been the first to which *capa y espada* members were appointed. Philip III in August 1600 ordered that whenever military matters were to be discussed, two members of the Council of War should join that of the Indies. This mixed board came to be known as the *Junta de Guerra de Indias*. A similar mixed board, the *Junta de Hacienda de Indias*, was set up by bringing together members of the Councils of Finance and of the Indies, the former trying to resolve the anomaly that the American Treasure, one of the most important sources of the royal revenue, was outside the control of the Council of Finance. Naturally, the Council of the Indies did not want interference from members of the other two councils and kept postponing the execution of the royal decision, until a new decree in October 1601 ordered them to implement the measure forthwith.

The next step was a decision that the *Junta de Guerra* should have two members from the War Council and two from the Council of the Indies under one president. Perhaps as a compromise or with the idea that military experts should sit permanently in the latter council, which should be able to delegate them to the Junta, a further order was given in 1604 appointing two *capa y espada* members to the Council of the Indies on equal terms with the gowned members; but they had to abstain from taking part in matters of justice.

In the following years the new councillors were gradually brought into all the councils.

The Council of Italy seems to have been rather late in receiving them. The first *capa y espada* councillor was probably G. Funes Muñoz, appointed in 1636 from his post as Keeper General of the Royal Patrimony in Italy. While the number of gowned (*togados*) councillors was restricted to two for each of the three Italian states and to natives of these states as experts on the law and traditions of their countries, the monarch could appoint as many *capa y espada* councillors as he pleased.

Capa y espada councillors also found their way into the Supreme Council of Flanders towards the end of the century. At least, to this period belong the appointments I have been able to find – those of the Marquis de Castelmoncayo (1689–92) and of D. García de Sarmiento y Toledo, Marquis de Montalvo (1690).

It will be noted that all the appointments recorded were of Castilian nobles, not Italian nor Flemish nor natives of the countries of the Crown of Aragon with the sole exception of Funes Muñoz, who was an Aragonese. The *capa y espada* councillors were, therefore, instruments for the hegemony of Castile over the other members of the Hapsburg Monarchy.

It is clear from the above paragraphs that the appointment of *capa y espada* councillors became a corrupt practice. Appointments depended solely on royal favour; there was no limitation of their numbers, nor standard for their ability, and the salaries of these new members nominated over and above the prescribed number of councillors of each council began to be a heavy charge on the treasury in the last years of rule of the count-duke of Olivares owing to the large number of appointments he made. As an instance, in the course of his reign Philip IV appointed 78 members to the Council of the Indies, 21 of them *capa y espada* over and above the legal number of councillors; and the imbecile Charles II appointed 72 members to the same council, 24 being *capa y espada*.

The appointments made so greatly exceeded the needs of the councils that Philip IV had to decree in 1661 that *capa y espada* councillors appointed to the War Junta should wait for a vacancy before joining it – though they received their salaries from the date of nomination.

Another step in this corruption was the appointment of supernumerary councillors, both gowned and *capa y espada*, who held other offices abroad and remained there, but drew the council salary as well.

A further development was the purchase of posts of councillor by means of a 'service' or donation to the crown. This was not seen as reprehensible; it was openly mentioned in the decree of appointment, and even praised as an act of patriotism.

If a post was bought, the purchaser was inclined to try to make it hereditary. Thus we find a boy of 9 inheriting a post in the Council of the Indies, being appointed as a *capa y espada* councillor but not allowed to sit until he was of age. The boy councillor was Don José Maria Francisco de la Cerda Manrique de Lara, Marquis de la Laguna and Count of Paredes, son of Don Tomás Antonio de la Cerda y Enriquez Afán de Ribera, Councillor of the Indies (actively 1675–89), Viceroy of Mexico, *Mayordomo Mayor* of the queen.

J. M. BATISTA i ROCA,

CAMBRIDGE, 1950

PREFACE

NEITHER Sicily under Spanish rule nor the organization of the Spanish Empire in Italy has ever been the subject of a comprehensive historical investigation. Ranke's chapter on Sicily in *Die Osmanen und die Spanische Monarchie, Sämtliche Werke*, vol. xxxv/vi (Leipzig 1877) is no more than a sketch, though a very brilliant one, based on the *Historia Siciliana* of the sixteenth century historian Buonfiglio e Costanzo (Venice 1604), on the short report of the Venetian Resident in Sicily, Placido Ragazzoni (in Albèri, *Relazioni degli Ambasciatori Veneti*, ser. 2. vol. v), and on Scipio di Castro's *Avvertimenti a Marc Antonio Colonna*, in the *Thesoro Politico*, vol. II (Milan 1601). Very recently V. Titone has published his *La Sicilia Spagnuola, Saggi Storici* (Palermo 1948), based on printed documents and MSS in Sicily. The sources at his disposal form only a part of the total available material, and his book is not so much a detailed account as an interpretation of the character of Spanish rule in Sicily.[1]

The remaining works on the subject may be divided into three groups: (*a*) General histories of Sicily in which the Spanish period constitutes one of the parts. The most important of these are Buonfiglio e Costanzo, *Historia Siciliana*; G. B. Caruso, *Memorie Istoriche* (Palermo 1744; part 3, vol. I, deals with the reign of Philip II); and G. E. di Blasi, *Storia Cronologica de' Vicerè* (Palermo 1790; vol. II deals with the 16th century). These are not so much histories as chronicles. The more modern general works of A. F. Ferrara, *Storia Generale della Sicilia* (Palermo 1830-38), and L. Natoli, *Storia di Sicilia* (Palermo 1935) add little to what is contained in the earlier works, nor are they remarkable for their historical judgment.

(*b*) Works dealing with particular aspects of Sicilian history. The best of these is R. Gregorio, *Considerazioni sopra la Storia di Sicilia*, in *Opere Scelte* (Palermo 1853). This history of public law was written at the beginning of the last century and is based on published and unpublished laws and governmental decrees. L. Bianchini, *Della Storia Economico-Civile di Sicilia* (Naples 1848) is a useful but unreliable work, dealing mainly with economic legislation. The history of the Sicilian Parliament is treated by C. Calisse, *Storia del Parla-*

---

[1] F. Braudel's *La Méditerranée et le Monde méditerranéen à l'époque de Philippe II* (Paris 1949) appeared when this book was already in the hands of the publishers.

mento in Sicilia (Turin 1887) and by L. Genuardi, *Parlamento Siciliano* (Bologna 1924). This latter is one of the best monographs on Sicilian history, but it is not primarily concerned with the sixteenth century. The history of the *Monarchia Sicula* has been written by G. B. Caruso, *Discorso istorico-apologetico della monarchia di Sicilia* (ed. Mira, Palermo 1863) and by F. Sentis, *Die Monarchia Sicula* (Freiburg i.Br. 1896).

(*c*) Monographs dealing with particular aspects of Sicilian or Spanish history in the sixteenth century. Of these there are a great number, many of them published as articles in the *Archivio Storico Siciliano*. Their greatest merit is often in the documents they publish. Among the best and most useful might be named C. A. Garufi, *Contributo alla storia dell'Inquisizione in Sicilia nei secoli xvi e xvii* (Archivio Storico Siciliano, new series, vols. XXXVIII-XLIII) and C. Giardina, *Il Supremo Consiglio d'Italia* (Atti della Regia Accademia di Scienze, Lettere e Belle Arti di Palermo, ser. 3. vol. XIX) and *L'Istituto del Vicerè di Sicilia*, by the same author (Arch. stor. sic. n.s. vol. LI). Garufi and Giardina are the only two Sicilian historians of the Spanish period to have worked in Spanish Archives. But Garufi confined himself to the documents of the Inquisition and Giardina was content to describe the structure and procedure of the Council of Italy without attempting to discuss its actual working or its place in the Spanish system of imperial administration. His treatment of the institution of the viceroy follows similar lines. Apart from Giardina's article, the Spanish side of the history of Sicily has been almost entirely ignored.

The present essay is based primarily on contemporary printed and manuscript sources. Of the printed sources the collections of sixteenth century diaries (di Marzo, *Biblioteca storica e letteraria di Sicilia*), the collections of laws (*Regni Siciliae Pragmaticarum Sanctionum,* 2 vols., Venice 1574; and *Pragmaticarum Regni Siciliae Novissima Collectio*, 3 vols., Palermo 1636-1700) and the acts of Parliament (Mongitore, *Parlamenti Generali del Regno di Sicilia*, Palermo, 1749; and Testa, *Capitula Regni Siciliae*, Palermo 1743) have been utilized by previous historians. Part of the correspondence of the duke of Terranova has been published by the *Società Siciliana per la Storia Patria* (C. D'Aragona, *Corrispondenza Particolare*, ed. Bozzo and Cozzo, in *Documenti per servire alla Storia di Sicilia*, ser. 1, vol. II). But, except by Genuardi, this valuable source has been left almost entirely unused. No copy of the *Colección de Documentos Inéditos para la Historia de España* exists in Sicily, with the result that the two volumes of Toledo's correspondence, (vols. XXIX-XXX), as well as many other documents, have remained unknown to Sicilian historians. The same applies to the correspondence of Granvelle, and in particular to the important letter of Juan de Vega to Philip II (*Papiers d'Etat du Cardinal de Granvelle*, ed. Ch. Weiss, vol. V; also *Correspondence de Granvelle*, ed. Ch. Piot, vols. IV, V, IX, XI). Of the relations of the Venetian ambassadors only the short account of Sicily by Ragazzoni has previously been quoted. But there are many relevant facts and observations on Spanish rule in Italy and on the workings of the Council of Italy, which have hitherto escaped the notice of historians.

The unpublished manuscript sources consist of the correspondence between the governments of Sicily and Spain (together with documents, such as budgets, naval accounts, etc., enclosed with official reports), and of formal relations of the government of Sicily for the benefit of new viceroys, written either by their predecessors or by a Spanish or Sicilian official with long experience of Sicilian government and politics. Copies of a number of these relations exist both in Sicily and in the British Museum, although the very important relation of Francesco Fortunato is to be found only in London (B.M. MS. Additional 28,396), the anonymous *Trattato di Sicilia* only in Naples (Biblioteca Nazionale di Napoli, MS. X.D.46), and the relation of Matute only in the Real Academia de la Historia of Madrid (Estante 21 gr. l.a. No. 3.).[1]

The official correspondence is even more important than the relations, and so far it has been almost entirely unknown. A surprisingly large number of viceregal and royal letters, as well as royal instructions to Sicilian and Neapolitan viceroys, have found their way into the British Museum. The bulk, however, is in the Archivo General de Simancas[2] and a portion is in the Biblioteca Nacional of Madrid. The existence of the Sicilian state papers in Spain was, of course, not unknown to Sicilian historians.[3] The viceregal court in Sicily possessed copies, but early in the seventeenth century they

---

[1] In the Archivio di Stato of Genoa are preserved some letters of Genoese consuls which, however, contain little of interest to the historian of Sicily.
In Venice there is another MS relation of Ragazzoni on Sicily, not published in Albèri.
[2] The senior archivist of Simancas, Don Ricardo Magdaleno, is at present engaged on the compilation of a catalogue of the Sicilian papers in the '*sección estado*.'
Titone's discussion of the instructions for the duke of Maqueda (*La Sicilia Spagnuola*, pp. 167–179) is based on my transcript of this document from Simancas.
[3] The Sicilian archivist, I. Carini, produced a very useful general catalogue of Spanish MSS referring to Sicilian history (*Gli Archivi e le Biblioteche di Spagna*, Palermo 1884).

PREFACE

were lost at sea while being transferred from Messina to Palermo.

This official correspondence forms the core of the material on which the present work is based. Even on topics previously treated by other historians a considerable amount of new material has been introduced and, in consequence, different conclusions have often been reached. This applies, in particular, to the chapter on the Council of Italy (ch. 2), and to the three sections of chapter 6, on the *Monarchia Sicula*, Parliament, and the Sicilian Inquisition. The remaining chapters are based almost entirely on new materials. For the first time it has been possible to see the detailed work of the Sicilian and imperial administration not only in generalized relations, but in the weekly reports and letters of the viceroys and in the *consultas* of the Council of Italy. Rather more than half the documents were concerned with military and naval matters connected with the defence of Sicily, Malta and Goletta, and with the naval war against the Turks. This part of the subject has been treated here only in so far as it was relevant to the understanding of the organization of the Spanish Empire and the administration of Sicily.

The subject of the Spanish government in Sicily was first suggested to me by the late Professor C. W. Previté Orton. It was he who first introduced me to the study of Renaissance Italy and to the peculiar fascination of Mediterranean civilization. Until almost the very day of his death he took an active interest in my research, always ready to make pertinent suggestions or to listen patiently to a young research student. I also owe a very great debt to Professor H. Butterfield, especially for his invaluable advice on the technique of historical writing.

In 1947 Gonville and Caius College made me a grant which enabled me to spend six months in Spain and Italy, and in 1950 The Queen's University of Belfast made me a grant towards the cost of publication. My thanks are also due to the officials of the British Museum, of the Bodleian Library, and of the archives of Simancas, Madrid, Palermo and Naples for their unfailing courtesy and helpfulness. It is a long time now since Bergenroth wrote his famous preface to the first volume of the Calendar of State Papers from Spain. The student who approaches Simancas with some apprehension will now find that there is hardly a place where it is more pleasant to work than the old archive-fortress of Castile.

Of the many friends who have helped and encouraged me, I am particularly grateful to Professor Virgilio Titone of the University of Palermo who, during my stay in Sicily, put much of his time and all his great knowledge of the island and its history most readily at my disposal. Mr. and Mrs. K. A. Usherwood and Mr. J. D. Hillaby have helped me in every possible way with suggestions, criticisms and typing.

H. G. K.

BELFAST, *April*, 1950

CHAPTER ONE

Introduction

HISTORIANS of Sicily have always shown a marked preference for a few periods in the history of the great Mediterranean island. They have concentrated on the brilliant civilization of Norman Sicily and they have studied the exciting career of that *stupor mundi*, the Emperor Frederick II, the sombre heroism of the Wars of the Vespers or, at the other end of the story, the revolutions and constitutional experiments of the nineteenth century with the patriotic climax of Garibaldi. The long intervening period of apparent decadence and humiliation has offered few attractions to the student in search of dramatic interest or patriotic edification. Only the revolts of Palermo and Messina, during the seventeenth century, have been studied more thoroughly, for both lend themselves to more picturesque treatment and both appear to show the survival of a spirit of nationalist independence. A similar bias is apparent in the study of the Spanish Empire. Here, too, historians have been preoccupied with the dramatic struggle in the Netherlands or the creation of a new civilization in the Americas, while interest in Spain's Italian Empire has been largely confined to the wars with France and with the Ottoman Turks. In consequence the history of Sicily under Spanish domination has been one of the most neglected fields of historical study. Sicilians themselves who have studied their country's history during that period have been, for the most part, antiquarians or lawyers, rather than historians. They have been content to chronicle events or to describe certain institutions of their country. At best we have been given a history of Sicilian public law, as in the work of Rosario Gregorio; but we look in vain for a comprehensive account of the story of Sicily during the period of the Spanish viceroys, or even for a more limited study relating Sicilian history to the wider setting of the development of European civilization. Turning to the historians of the Spanish Empire, we fare no better. Only Ranke, writing more than a century ago, has been able to see Sicily and the other Spanish dominions in Italy in their true perspective; not simply as passive objects of Spanish domination, but as vital integers in a great empire.[1]

The Spanish world-empire had come into existence at the very moment when the reformation movements in central and northern Europe were breaking up the last vestiges of the unity of medieval Christendom. It was not immediately obvious that the Hapsburg collection of states could fill the void. Marriage alliances and conquest had made Charles V and Philip II rulers of a large number of states both in Europe and in the New World. These states were bound together neither by interest nor tradition; yet the mere fact of union under one crown imposed upon them common functions, invested them with a collective duty and made them share a common historical destiny.

Throughout Hungary and over the whole length and breadth of the Mediterranean, the Hapsburg states were assailed by the Ottoman Turks, and in defending themselves they were 'protecting the whole of Christian Europe.' Or thus it appeared to the viceroy of Sicily, García de Toledo, when he urged that France and Portugal should be induced to lend galleys for the defence of Malta,[2] while Spain and Italy were stretching their resources to the limits; and thus the position presented itself to Philip II when he ordered the capture of English ships carrying war-materials to Constantinople.[3] In central and western Europe the rise of Protestantism threatened the very basis of the heterogeneous monarchy by destroying the religious unity which was essential for its cohesion. When the Prudent King sent his galleons to protect the Spanish monopoly of trade with the Indies against English and Dutch interlopers and competitors, they were at the same time 'safeguarding the Catholic World from the contagion of Protestant heresies.'

This oecumenical task of defence against the dual threat of Protestantism and Islam forced the Hapsburg states into a union which tended to become a universal Catholic state in the tradition of the medieval Roman Empires, but with an essentially different political orientation and an entirely novel administrative organization. France and Germany had been the kernels of the political

---

[1] L. von Ranke, Die Osmanen und die Spanische Monarchie; Sämtliche Werke, vol. xxxv/vi (Leipzig 1877).
[2] Toledo to Philip II, May 16th, 1565; Colección de Documentos Inéditos para la Historia de España, vol. xxix, pp.144 ff.
[3] Philip II to Marc Antonio Colonna, viceroy of Sicily, May 29th, 1580; Archivo General de Simancas, Sección Estado, legajo 1149. Same to same, January 24th, 1583, ibid. leg. 1152. – Most of the Simancas legajos, or bundles of documents, have no folio numbers.

structure of medieval Europe. Spain became their heir in the sixteenth century. For eight centuries the peninsula had been the scene of the most constant and bitter fighting between Christian and Moslem. While in the east the Turks overran one Christian province after another, in Andalucia the crusading spirit was still alive, and the capture of Granada from the Moors deprived Islam of its earliest foothold in Europe. In the first half of the fifteenth century it had been possible for Alfonso of Aragon to establish the capital of his purely Mediterranean Aragonese Empire in Naples. His greatest enemies had been the Genoese and the duke of Milan who had concluded an alliance with him after taking him prisoner. But in the sixteenth century Naples and Sicily had become frontier provinces fighting desperately for their existence in a war *à outrance* against the most powerful armies and navies of the time. On the other hand, the empire had expanded westward. Having overthrown the Moslem kingdoms on the Iberian peninsula, the Castilians and Portuguese continued their tradition of Christian conquest by the colonization of America and the East Indies[1]. Lisbon and Seville replaced Naples, Genoa and Barcelona as the focal points of world trade from which Indian spices and Peruvian silver flooded the courts and cities of western Europe. Only Spanish galleys could still take offensive action against the corsair nests of the north African coast; Spanish infantry remained undefeated on all great battle fields of Europe, from the days of the Great Captain, Gonzalez de Córdova, until the final catastrophe of Rocroi which marked the end of Spain's military power. Torquemada's Inquisition and Loyola's Society of Jesus became the most powerful weapons of the Counter-Reformation, and with the material basis for the Catholic revival, Spain also produced its most distinguished spiritual exponents.

The preponderance of Spain was not, however, clearly apparent from the beginnings of the Hapsburg Empire. During the reign of Charles V, the fortuitous and personal elements in the Hapsburg inheritance were still predominant. Moreover, the true functions of the empire were to some extent obscured by the long struggle with France, a struggle which Charles V fought more as a Burgundian than as a Spaniard. But during the reign of Philip II the character of the new union of states as a predominantly Spanish empire was

[1] A. J. Toynbee, A Study of History, vol. II (London 1945), p. 204, 'The Portuguese and Castilian seafarers who made their presence felt throughout the World in the first century of our modern age (*circa* A.D. 1475–1575) were the heirs of frontiersmen whose spirit had been tempered by thirty generations of strenuous warfare against the Moors on the Iberian marches.'

firmly established and its organization was given the essential form which it preserved for the remainder of its existence. Ferdinand and Isabella had laid the foundations for the future strength of the monarchy by applying in Castile the principles of the new and more efficient organization developed by the city-states and small principalities of northern Italy. 'The state as a work of art',[1] centralized and bureaucratic government, had now to be introduced in those provinces where it did not yet exist and, at the same time, the empire as a whole had to be organized in harmony with the new political principles.

Sicily provides perhaps the best example for the practical application of these principles. The internal history of the Spanish Empire, as Ranke clearly saw,[2] was the story of the struggle between the centralizing forces of the monarchy and the centrifugal forces of the particularist interests of the states and provinces composing the empire. In the Netherlands the policy of centralization led to revolt and the eventual defeat of the monarchy. In Milan and Naples the struggle between estates and central government had already been decided in favour of the latter when Spain took control. But in Sicily all fundamental questions were still unresolved. It was in the reign of Philip II that Spaniards and Sicilians worked out the balance of power by which the island could play its part in fulfilling the Catholic obligations and imperialist aspirations of the Spanish Monarchy while, at the same time, it was able to preserve many essentials of its former independence.

---

[1] J. Burckhardt, The Civilization of the Renaissance in Italy, transl. S. G. C. Middlemore (Vienna and London); Heading of Part I.
[2] L. von Ranke, Die Osmanen und die Spanische Monarchie, pp. 88 f.

CHAPTER TWO

The Spanish Theory of Empire in Sicily

CRISTÓBAL DE VILLALÓN, Spanish adventurer and writer, relates a small incident which illustrates clearly the attitude of both Spaniards and Italians towards the Hapsburg Empire. During a voyage in the Mediterranean Cristóbal had been captured by Turkish pirates and sent as a slave to Constantinople, but had finally managed to escape. Returning to Spain by way òf Sicily he heard that Turkish corsairs were lying in wait outside the Straits of Messina. At all costs he had to avoid renewed capture. Inventing some pretext he borrowed the ship's boat, rowed ashore and jumped on to the beach, determined to continue his journey by land. But on touching ground he was immediately set upon by the Messinese guards. 'And when they asked me who had given me permission to disembark,' he recorded, 'I answered that I did not need permission, for as this was the emperor's land, and I his vassal, I had as much right to be in it as they themselves.'[1] The Messinese authorities, however, were not impressed by this argument. Cristóbal was kept in quarantine for several weeks.

For the Spaniards Italy was an extension of their own country. By virtue of their ruler's position as king of Naples and Sicily, they expected the same rights of citizenship which they enjoyed in Spain. For the Neapolitans and Sicilians, on the other hand, Charles V and Philip II were their own kings. If they were rulers also of other kingdoms – that was incidental. The Italians found nothing incompatible with their loyalty to their sovereigns if they maintained their local laws and privileges against all foreigners, vassals of the king or not.

Most important of these privileges, to their mind, was the right to have public offices filled only by natives. It is natural for all nations to exclude foreigners from offices, wrote Francesco Fortunato, president of the Court of the Holy Conscience,[2] and one of the most faithful supporters of Spanish rule in Sicily. The French had failed

[1] C. de Villalón, Viaje de Turquía, vol. II (Madrid-Barcelona 1919) p. 60. The incident took place about 1550.
[2] The Sicilian court of appeal; cf. below, p. 87.

47

to maintain themselves in Italy precisely because they had neglected this fundamental rule whereas, during the war against Paul IV, the duke of Alva had reaped handsome dividends from his policy of giving the captaincies of the Naples militia to Neapolitan nobles.[1] In session after session the Sicilian Parliament petitioned the king for strict observance of the rule that all except a very few appointments should be made from Sicilians.[2] Yet all those Spaniards who knew Sicily well were agreed on the desirability of appointing their own countrymen to as many offices as possible,[3] convinced though they might be of the ability and personal loyalty of the King's Italian ministers. Yet in the last analyses the Spaniards were the conquerors and the Italians the conquered. This attitude was expressed quite plainly in a letter to the king from Milan:[4] '... in Italy there is no state, no power, no prince, no man who owns a castle... nor one who does not, who desires the maintenance and increase of Your Majesty's states; and all are past masters in giving good words and pretending the contrary... I do not know whether there is any one in the world who is subject to the Spanish nation and empire and who is devoted to them, but does not rather abhor their name... And this is much more the case in Italy than in any other part of the world...' The writer's view was endorsed by an unsigned comment, scribbled on the back of the letter and probably intended for the benefit of Mateo Vázquez, the king's secretary: 'For these Italians, although they are not Indians, have to be treated as such, so that they will understand that we are in charge of them and not they in charge of us.' A typical note of a Master Race.

Whatever the private opinions of Spanish ministers, Sicily could not be governed along such lines without arousing fierce opposition, and the monarchy was careful not to press Spanish imperialistic claims too far. Even from high ministerial positions, normally occupied by Spaniards, the *Rey Prudente* thought it wise not always to exclude Sicilians.[5] Towards the end of the reign the Council of

---

[1] 'Los avertimentos del doctor Fortunato sobre el govierno de Sicilia', written in 1592 for the count of Olivares; Letters and Papers relating to Sicily, 1572–1603; British Museum MS. Add. 28 396, fo. 410–11.
[2] F. Testa, Capitula Regni Siciliae, vol. II (Palermo 1743), pp. 251, 287, 302, 307.
[3] e.g. Pedro Velázquez, favourite of the duke of Medinaceli, in an abstract of a memorandum on the defence of Sicily; Letters and Papers... Sicily, B.M. MS. Add. 28 396, fo. 218. Also the *consultore*, León, to Philip II, Nov. 1574, ibid. fo. 16.
[4] Probably from the marquis of Ayamonte, governor of Milan, Febr. 2nd, 1570; Letters and Papers relating to Italy, I, B.M. MS. Add. 28 399, fo. 7–9.
[5] e.g. the appointment of the marquis of Geraci to the post of *straticò* (or chief executive officer and judge) of Messina. Answer to a *consulta* of the Council of Italy, Oct. 26th, 1587. Simancas, Secreterías Provinciales, leg. 984.

Italy advanced towards a more comprehensive view of appointments. 'In general,' so ran a *consulta* of the year 1592, 'men serve better in those offices and positions which they occupy outside their own countries and where they have fewer vested interests. Thus the Sicilians serve better in Naples and Flanders, and the Neapolitans in Sicily, rather than in their own country.'[1] As always happened in statements by a body occupied in the concrete tasks of government, the emphasis was on the practical problem of appointing officials who might be immune from influences apt to corrupt the best executives. Yet it did contain the germ of a theory of empire according to which members of all constituent nations shared on equal terms in the administration. It is, moreover, significant that this theory was conceived in a council composed both of Spaniards and Italians.

The Sicilians were less successful when it came to preventing ecclesiastical benefices and the material benefits attaching to them from swelling the income of members of the dominant nation. Church patronage was one of the crown's most effective and jealously guarded weapons for maintaining control over the empire.[2] There was no better nor cheaper way of rewarding faithful service of soldiers and councillors than by granting them a share in the income of an episcopal see, or of binding a great noble to the royal house by making one of his sons abbot of a wealthy monastery. The tables of the Council of Italy were always piled high with petitions by persons who thought themselves entitled to the rents of religious foundations.[3] Of these the Spaniards both expected and received the lion's share. The viceroy Colonna suggested that the low standard of the Sicilian clergy was due to their poverty and their very small hope of advancement, since most benefices were given to the king's chaplains. The Council of Italy did not disagree with this view but was firm in its opinion that preference should always be given to those serving the king's person.[4] In 1503 Ferdinand the Catholic had issued a law by which any benefice held by a foreigner had to be given to a Sicilian when a vacancy occurred.[5] But the Spaniards

---

[1] *Consulta* of Nov. 12th, 1592; Simancas MS. Secret. Prov., leg. 985.
[2] Colonna to Philip II, Nov. 22nd, 1577, giving historical and legal justifications for the crown's ecclesiastical rights against papal claims. – One method of obtaining a benefice seems to have been to write a learned thesis proving the king's right to grant them. There are many such theses.
[3] Among the papers of the Council of Italy, at Simancas, there are whole bundles of *consultas* on requests for 'ventajas' and 'mercedes.'
[4] *Consulta* of March 26th, 1580, Simancas MS. Secret. Prov. leg. 982.
[5] Correspondence relating to Naples and Sicily, I. B.M. MS. Add. 28 394, fo. 66.

were not satisfied with this 'law of the alternative' which allowed them half the total income of the island's wealthy church. It was, in fact, almost the only material benefit which the Castilian ruling classes reaped from their master's sovereignty over Sicily; for captains and adventurers could win no American treasures in the island, and the hidalgos from the arid plateau of Old Castile, the men who sailed round the world and captured vast empires, had neither the desire nor the capacity to break the Italian and Catalan monopoly of the island's lucrative traffic in grain and silk. In consequence there was strong pressure on the government at Madrid to interpret the 'alternative' as applying only in cases of vacancy by death;[1] and despite the constant protests of the Sicilian Parliament,[2] Philip continued to appoint Spaniards on all other occasions, such as the promotion of an abbot or the transference of a bishop.[3]

However strong the legal claims of Aragonese and Hapsburg kings, Spanish rule in Italy was eventually based on military conquest. It was therefore to be expected that the Spaniards should seek to keep a tight hold on all military positions of strategic importance. The captaincies of the local militia and the feudal levies, indeed, were generally reserved to natives, for it was one of Philip's maxims to keep the Italian nobility contented.[4] But only Spaniards were employed in the command of the regular *tercios* and of castles and fortresses. The Venetian ambassador in Madrid, Leonardo Donato, tells how a Neapolitan gentleman with a long record of faithful service petitioned for a castellanship. For a long time he vainly importuned the Council of Italy until finally, in order to be rid of him, one of the councillors 'let the cat out of the bag' (*si lasciò uscir di bocca*) by telling him bluntly that His Majesty was determined never to give a castle to an Italian[5] and, added the ambassador, this rule was in fact followed with only one or two insignificant exceptions.

It is clear that the empire was governed according to some more

[1] Ibid. The Sicilian interpretation in a letter by the regent Ramondetta to Philip II, Sept. 5th, 1578.
[2] Testa, Capitula..., II, pp. 234, 246. f., 268.
[3] The Spanish regent León to Philip II; Correspondence... Naples and Sicily, I, B.M. MS. Add. 28 394, fo. 50; also Vázquez' correspondence about the abbey of Parco, Letters and Papers... B.M. MS. Add. 28 396, fo., 159.
[4] e.g. Instruccion... al duque de Maqueda, Simancas MS. Secret. Prov. lib. 803, fo. 31. 'Terneis assi mismo cuydado que el que se huviere de nombrar por Capitan del dicho servicio Militar sea de los principales y mas qualificados titulados del Reyno por que de otra manera se les daria causa de poca satisfaccion.'
[5] E. Albèri, Relazioni degli Ambasciatori Veneti, ser. 1, vol VI (Firenze 1858 etc.) p. 415.

or less definite maxims. But these constituted an attitude rather than clearcut principles, opinions rather than well-defined theories. 'The deliberate and self-conscious purpose',[1] so characteristic of Spanish imperialism in America, could not develop in the totally different atmosphere of the old-established Italian states. Here the conquerors were confronted not with a heathen people, 'living like animals,' men who might be regarded as 'by nature servile,'[2] but with Christians and Catholics whose civilization was in no respect inferior to their own. Here the Spaniards were neither colonial settlers on virgin soil nor despots among primitives. They were living in an urban and feudalized society which had laws and institutions of its own. The Spaniards never thought of imposing their whole legal system in their Mediterranean dominions as they had imposed it on the Indians of Mexico and Peru. It was sufficient that Charles V and Philip II should found their pretensions to the thrones of Naples and Sicily on the laws of these states; and Sicilian and Neapolitan jurists were not lacking to prove Hapsburg rights by learned legalistic treatises. It did not occur to either Spaniards or Italians that any other justification for Spanish rule was needed. No Las Casas nor Sepúlveda debated the laws and forms of government to be imposed on Neapolitans, Milanese and Sicilians, as they had debated them for the benefit of Mexican and Peruvian Indians.[3] Nor were the Italians themselves anxious to start the discussions against a background of burnt harvests and the sacked cities of a sixty years-old war, when the common danger from the Turks increased year by year.[4] The country would never have peace, wrote Cardinal Burgos, until one prince was absolute ruler of the whole peninsula or, at least, until one prince was sufficiently strong to nullify any hope of overthrow, even with foreign help; and, fortunately, it had now pleased Almighty God to place King Philip in this position.[5] Machiavelli's political writings were attacked or imitated, but his patriotic call to overthrow the foreign invader was forgotten.[6]

[1] J. H. Parry, The Spanish Theory of Empire in the Sixteenth Century (Cambridge 1940) p. 2.
[2] Ibid. p. 18.
[3] Ibid. pp. 32 ff.
[4] Cf. V. de Tocco, Ideali d'Indipendenza in Italia durante la Preponderanza Spagnuola (Messina 1926), p. 326. 'Sentimento quasi universale degli spiriti indipendenti fu il desiderio non di cacciare gli stranieri ma di unirsi tra italiani per conservare intatta la pericolante libertà che ancora restava...'
[5] Discorso del Cardinal Burgos al Ré Filippo sopra le cose d'Italia; B.M. MS. Egerton 534, fo. 96.
[6] Cf. I. Ferrari, Histoire de la Raison d'Etat (Paris 1860), for Italian political thought of the period.

The monarchy, in turn, was careful not to accentuate claims based on the rights of conquest, preferring (as Donato's anecdote shows) to keep dark even the principle of maintaining all-important strategic positions for itself. In Sicily this was even more important than in Naples and Milan. The Sicilians never recognized any right of conquest which the Aragonese kings put forward ever since Peter III helped the islanders to overthrow the rule of the French Angevins.[1] Foreigners who came to Sicily were impressed by the unanimity with which the natives insisted on the voluntary nature of their allegiance to the king.[2] The Sicilian Vespers, and the wars of independence which followed them, were the heroic period of the island's history. But as the spirit of national unity receded into the past and the Sicilians lost almost completely their ability for united action, they cherished all the more fiercely the legend which grew up around their supreme assertion of national will. The Vespers and John of Procida became the bugbear of all Spaniards in the kindom, for the Sicilians were not slow in hinting that what had been done once could be done again.[3] Yet, because of the hollowness of the threat, the legend strengthened conservative rather than revolutionary tendencies. As long as the king left their rights and privileges untouched he could be assured of their allegiance; for on allegiance the Sicilians prided themselves; they were giving it of their own free will.

The intervention of Peter of Aragon in Sicily nevertheless resembled the conquests of the Norman count Roger and of the Angevin Charles in that the conqueror was followed by great feudal vassals who had to be rewarded by grants of land. In this way there arose, side by side with the old Norman and Angevin families, a new feudal aristocracy, Argonese in origin, and strengthened a century later by the second 'conquest' of Sicily by Martin I. More than fifty Catalan families settled in the island[4] and, in the sixteenth and seventeenth centuries it was the nobles of Aragonese descent who obtained the majority of the ducal and princely titles.[5] These families inter-

[1] e.g. Francesco Fortunato, Avertimentos . . . ; Letters and Papers . . . Sicily, B.M. MS. Add. 28 396, fo. 399–402.
[2] L. Cabrera de Córdoba, Filipe Segundo Rey de España, vol. I (Madrid 1876), p. 417; also Placido Ragazzoni, Relazione di Sicilia, Bodleian MS. Rawlinson D.616, f. 191. This MS. copy is fuller than the relation printed in Albèri, Relazioni . . . , ser. 2, vol. v.
[3] Letter of Pedro Velázquez to Philip II on Febr. 5th, 1572; Letters and Papers . . . . Sicily, B.M. MS. Add. 28 396, fo. 6–28.
[4] Ranke, Die Osmanen . . . p. 210, quoting Capmany, Memorias sobre la marina, vol. II.
[5] See the list of noble families of Palermo in V. di Giovanni, Del Palermo Restaurato, in G. di Marzo, Biblioteca Storica e Letteraria di Sicilia, 2nd ser. vol. II (Palermo1869 etc) pp. 283 ff.

married with the older Sicilian nobility; although their outlook became more Sicilian than Aragonese, their loyalty to the crown of Aragon was beyond question. Nor was there, as in Naples, a large Angevin party which might want to turn the country over to France. Indeed, the legend of the Vespers kept alive anti-French sentiment which was a political force even when, centuries later, it had completely lost any basis in practical experience.

Since there were neither fundamental problems of loyalty, nor obvious contrasts between a master and a subject race, as there were in the Americas, the need for a consistent theory of empire was not immediately felt either by Spaniards or by Sicilians. The basic class structure of society in Italy and Spain was similar, and in Sicily its justice did not come to be seriously questioned until the middle of the seventeenth century.[1] Only gradually did the practical demands of imperial administration compel the king and his ministers to face the fundamental problem of the true nature of the relationship between Spain and her Italian dependencies. Thus the theory of empire, which came into existence by force of circumstances, was never a coherent body of carefully thought-out principles. It was little more than a number of rules of conduct or *ad hoc* justifications for imperial actions based on certain generalized patterns of political thought.

Rooted in the tradition of political independence and local self-sufficiency, the Sicilians were concerned only with their own problems and needs, and the king fully approved of this attitude. For Philip reigned in the island as king of Sicily and not as king of Castile nor did he have his father's title of Holy Roman Emperor. Unlike his great antagonist, Suleiman, he was not the sultan, the padisha of all his lands. The essentially western and medieval conception of kingship implicit in Philip's attitude was now beginning to break down and make way for a wider sense of political obligation, the Turkish fleet acting as a catalyst in this process. In 1565 Malta had been defended against Dragut and Ali Pasha by the combined efforts of Philip's Mediterranean states.[2] With the island's defences wrecked by some of the fiercest fighting which ever took place between Christians and Moslems, and with Goletta denuded of supplies, the King had to look forward to a renewal of Suleiman's assault. On December 31st he wrote to the viceroy of Sicily, asking him to call a special session of Parliament in order to obtain some 150,000

[1] cf. Koenigsberger, The Revolt of Palermo in 1647, The Cambridge Historical Journal, vol. vIII, No. 3, 1946.
[2] Correspondence of the viceroy Toledo with Philip II, Colección de Documentos Inéditos para la Historia de España; ed. Marqu. de Pidal etc., vol. xxix.

scudi as a Sicilian contribution towards the estimated defence cost of 1,400,000.[1] The Turk was the common enemy of Christendom, so ran the letter, and neither the Order of St. John nor the garrison of Goletta could by themselves resist so powerful an enemy. Malta was the bastion (*antemuralla*) of Sicily, and Castile was already contributing heavily towards its defence. If the royal patrimony could have supplied all needs, and if it had not been entirely exhausted by previous efforts, both for the public weal and for the particular interests of his provinces, the king would have preferred to relieve his vassals of this burden. But he had no doubt that the affection and readiness to serve, which his loyal subjects had always shown on similar occasions, would not fail him in this hour of urgent necessity. With his own hand he added a postscript: 'I would not ask you this if here (i.e. in Castile) some form could be found of supplying the needs which I have explained, just as was done last year; but as this is impossible, there is no choice; and thus I request you urgently that you will arrange this since you see that it is necessary, because of the great importance of these two places (i.e. Malta and Goletta).'

It is evident that Philip still accepted the medieval principle that the king should 'live on his own' – an idea which in England had not died entirely even in the reign of James I. But the assumptions on which this principle were based were no longer valid. As the Turkish war grew in intensity, all the resources of the empire had to be called upon. From 1571 to 1577 the duke of Terranova's government in Sicily spent more than $1\frac{1}{2}$ million scudi both on Sicilian defence and on supplies for the whole Spanish armada.[2] This was during the Lepanto campaign and the dark years following the defection of Venice from the League, when Tunis and Goletta were lost and the danger of invasion seemed as menacing as at the time of the great Suleiman. As it had done on the occasion of the king's earlier appeal,[3] Parliament responded with extraordinary grants,[4] and the president of the kingdom, himself a Sicilian, regarded it as natural that Sicily should fulfil her imperial obligations.[5] In proportion to her size,

[1] Simancas MS. Secret. Prov. leg. 1597, fo. 258–9.
[2] Terranova to Philip II, April 30th, 1577, Simancas MS. Estado leg. 1147; corroborated by Colonna to Philip II, June 10th, 1577, ibid.
[3] A. Mongitore, Parlamenti Generali del Regno di Sicilia, vol. I (Palermo 1749) pp. 340 ff.
[4] Ibid. pp. 361 f; 370 ff.
[5] Terranova, letter cit.; cf. also his published correspondence in Società Siciliana per la Storia Patria, Documenti per servire alla storia di Sicilia, ser. 1, vol. II. Carlo d'Aragona, Corrispondenza particolare con Filippo II.

he wrote to his master, he could not believe that any other kingdom had done as much as Sicily.¹

During the Turkish wars Sicily was in the front-line of military and naval operations, and her own immediate interests coincided with those of the empire as a whole. When Don John of Austria's victorious galleys crowded into the harbour of Messina, it was obvious to all Sicilians that the empire was supporting them as much as they were supporting the empire. When the fall of Tunis and Goletta led to an immediate increase of corsair activities around the island's coast, it was easy to see that only generous contributions to the cost of imperial defence could save Sicily from worse disasters. From about 1580, however, the strategic situation changed completely. African pirates continued to prey on merchant shipping while the Sicilian squadron did little to deter them, but the king and the sultan had concluded a truce. For many years to come no full scale invasion had to be feared, yet the strain which Philip's imperialist policy imposed on the empire's resources increased rather than diminished. Galleys from the Sicilian navy had to support the invasion of Portugal; grain and armaments were required in Spain to fit out the Invincible Armada; and the unpaid *tercios* in Flanders were ever clamouring for money which neither the treasury of Castile nor the silver mines of Peru could provide in sufficient quantities. A more comprehensive theory of empire was now needed to justify demands for contributions no longer used for the immediate and obvious benefits of Sicily. This was all the more important as the once ready acceptance of imperial obligations by the Sicilians had changed to an attitude of resentment and obstruction. Colonna complained that the members of the Court of the Royal Patrimony, in charge of the country's financial administration, objected to a single *real* being sent out of the country 'as if ... (the government in Madrid) simply pocketed what was given for the fleet.' He asked to be allowed to send money without the approval of his ministers which was normally necessary for all government expenditure.²

In 1589 the king's Spanish advisers joined the Sicilians in their protests. Following strong representations by the viceroy, the count of Alvadeliste, about the financial exhaustion of the kingdom and

¹ Terranova to Philip II, 1573, together with the accounts of military expenditure for 1571-73, Simancas MS. Estado, leg. 1141.
² Colonna to Philip II, Febr. 25th, 1580, ibid. leg. 1149.

the demands made upon it,[1] the Council of Italy submitted to the king that Sicily should be spared further contributions for causes 'which were not her own.' The complete failure of his advisers to consider the interests of all his dominions in terms of his empire policy, roused Philip to give a clear statement of his own ideas on colonial obligations to the crown. They were modest enough, perhaps coloured still by recollections of Spanish objections to his father's neglect of the peninsula – an attitude to which Philip's Spanish upbringing could not fail to make him sympathetic. 'Except in the most urgent cases,' he wrote in reply to the council's *consulta*, 'it is not the custom to transfer the burdens of one kingdom to another. And since God has entrusted me with so many (kingdoms), since all are in my charge, and since in the defence of one all are preserved, it is just that all should help me; and the council has done its duty in saying what it did in this consulta.'[2]

The clearest formulation of a theory of empire came not from a Spaniard but from an Italian, Marc Antonia Colonna.[3] His arguments were those of a general and strategist. The Sicilians might haggle about money to be sent to Spain, yet in case of a serious attack, the defence of the island would not depend on some 200,000 ducats more or less; thus Colonna argued. For such a sum would

[1] Alvadeliste to Philip II, March 31st, 1589. Simancas MS. Secret. Prov. leg. 984. Money and goods to a total value of more than 533,000 scudi had been sent out of the kingdom in one year, only about half of this was covered by revenue.
[2] *Consulta* of June 12th and answer of Nov. 11th, 1589. Ibid.
[3] It is, perhaps, not surprising that this should have been so. Members of old and famous Italian families, like the Colonna, Doria and Pescara, would feel the necessity of justifying their position in the service of the king of Spain. As they naturally would not accept for themselves any inferiority of status to the Spanish Grandees, it followed that they must regard Milan, Naples and Sicily as states ranking equally with the Spanish kingdoms in an international, rather than a Spanish, empire. This may well have been unconscious reasoning, but it was sufficiently general to create an attitude which aroused the uncomprehending astonishment of Italians normally living outside the Spanish sphere of influence. The Venetian Alvise Lando wrote in his *Relazione di Napoli* of 1580 (Albèri, Relazioni..., ser. 2, vol. v, p. 450): 'Many have been the kingdoms and republics which, by their own deaths, have given birth to other kingdoms and dominions, and which have transformed themselves into these latter with the extinction of their own name; and many others, troubled for a time by invasions and hostile assaults, have finally either lost their liberty or reconfirmed their natural greatness; but there has never been a kingdom, like this kingdom of Naples, which has fallen so often without having fallen and which, in perpetual bondage and having become so many times its own enemy, should with the greatness of its own foes have always boasted liberty and dominion.' An acute observer, like Lando, would undoubtedly have found a similar paradox in Sicily. The origin of the process of subconscious rationalization of subjection into an appreciation of empire has been noted by Toynbee, A Study of History, vol. v, p. 620: '... we find in general that as a matter of fact an empire is apt to play a less important part in the lives of the empire-builders who have exerted themselves to erect it as a monument to their own egotism than it plays in the lives of their involuntary subjects who have been annexed by force of arms and who have been chafing under a yoke which they feel both cramping and humiliating.'

never be sufficient to build a fleet strong enough to defend Sicily; only the combined resources of all Hapsburg provinces could provide the means for this purpose. If Malta could be relieved, how much easier would it not be to relieve Sicily in case of need?[1] All the king's dominions formed one body and the members must help each other as much as they could, the more so as long distances between them made defence more difficult. The ordinary expenses of each kingdom had, indeed, to be met first; but, concluded, the viceroy, 'I have never seen Your Majesty's affairs in danger, or lost, for lack of money, men or munitions, but because there was an abundance in one part and want in another' and because the vanity of ministers prevented them from giving full support to their colleagues.[2]

Colonna had thus arrived at a conception of the empire as a political unit, the resources of whose component parts should be shared for the benefit of whichever was in most need of them. Yet his view was not fundamentally different from that of the king. Like most of his contemporaries he did not even use the term 'empire'. If the king's formulation of the concept of imperial obligation was not as advanced as the observations of his viceroy, this was due to Philip's inability to emancipate himself from the traditional view of the financial independence of each dominion, an independence to be set aside only in cases of the most urgent necessity. It is precisely because Philip thought of himself as the only connecting link between the component states that he could not conceive the idea of an empire as a living organization with an inherent purpose, transcending the unity provided by the crown. But in practice his oblique conception had little effect on his policy. Since the empire was in an almost continual state of emergency, demands by the central government for support from the Italian Provinces became an established practice; nor was this a one-sided process, for Castile contributed more than any other kingdom.[3] The sums of money and the number of ships and soldiers extracted from Naples, Milan and Sicily depended eventually not on more or less clearly formulated theories of imperial obligation, but on the rights and powers of the crown in

[1] Colonna to Philip II, Feb. 25th, 1580, Simancas MS. Estado. leg. 1149.
[2] Colonna to Philip II, May 24th, 1582; ibid. leg. 1152. Colonna always emphasized that he tried to co-operate with the governors of the other Italian dominions (e.g. Letter to Philip II, June 10th, 1577, ibid. leg. 1147), but often complained of lack of reciprocity (e.g. letter of Oct. 14th, 1577, ibid.).
[3] e.g. Colonna letter cit. of Feb. 25th, 1580. 'Hé querido decir esto ... que à mi juycio son consideraciones necessarias, y no, que el dinero de Vuestra Magestad no vaya de una parte à otra, cumpliendo assi su Real servicio como si de España no se sacasse la gran cantidad que se sabe...'

each particular state and on the resistance which the Italians put up against Spanish demands. Yet the failure to develop empire theory beyond a few statements of principle was to prove a grave weakness in the structure of the Spanish Monarchy. The absence of a coherent and comprehensible justification of the empire, beyond the monarchical principle and administrative necessity, left Spanish rule in Italy an alien institution. At best, it was supported by the vested interests of a large section of the nobility and liked or disliked by the mass of the people according to the good or bad governments of successive viceroys.[1] The Spanish Empire in Italy never succeeded in creating that feeling of veneration which was so striking a feature of the Roman Empire even when it was no more than a memory. When the treaty of Utrecht finally put an end to the Spanish Empire, there were few in Italy who mourned its passing.

[1]Cf. Leonardo Donato, Relazione di Spagna, 1573, in Albèri, Relazioni..., ser. 1. vol. VI, p. 415. 'Non mancono ai regnicoli (i.e. in Naples), così grandi come piccoli, occasioni di mala affezione cogli spagnuoli, oltra la universale che in cadauno è di veder mal volentieri il dominio delle cose sue in poter di stranieri. I piccoli per le eccessive gravezze li odiano, e i grandi ne stanno mal contenti perciocchè nel godimento degli onori e carichi hanno poca parte. Ma con tutto questo ha S.M. una gran banda di parziali suoi, che per il proprio interesse la sostentariano, quelli cioè che godono i beni dei fuorusciti e le infinite confiscazioni che per tempora sone state fatte nelle guerre passate.' The Venetian ambassadors are not always entirely trustworthy witnesses; yet it is significant that (apart from the general dislike of foreigners) Donato mentions only material advantages and disadvantages as reasons for loyalty or disloyalty to the king.

CHAPTER THREE

Imperial Administration at the Centre

AGAINST the conservatism of Spanish political thought, Philip the Second's improvements in the technique of imperial administration stand out as a revolutionary advance. In the vast and unprecedented imperial problems facing the king and his advisers, the experience of the Aragonese Empire could provide but little guidance. This medieval union of Mediterranean kingdoms had primarily served the mercantile interests of Catalonia. Direct administrative control offered few advantages either to the merchants of Barcelona or the kings of Aragon who profited by the latter's trade. As late as 1522, when Charles V confirmed the authority of the Council of Aragon,[1] he restricted its activities to those of a supreme court for Valencia, the Balearics and the Spanish dominions in Italy: Sicily, Sardinia, Naples and Milan.[2] Administratively, the council acted only as a link between the king and the governors of these dominions, and politically its influence remained slight.[3]

In the sixteenth century, however, the trade of Barcelona was already in deep decline. Naples and Milan had been conquered for reasons more political and dynastic than economic. The sectional considerations of a declining class could not form the basis of an empire of the dimensions of Philip's domain, and the Hapsburg ruler had no desire to see the Aragonese Empire continue as a separate entity within his possessions. Philip, therefore, preferred not to extend the competence of the Council of Aragon, compromised as it was in his eyes by its Catalan traditions and not entirely trustworthy for the simple fact that its president and five councillors were never Castilians. They were Aragonese, Valencianos and Catalans. It was, therefore, infinitely preferable to create a completely new organ for the control of Milan, Naples and Sicily, a

[1] Established by Ferdinand in 1494.
[2] C. Giardina, Sul governo centrale spagnuolo e sull' anno di fondazione del supremo consiglio d'Italia; Archivio Storico per la Sicilia, vol. IV/V (Palermo 1938/39) pp. 252 f.
[3] R. B. Merriman, The Rise of the Spanish Empire, vol. III (New York 1925), p. 153. Merriman thinks it likely that the Council of Aragon did, in fact, extend its authority into the political sphere during the reign of Charles V. But this development probably did not go very far.

body, moreover, in which the principal administrators were from Castile.[1]

So important did Philip consider the break with the Aragonese tradition that he set up the Supreme Council of Italy even before he returned to Spain from the Netherlands.[2] On July 26th 1558,the Duke of Francavilla was appointed president of the newly-formed council,[3] and in January 1559 the viceroys of Naples and Sicily were informed of the appointment of Gonzalo Pérez and Diego de Vargas as secretaries for Italy.[4] Pérez was designated secretary of state for Italy. Vargas' province was judicature, the administration of the Italian provinces and royal patronage. The Council of Aragon, having lost control over Italy, retained authority over Aragon and Catalonia, thus preserving the unity of the medieval (but not the more modern) Aragonese Empire, and emphasizing the union of the crowns of Aragon and Castile.

The first set of instructions for the Council of Italy, establishing its organization, powers and functions, was issued by Philip from Toledo on the 3rd December, 1559.[5] In essentials the structure of the body resembled the other ten councils which had been developed since the times of the Catholic Kings, and by which Spain and the Spanish Empire were governed.[6] The six councillors, called regents, were all lawyers; each of the three Italian provinces, Sicily, Naples and Milan, having one Spanish and one local regent. The president was never a lawyer and had no vote in legal matters. This post was always held by a man of great political experience, a distinguished grandee such as Francavilla,[7] the father-in-law of Ruy Gómez de Silva, or a high ecclesiastical dignitary such as Cardinal Granvelle and Cardinal Quiroga. Under the president and the regents was a host of minor officials of varying importance. Some, like the treasurer-

---

[1] S. A. Riol, Creación de todos los Tribunales de España; MS. of 1726; Madrid, Biblioteca Nacional, MS. 10, 558.
[2] For the sake of convenience, the council will from now be called the Council of Italy.
[3] Letters and Papers relating to Italy, vol. I, British Museum MS. Add. 28 399, fo. 196.
[4] Letters and Papers ... Add. 28 399, fo. 2. For a discussion of the date of the establishment of the Council of Italy cf. Giardina, Sul governo .... His conclusions are borne out by the letter of appointment of Francavilla. On the way back from Flanders to Spain, the registers of the dispatches establishing the council were lost (Philip II to Pescara, Jan. 25th, 1571, Simancas MS., Secret. Prov. leg. 1598 fo. 25). This may well be the reason why Philip wrote as late as December 1560, informing Medinaceli of the setting-up of the Council of Italy (ibid. leg. 1597, fo. 12).
[5] They are printed in C. Giardina, II Supremo Consilgio d'Italia, in Atti della Reale Accademia di Scienze, Lettere e Belle Arti di Palermo, 3rd ser. vol. XIX (1936) Appendix 1.
[6] Merriman, The Rise of the Spanish Empire, IV (New York 1934) ch. 36.
[7] His full name was Diego Hurtado de Mendoza, Duke of Francavilla and Prince of Melito.

general, the count of Chinchón, were taken over from the Council of Aragon, and had, like the regents, a vote in the council;[1] but not all were established immediately, and the council continued to experiment with the organization of its staff. As in the case of all the other councils, the king never attended their meetings, but communicated with the councillors through secretaries.

The remainder of the council instructions of 1559 related to functions and minute details of procedure which, according to Philip's usual custom, received as much emphasis as the work of the body itself. The Council of Italy took the place of the Council of Aragon as the supreme court of appeal for the Italian dominions. For Sicily this function was limited to cases involving foreigners[2] and to feudal cases; the Sicilians enjoying the privilege of having all other cases tried up to the final instance inside their own kingdom. Even the trial of feudal cases by the Council of Italy was strictly contrary to Sicilian privileges[3] which the king's representative had sworn to observe in his name;[4] but Philip was peculiarly sensitive of his rights as feudal overlord,[5] and Sicilian litigants were often well pleased to have another court of appeal when their claims had failed in Sicily. As all Sicilian courts were influenced either by family and political interests, or else were accused of being so influenced, it was often worth the great expense and delay involved in transferring a case to the very different political atmosphere of Madrid where anything might happen.[6]

Apart from its functions as a court of law, the council supervised all aspects of the administration of the Italian dominions, especially finance, trade and customs, the appointment to military and civil offices, and the grant of privileges, titles, and benefices. The regents dealt with dominion petitions, and drafted royal orders and laws for transmission to the viceroys. Short of interfering in the day-to-day government of the provinces, the king clearly meant to supervise all

[1] Giardina, Il Supremo Consiglio ... pp. 37 f.; E. Albèri, Relazioni degli ambasciatori veneti, 1st ser. vol. v. p. 66.
[2] e.g. the case of 'The Trial', in my article, English Merchants in Naples and Sicily in the 17th century, in English Historical Review, vol. LXII, No. 224, July, 1947, pp.308ff.
[3] V. La Mantia, Storia della Legislazione civile e criminale de Sicilia, vol. I (Palermo 1874) p. 214.
[4] A. Mongitore, Parlamenti Generali del Regno di Sicilia, vol. II (Palermo 1749) pp. 285 f.
[5] e.g. Philip's instructions to his ambassadors in Rome, on the occasion of an attempted interference in a feudal case by Cardinal Alessandrini; Philip stressed 'el notable prejuyzio que se hizo a nuestra real jurisdiction ... en especial que es feudal, y cuyo juyzio nos toca como a directo y supremo señor del feudo ...' C. Piot, Correspondence du Cardinal de Granvelle, V (Brussels 1886) pp. 116 f.
[6] V. La Mantia, Storia della legislazione ... p. 214.

aspects of their administration in a way which would not have been possible through the old Council of Aragon.[1] It was in keeping with this policy that the organization of the council developed almost entirely on the administrative and not on the judicial side. In 1579 a new set of royal instructions provided for the systematic collection of information from the Italian provinces and for the registering of all work done by the Council of Italy.[2] Books were to be kept recording all judicial, financial and military appointments with the recommendations of the viceroys; all presentations to ecclesiastical benefices, from the archbishop of Palermo to the prior of the smallest monastery, were to be duly noted, and the viceroys were to search for documents establishing all the ecclesiastical rights of the crown, all royal titles, and all its papal investitures; copies of these were to be registered in the council, and finally the municipal laws and constitutions of all towns of the Spanish provinces in Italy were to be collected and classified.[3] In the last decade of Philip's reign the office of conservator-general of the Patrimony of Italy was established, probably at first only to deal with this vast amount of information and to make it available to the councillors.[4] Characteristically the new officer's powers increased rapidly to include the supervision of the whole financial administration of the Italian provinces, and a decree of 1601 accorded him the decisive vote in the council on all matters concerning the king's 'patrimony'.[5]

Nevertheless, during the whole of Philip the Second's reign, the council's judicial business was still considered its most important

---

[1] Philip developed but did not initiate this policy. There are indications that even the Council of Aragon made itself very unpopular with the viceroys by interfering with their actions. Thus Vega complained that the council had ordered the release of the *pretore* of Palermo whom he had imprisoned for fraud (Vega to Philip II, June 8th, 1558(?), in Papiers d'Etat du Cardinal de Granvelle, vol. v, ed. Ch. Weiss, Paris 1844, pp. 159 ff).But this, too, was a legal case. Unfortunately the early history of the Council of Aragon is virtually unknown. In the latter part of Philip's reign its functions were largely parallel with those of the Council of Italy. Cf. C. Riba, El Consejo Supremo de Aragón en el Reinado de Felipe II (Valencia 1914).

[2] Papers relating to Italian States . . . I, B.M. MS. Add. 28 465, fo. 6-7.

[3] I have not been able to find these books either in Madrid or Simancas. While I am fairly certain that they really do not exist in Madrid, it is quite impossible to be certain of the non-existence of any document in the vast and largely un-catalogued archives of Simancas.

[4] The earliest reference to the office which I have been able to find is in a list of salaries for the Council of Italy in 1591. Letters and Papers . . . Sicily, B.M. MS. Add. 28 396, fo. 489–97.

[5] Giardina, Il Supremo Consiglio . . . , p. 109, note 3.

activity.[1] Even when the lay councillors had attained to a position of equality with the lawyers in the seventeenth century,[2] the council remained basically a court of law performing administrative as well as judicial functions. It was as if the judicial committee of the Privy Council in London had been fused with the Colonial Office to do the work of both.

In contrast with its wide administrative powers, the Council of Italy was never intended to be a policy-controlling body; although it was allowed to deal with routine matters of diplomacy, such as relations with Venice,[3] all important 'matters of state' were expressly reserved for the king and the Council of State.[4] If questions of high policy alone were reserved for the king and his principal advisers, the Council of Italy might have been a very efficient organ of government. The king, however, insisted on being consulted on practically the whole of the Council's business. In particular, he kept close control over official appointments and over the granting of all types of privileges and advancements. Most offices in Sicily were tenable for only one or two years, and every year, in March, the Viceroy sent lists to the council of suitable entrants, stating their qualifications, and in September his own recommendations for the appointments. These lists, endorsed with the comments of the council, were transmitted in the form of a *consulta* to the king for final decision, and often enough, at the end of August, there was a minor crisis at the viceregal court of Palermo when the answers from Madrid had not arrived in time. Apart from these official appointments, there were innumerable private requests for advancement. Of fifty-four *consultas* from the Council of Italy which were in the king's hands on one day in 1583, no less than thirty-seven were private petitions.[5] Granvelle, who had to deal with these *consultas* in the king's absence, complained bitterly that it was impossible to work through the ever-

---

[1] Correspondence relating to Naples, II, 1583–1609, B.M. MS. Add. 28 398, fo. 174. The regent Juan Francisco de Ponte to the King, Dec. 8th, 1595. 'Las causas principales por las quales Vuestra Majestad se sirve tenernos en este su supremo consejo de Italia son, La primera, para prover las cosas de Justicia y las demas pretensiones de particulares. La segunda, para mirar a la conservacion y crecentamiento de su Real Patrimonio, y La tercera, para el govierno y conservacion de sus estados y Reynos de los quales se tracta en el advertiendo y proveyendo lo que conviene.'
[2] Giardina, Il Supremo Consiglio . . . , pp. 31 f.
[3] Relazione di Spagna by Paolo Tiepolo in 1563. Albèri, Relazioni . . . , ser. 1, vol. v, p. 66.
[4] Giardina, Il Supremo Consiglio . . . p. 130. 'Que los cartas de Ministros que fueren de negocios ordinarios se lean en Consejo, salvo quando en ellas hubiera cosas de estado, que entonces se saquen los puntos, que se hubieran de ver en Consejo, y se apunte alli lo que no fuere de calidad que se haya de remitir á consulta.'
[5] Correspondence relating to Naples and Sicily, vol. II, B.M. MS. Add. 28 395, fo. 34-36.

increasing mountain of papers.[1] The king repeatedly issued strict orders that the regents were not to accept presents from the viceroys or from private persons nor were they to try to further the interests of their relatives: but the regents openly continued to petition the king or induced the viceroys to petition for benefices for themselves and for members of their families. The king's own secretary, Mateo Vázquez, maintained a lengthy correspondence with nearly all the members of the council and with other important ministers, to secure for himself the income of the rich Sicilian abbey of Parco.[2]

Philip's personal administration of the patronage did not give him the degree of control over his servants which he hoped to exercise.[3] It was in most cases impossible, even for such a hard-working and well-informed ruler as the king, to do anything but follow the advice of his council. The result of this system was that those whose requests were not granted blamed the king for having specially invented the procedure of the *consulta* to be able to refuse them more easily, while those who obtained what they wanted were more grateful to the ministers than to the king. It was considered more useful to please the ministers than to serve their master.[4]

While the system of government by *consulta* had the effect of increasing rather than diminishing the control of the council over patronage, it also resulted in increasing the importance of the secretary of the council as against the regents.[5] The secretary received all dispatches from Italy and every Saturday opened them in the presence of the president of the council. Together they decided what subjects had to be sent to the Council of State and the order in which the remainder were to be dealt with in the Council of Italy. It often happened that the president and the secretary would on these occasions decide important matters between them without reference to the regents. The secretary attended the meetings of the council and, although he was nominally dependent on the regents, he had a vote in some matters, and his close contact with the king often gave his views a decisive importance even in questions where he did not vote. He prepared the *consultas* for the king and would discuss

[1] Ibid. fo. 32.
[2] Letters and Papers relating to Sicily 1572–1603, B.M. MS. Add. 28 396, fo. 90–110, 147–216, 307–321. The abbey is situated a few miles to the south west of Palermo.
[3] Giardina, Il Supremo Consiglio . . . p. 131. Philip expressly stated '. . . que de me solo han de depender, y recebir merced por los servizios que me hizieren.' It might have been his motto.
[4] Paolo Tiepolo in Albèri, Relazioni . . . p. 66.
[5] It seems that after Gonzalo Pérez' death, and possibly before, Vargas was the sole secretary of the council, with Gaitan acting as his assistant. Antonio Pérez dealt with Italian problems in the Council of State.

difficult problems arising out of the dispatches from Italy with the regent who dealt with the particular province. During a 'visit' of the Council of Italy – a one-man commission of investigation to which all officials of the Spanish Government, from the most humble clerk to the viceroys themselves, were from time to time subjected – it was stated that the ministers had practically become servants of the secretary.[1] Between 1576 and 1578 the whole position of the office and of its staff came under review. Antonio Padilla, the visitor, found that while Vargas could be exonerated from taking bribes, Gaitan, his assistant, had accepted large gifts from Italy. Francisco de Idiáquez, his other assistant, had a reputation for honesty, but he, too, had not been above accepting small favours.[2] In the seal and register offices there was great confusion. The seal of Sicily and the financial rights attached to it, had been sold to the count of Buscemi who in turn sold them to Ottavio del Bosco. Bosco, a Sicilian noble, paid Vargas thirty ducats a year to use the seal and Vargas paid one of his officials six ducats to do the work. There was a similar arrangement with the seal of Naples, and the emoluments of the seal of Milan were shared by four different parties.[3] Such political simony was typical of the Spanish system of government which regarded offices and rights as sources of financial profit, and it was equally typical that nothing was said about the seals in the new set of instructions for the Council of Italy which the king issued in 1579.[4]

The control of the register office was also divided between different persons, and its work was done partly by officials from Vargas' office and partly by officials from the Council of Aragon – an overlapping of staffs which caused considerable confusion.[5]

Yet after the death of Vargas the appointment of the new secretary and the limits of his competence were decided on political and not on administrative grounds. Antonio Pérez claimed the office with its large emoluments over and above the regular salary of two thousand ducats. He was supported by the Marquis de los Vélez, by the Inquisitor-General Quiroga and by the king himself. But the Count of Chinchón, the treasurer of the council, and all the other enemies of Pérez insisted on the reformation of the office and the limitation of its powers as against those of the president; not, primarily, because

[1] Letters and Papers . . . vol. I. B.M. MS. Add. 28 399 fo. 182.
[2] Ibid. fo. 192–5.
[3] Ibid. fo. 188.
[4] Printed in Giardina, Il Supremo Consiglio . . . Appendix II, also in Papers relating to Italian States in the 16th and 17th cent. vol. I, B.M. M.S. Add. 28 465, fo. 2–7.
[5] Letters and Papers . . . vol. I, B.M. MS. Add. 28 399, fo. 189–191.

they wanted to increase the efficiency of the council, but because they feared a further increase in Pérez' power. Under these circumstances Pérez refused to accept the appointment.[1] There seems to have been some difficulty in filling the post, for Cutinario, the experienced Neapolitan regent, also refused;[2] but in August 1579 Gabriel Zayas was appointed with Idiáquez as his assistant. Since the predecessors of Zayas had on their own authority made appointments to some of the best-paid offices in Sicily, such as the Pretore and Capitan of Palermo,[3] the instructions given him laid special stress on the duty to refer appointments to the king and also emphasized that he should give his opinion in council only when asked – except when he should feel it his duty to intervene in the interests of the king.[4] This last was probably the operative clause which left a skilful secretary sufficient room to assert himself. His salary, which was twice that of the regents, was in any case enough to indicate their relative importance. Yet even these limitations of the secretary's powers were not all advantageous. A few months after the issue of the new instructions Idiáquez complained that there was great confusion in the distribution of dispatches, that Zayas opened them and sent them directly to the acting president, Francisco Hernández de Lievana, and that the regents did not see them all. *Consultas* which were sent to the Council of State used to be taken there by Vargas and Gaitaín who then acted as secretaries in the Council of State during the discussion of these *consultas*. They were now taken there by Lievana himself or handed over to Zayas or Antonio Pérez. Zayas was inexperienced; matters which should have taken four or five days took as many weeks; and when dispatches were assigned to Pérez, they were dealt with by secretaries of the Council of State who were not interested in them and from whom it was difficult to retrieve papers.[5]

Not unnaturally, the regents were intensely jealous of the secretary's power. Already in 1578 they had pressed for his replacement

[1] A. de Herrera y Tordesillas, Historia General del Mundo ... del Tiempo del Rey Felipe II., vol. III (Madrid 1606 etc) pp. 276 f. Also quoted by Ranke, Die Osmanen und die Spanische Monarchie, pp. 152 f.
[2] In Letters and Papers ... vol. I, B.M. MS. Add. 28 399, there is a letter by Vázquez to Cutinario, dated August 8th, 1579, offering him the 'Secreteria de Italia toda entera' (fo. 267). Only a week later, on the 14th, Zayas thanks Vázquez for his promotion to the secretaryship (fo. 265). If Cutinario refused, the appointment of Zayas was quite unusually quick.
[3] Letters and Papers ... vol. II, B.M. MS. Add. 28 400 fo. 63.
[4] Giardina, Il Supremo Consiglio ... Appendix III. p. 139. Instructions to Zayas: ... salvo quando se os ofreciere advertir alguna cosa tocante a mi servicio que entonces terneis obligacion de hacerlo (i.e. to speak up).'
[5] Letters and Papers ... vol. I, B.M. MS. Add. 28 399 fo. 298–305.

by three clerks entirely dependent on the council (a system which prevailed in the Council of Aragon). The visitor, Padilla, had advised against this, stressing the difficulty of preserving secrecy in the council's deliberations when these were attended by a number of minor officials. Philip had followed his opinions which coincided with his own preference for powerful secretaries more dependent on himself than on the council.[1] But after the death of Zayas in 1595 he consented to have the office divided between Martin de Gante for Sicily, Francisco de Idiáquez for Naples and Juan López de Zárate for Milan, both de Gante and Idiáquez having two, and Zárate one assistant.[2] Not content with this compromise, the regents now followed up their advantage by drafting *consultas* without the intervention of the secretaries and by trying to obtain control over all incoming dispatches. Idiáquez protested vigorously in the name of the secretariat, but the old balance was not restored until the reign of Philip III.[3]

Confusion and a certain degree of corruption could never be entirely avoided. For how could this have been possible if those in the highest position and nearest the king were involved? Vázquez' behaviour has already been mentioned.[4] Chinchón was considered to be 'free from personal interest', but it was well known that his private business interests were not inseparable from the interests of the state.[5] Or what could be expected of Philip's last president of the council, the count of Miranda, who had employed his nine years as viceroy of Naples in amassing a fortune of a million gold ductas[6]? Padilla's visit of the council consisted of an initial period of great vigour, resulting in the fall of Gaitan and in the promulgation of the orders of 1579, but then dragged on without making any further impression. In 1583 Granvelle wrote despondently that after twelve years those who had been thought the most guilty had died and yet no end of the visit seemed in sight although he had been assured that it would finish soon.[7]

[1] Letters and Papers..., I. B.M. MS. Add. 28 399, fo. 182, 192–5.
[2] Papers relating to Italian States, I. B.M. MS. Add. 28 465, fo. 8–9. The reason for the reorganization stated in the royal order was that Idiáquez could not manage all the work by himself, much as the king would have liked him to do so.
[3] Riol, Creación..., Madrid, B.N. MS. 10, 558.
[4] Above, p. 64.
[5] The Venetian ambassador, Simone Contarini, quoted by Riba, El Consejo..., p. xix.
[6] Provided, always, that the testimony of the gossip-loving Venetian ambassadors may be believed. But their accusations were often true enough. Girolamo Ramusio, Relazione di Napoli, 1597, in Albèri, Relazioni..., Appendix, p. 324.
[7] Granvelle to Margaret of Parma, Nov. 30th, 1583; Piot, Correspondence..., vol. x, p. 416.

The count of Barajas' description of the confusion and lack of regular rules of procedure in the Council of Castile[1] applied no less in the Council of Italy. All litigants tried to hand their memorials to the president and for this purpose bribed his servants without his knowledge. There was no knowing when a case might be called, and poor priests had been known to wait for months in the court yard only to find that their lawyer was not available at the decisive moment. Even if the hearing of a case had started it might be shelved and another taken up so as to be fair to all, and then the first case would have to wait until the same judges happened to sit together again. Decisions in the Council of Italy were often given before all judges concerned had seen all relevant papers of a case, and judgments were published before being announced to the parties in the action.[2] As a result of these shortcomings, accusations against the personal integrity of the regents became increasingly frequent, and cases were held up more than ever. In 1586 the king was obliged to introduce a system of deposits to be forfeited to the accused regent and to the government if the accusations could not be substantiated.[3]

Yet with all its muddle, with its interminable delays and with the doubtful honesty of many of its officers, the Council of Italy proved itself vastly superior to most of the courts in the provinces under its control. By the beginning of the seventeenth century it had built up a fine reputation for impartiality as a court of law, recognized even by neutral and hostile observers.[4]

While the Council of Italy as a body was not called upon to discuss vital matters of policy, its influence thereon was still considerable. Its practical control of patronage and appointments largely determined the nature of the administration of the Italian dependencies. The viceroys themselves were appointed by the Council of State, but the Council of Italy, because of its closer contact with the king and his chief advisers, could further or hinder the viceroy's policy and might even effect his recall. Owing to the special conditions of government in Sicily, the viceroys there were far more dependent on the goodwill of the council than the viceroys of Naples or the

---

[1] Papers relating to Ceremonial, 1579–88. B.M. MS. Add. 28 361, fo. 236. Partly quoted in Merriman, Rise . . . , vol IV, pp. 417 f.
[2] Idiáquez to the king, 1579; Letters and Papers . . . , I, B.M. MS. Add. 28 399, fo. 298–300.
[3] Giardina, Il Consiglio Supremo . . . , pp. 96 f.
[4] In nearly all cases in which English merchants were involved the Council of Italy gave decisions in their favour although it sometimes took them several years to do so. Cf. my English Merchants . . . , E.H.R. No. 244, pp. 309 f.

governors of Milan.¹ Moreover, the division between 'matters of state' and 'matters of government' was far from rigid, and this not only because in the dispatches of the viceroys matters of high policy and administrative detail were often inextricably confused. Thus while both the Sicilian corn trade and relations with Venice would normally lie within the province of the Council of Italy, the Council of State would take over all negotiations when they become involved in the vitally important question of the League against the Turks.² The Council of Italy discussed as important an issue as the recall of the viceroy Medinaceli,³ while the question of the extradition of a common bandit from Tuscan territory was handled by the Council of State.⁴ So vague were the dividing lines between the functions of the king's councils that suggestions for the appointment of a commander of a Sicilian castle might even be sent to the president of the Council of the Indies.⁵

The absence of a clear demarcation of functions was not uncommon among the organs of government within the Spanish Empire.⁶ It increased the confusion typical of Spanish administration and, in the seventeenth century, led to fierce quarrels over competence between the Council of Italy and the Council of State.⁷ Yet it also provided some welcome elasticity in a system otherwise noted for its rigidity. With councils composed almost wholly of lawyers such rigidity was inevitable. The Venetian ambassador, Lorenzo Priuli, has left some penetrating observations on these 'men of long robe, doctors (i.e. lawyers) and prelates of low birth.' The king made use of these men for two reasons, he wrote,⁸

'one, to have in his councils men completely dependent on him who will serve him with greater loyalty, knowing their greatness to derive from him; the other, because the nobles and great lords are little qualified in this service, not having been brought up in the honourable study of letters. But his arrangement, while leaving the gentlemen and great lords ill satisfied, does not at the same time bring forth the good effect which the king desires; for in these doctors, who have applied themselves to study primarily for the end of gain, there is

¹ See below, ch. 7.
² Simancas MS. Secret. Prov. leg. 981.
³ *Consulta* of 1563, ibid. leg. 980.
⁴ Colonna to the Council of State, Sept. 20th, 1577, ibid. Estado, leg. 1147.
⁵ Pedro Velázquez, one of the most senior Spanish ministers in Sicily, to Juan de Ovanda, President of the Council of the Indies, Sept. 1st, 1574. Letters and Papers..., Sicily, B.M. MS. Add. 28 396, fo. 11.
⁶ Cf. the relations between the government of Sicily and the Sicilian Inquisition and between the Council of Italy and the 'Suprema.' Below, ch. 6. sect. 3.
⁷ Giardina, Il Supremo Consiglio..., pp. 116 ff.
⁸ Albèri, Relazioni..., ser. 1. vol. v. p. 251.

not to be found that desire for the public weal which is necessary; and, as persons of low birth who do not know how to use their authority with moderation, they carry out their duties with great arrogance and pride, for it seems to them that with cruelty they will acquire a great reputation for justice with the king... and if the king's goodness and justice did not console and curb everyone, there would be danger that some disaster might one day befall.'

The Spanish and Italian nobility shared the patrician ambassador's disapproval of middle class officials, and not without reason. The narrowness of the councillors' outlook and their excessive concern with the details of law and of administration made them incapable of appreciating the wider problems of empire or of evolving a coherent theory of imperial administration. Even their general hostility to the old nobility came to the surface only at intervals, and the king was careful not to let it develop into a systematic policy.[1] When faced with the opposition of the Supreme Council of the Inquisition in the dispute over Sicilian jurisdiction, the regents failed to hold their own against men who were prepared to press ruthlessly a line of action which was both well defined and clearly understood.[2] Much depended on the personality of the president, for on the one hand he acted as the link with the Council of State (of which he was an *ex officio* member) and on the other hand he could, if he chose, dominate the deliberations of the Council of Italy.[3] The duke of Francavilla does not seem to have been very effective in either body and left the Council of Italy to be run by its secretaries. His successor, Hernández de Lievana, was not a sufficiently distinguished person to play a dominant part among the Prudent King's closest advisers on matters of war and diplomacy,[4] but his behaviour in the Council of Italy was so dictatorial that it evoked violent protests by the regents to the king.[5] Lievana, in fact, fitted perfectly Priuli's description of the Spanish civil servant. Granvelle who was president from 1579 to 1586 was for most of this period the king's principal adviser and concerned mainly with the Spanish occupation of Portugal, the

---

[1] e.g. in 1588 the council supported a proposal by the Sicilian viceroy for the wholesale abolition of baronial jurisdiction. The king answered, 'Antes de ordenar que este se exequte (sic) sera bien que el Virey informe con mucha particularidad si toca a muchos y el inconveniente que por la una y otra parte puede haver, y que avise de lo que parecera...' *Consulta* of Sept. 7th, 1588, Simancas MS. Secret. Prov. leg. 984.
[2] Cf. below ch. 6. sect. 3.
[3] Padilla's report of 1577 stated that the president often gave his opinion before the vote was taken and that the regents then conformed, a practice detrimental to free discussion.
[4] Cf. Idiáquez' opinion, above, p. 45.
[5] Letters and Papers..., II, B.M. MS. Add. 28 400, fo. 216-9.

intrigues of Philip's French policy, Parma's reconquest of the southern Netherlands and the preparations for the invasion of England. Yet this brilliant and incorruptible administrator managed to find time for an unusually close attention to Italian affairs and was always helpful and sympathetic to the problems of his collaborators and subordinates.[1] For advice on Sicily he relied mainly on the regent Pedro de León who had had five years of first-hand experience in the tortuous politics of that country.[2] For the few years of the cardinal's ascendancy at the court of Madrid it seemed as if an effective integration of administrative and state policy might be possible. But with the presidency of Quiroga a new problem arose. The Inquisitor-General was directly interested not only in the representatives of the civil government of the king in Italy, but also in his ecclesiastical representatives, the Inquisition of Sicily; and with these latter the viceroys had come into serious conflict.[3] The result of Quiroga's dual position was to increase in the Council of Italy the tendency to put off decisions and to pursue a vacillating and flabby policy whose main object was to give offence to no one and to take no definite line which might run counter to the king's wishes. Philip might send an unusually strongly worded note to a joint committee of the Supreme Council of the Inquisition and of the Council of Italy after they had presented him with three or four different decisions in the course of only a few months of the year 1590.[4] But this was no remedy for a system whose results showed themselves to a greater or lesser degree in all the king's councils. In a court where everyone had a personal enemy and where the most trusted were not immune from slander, the king's refusal to attend the meetings of his councils had the opposite effect to the one he intended.[5] So far from making the councillors speak more freely, it made them afraid of opposing the unknown policy of the king. They could not even rely on their fellow members offering the same advice to the king in private which they had given at the council meeting. Chinchón sent private notes to the king, contradicting the

[1] Cf. his many holograph letters to the visitor Bravo (Simancas MS. Estado, leg. 1155) and his very fair treatment of the Colonna-Miserendino case (ibid. leg. 1154; also Letters and Papers . . . Sicily, B.M. MS. Add. 28 396, fo. 138, 141–3; Letters and Papers . . . , II, Add. 28 400, fo. 44–47). Cf. below ch. 7.
[2] Idiáquez to Zayas, May 1st, 1581; Simancas MS. Secret. Prov. leg. 982.
[3] See below, ch. 6. sect. 3.
[4] Papeles del Consejo de la General Inquisicion, I, B.M. MS. Egerton 1506, fo. 169-72 and passim.
[5] Ranke, Die Osmanen . . . , p. 215. 'Man kennt diesen Hof, wo für einen jeden ein Feind gefunden ward; wo sich die Verläumdung sichere Wege zum Ohre des Königs öffnete; wo schon das Misstrauen zum Verderben wurde.'

advice he had given in the official *consulta*,[1] and the king himself reversed the council's decision without informing it of this fact.[2] The lack of confidence which this produced between the king and his advisers made it impossible for the Council of Italy to develop a clear-cut policy even within its own limited sphere of competence.

The establishment of the Council of Italy had been a radical innovation. The powers with which this body was endowed, and the character of the functions which it had to perform, manifested a revolutionary change in the conception of the role of the central government in an international empire. Since the days of Imperial Rome, no European government had been so well informed about its dependencies or had been able to supervise their administration with such attention to detail and such concern as to the welfare of its subjects. Yet the mediocrity and conservatism of most of the council's members eventually produced the same ossifying and enfeebling effects which occurred in all the other Spanish governmental institutions. The evil results of this process projected themselves into the provinces under its control. In Sicily they were more marked than in either Naples or Milan. The council failed to counteract Philip's personal slowness in making decisions and left the governors of that most difficult province without adequate guidance and yet without sufficient authority to act independently. The Sicilian opposition to the viceroy was thus enabled to form a party within the Council of Italy which, sooner or later, brought about his recall.[3] The central control of the Spanish administration tended to degenerate into a tug-of-war between two rival parties at the court of Madrid, undermining Spanish reputation in Italy and making a mockery of the good intentions of the king's most capable and loyal servants.

---

[1] Correspondence relating to Naples and Sicily, I. B.M. MS. Add. 29 394, fo. 59.
[2] Ibid. fo. 161.
[3] Ranke, Die Osmanen . . . , pp. 215 f.

CHAPTER FOUR

Imperial Administration in the Provinces

THE DEVELOPMENT OF CONCILIAR GOVERNMENT IN SICILY

1. *Introduction*: *The Economic Background*
Of the three great dominions under the authority of the Council of Italy, Sicily was the one which presented the most baffling contrasts to its rulers. To the Spaniards from the bare table land of Castile the island appeared as a garden of enchantment. Instead of an arid Iberian plateau where only constant irrigation and hard toil could win a livelihood from the unwilling soil, there were gentle plains by the sea where olives, fruit and vegetables grew almost by themselves. No extremes of climate made life a misery in winter and a burden in summer. The bandit-infested mountain ranges were indeed as forbidding as the bleak sierras, but in the valleys the finest wheat could be grown earning for Sicily the name of 'granary of the Mediterranean.' Pedro de Cisneros, Spanish soldier and secretary of Marc Antonia Colonna, has left a glowing account of such impressions. He was particularly enthusiastic about the magnificent opportunities for hunting, about the fruit and honey of the *Conca d'Oro* around Palermo, about the island's wine which was 'perfectissimo', and about its meat which was 'as good as Spanish' – the highest praise a Castilian could bestow on the product of another country.[1] Italians from the north were no less impressed by the fertility of the island. 'Sicily produces all things necessary for human life, so that she does not need to import anything,' wrote Placido Ragazzoni, Venetian Resident in Messina from 1570 to 1574.[2]

Yet the island's appearance of wealth was deceptive, as it is today to the modern traveller. Once the richest and most advanced part of Italy, it had by the sixteenth century become one of the poorest.

---

[1] 'Relacion de las cosas del Reyno de Sicilia', written by Pedro de Cisneros for the viceroy Alvadeliste; Letters and Papers..., Sicily, B.M. MS. Add. 28 396, fo. 333.
[2] Albèri, Relazioni..., ser. 2, vol. v, p. 477.

From the eleventh century until the Black Death, in the middle of the fourteenth, the population of Italy had been steadily increasing.[1] Only in Sicily was there a steady decline from the two million mark, at the end of the Arab period, to less than half this number at the time of the Catholic Kings. The most catastrophic decrease, of 400,000, took place between the years 1282 and 1392.[2] During most of the fourteenth century, while Sicily was ruled by women, boys or half-wits, of a junior branch of the house of Aragon, there were fierce factions among the nobles and bitter rivalry between the towns.[3] The Norman-Sicilian or 'Latin' party fought the Catalans and Aragonese; the Chiaramonte, the Palizzi and the Alagona struggled for control over the person of the sovereign; the rivalry between Palermo and Messina for pre-eminence in the kingdom created a bitterness of feeling between these two cities which blighted all hope of co-operation against the Spaniards,[4] and which remains a not unnoticeable feature in the writings of modern Sicilian historians. Inside the towns the class struggle between the popular and the noble parties was at its height, and in the country the personal and family feuds became even more wide-spread and savage than in the rest of Italy.

In the last decade of the fourteenth century royal power was reestablished by the second Aragonese invasion. The whole country was so tired of civil war and anarchy that a certain degree of power was willingly conceded to the central government. But locally the barons and the larger towns maintained a degree of immunity from royal interference which went far beyond that enjoyed in Norman times. Even in the sixteenth century, while they could no longer

[1] A. Doren, Italienische Wirtschaftsgeschichte, vol. I (Jena 1934), pp. 632 ff.
[2] F. Maggiore-Perni, La Popolazione di Sicilia e di Palermo dal X al XVIII Secolo (Palermo 1892), p. 113. Unfortunately there are no figures for the years just before the plague. Sicilian population figures earlier than the sixteenth century are, in any case, very problematical. Thus Maggiore-Perni gives a figure of over 120,000 for Palermo in the fifteenth century, while Doren (p. 636) puts it at 25,000, which is almost certainly too low, just as M.-P's. figure is far too high. It is not quite clear why Doren has not accepted G. Pardi's estimate of 30,000 in 1402 and 48–50,000 in 1505 (Storia demografica della città di Palermo; Nuova Rivista Storica, An. III (Milano 1919) p. 602). In 1570 the population of Palermo was officially estimated at 70,000 (Simancas, MS. Estado, leg. 1124, fo. 63) and in 1593, unofficially at about 90,000 (Trattato di Sicilia, Anon. MS. Biblioteca Nazionale de Napoli, MS. X.D. 46, fo. 5). Even if this latter figure is discounted Doren's estimate would mean an increase of nearly 300 per cent in less than a century, which is inconceivable.
[3] R. Gregorio, Opere Scelte (Palermo 1853), Considerazioni sopra la storia di Sicilia, lib. V.
I. La Lumia, Matteo Palizzi ovvero I Latini e i Catalani, Storie Siciliane, vol. 2 (Palermo 1882).
[4] e.g. in the revolt of Palermo in 1647 and in the Messinese war of 1674–78.

involve the whole country in civil war, the nobles could wreak devastation on a provincial town and its surrounding countryside. In 1529 the longstanding feud between the Luna and the Perollo came to a head when Sigismondo de Luna with his retainers stormed and sacked Sciacca, the Perollo Castle, and killed Giacomo Perollo and many of his family. It was the last great feud to be fought out in open war. Sigismondo de Luna had to flee, and ended by drowning himself in the Tiber after he had failed to obtain pardon from the emperor or absolution from the pope. Heavy punitive taxes were laid on Sciacca, and the whole south-west of Sicily did not recover for many years.[1]

Thus, at a time when the city states of northern and central Italy enjoyed a period of rapid economic expansion, fruitful political experiments and vigorous social life, which formed the basis of the civilization of the Italian Renaissance, the energies of Sicily were spent in desultory feudal strife and class warfare.[2] Apart from a few brilliant figures, such as Panormita and Antonello da Messina, Sicily's contribution to the intellectual and artistic life of the Renaissance was slight and did not compare with the brilliance of the Arab-Norman civilization during the earlier middle ages. In the sixteenth century the effects of the *pax austriaca*, which Hapsburg rule was eventually able to impose on the turbulent islanders, were more than counterbalanced by the almost continual threat of Turkish invasion and the great increase of corsair raids on the coast, paralysing trade and rendering impossible successful competition by Palermo and Messina with their commercial rivals of the north.

Agriculture, therefore, was destined to remain the basis of Sicilian economy. By far the greatest part of the country was divided into large estates owned by the barons, the church or the communes.[3] The laws of feudal inheritance (systematized during the reign of Charles V) were so designed as to keep large properties intact,[4] and the *latifondi* continued to grow. During the reign of Philip II the entailed estates of the dukes of Terranova and of the princes of

[1] The story is brilliantly told by La Lumia in his La Sicilia sotto Carlo V Imperatore (1515–35); Storie Siciliane, vol. III (Palermo 1882/3) pp. 237–282.
[2] Cf. the vivid description of the state of Sicily in 1500 by La Lumia, ibid. p. 13.
[3] L. Bianchini, Della storia economico-civile di Sicilia, vol. I (Napoli 1841), p. 251, puts the proportion of feudal land held by the Parliamentary nobility as high as three quarters of all Sicilian land.
[4] F. Testa, Capitula Regni Siciliae, vol. II (Palermo 1742), Capitoli of Charles V, caps. 118, 204 and 258.

Paternò and Butera were joined together by marriage.¹ From the sixteenth to the eighteenth century the family of the Gioeni, in eastern Sicily, added no less than nine baronies to their estates; and the lords of Buscemi, of the old Ventimiglia family, started with the single fief of Casale and managed to acquire another five.²

Side by side with the *latifondi* there were, however, also smaller holdings, especially in eastern Sicily. Of these there were broadly two types; those of the well-to-do peasants, the *burgesi* or *padroni* who owned freehold land for which they were not obliged to any feudal overlord, and those of the tenant farmers on the large estates, the *garzoni or massariotti* who had to render such services to their landlords as were common in all feudal countries.³ Villeinage in Sicily had disappeared as early as the thirteenth and fourteenth centuries, but the tenant farmers remained subject to a great number of restrictions. The lords claimed a certain percentage of their crops, work without payment, the exclusive use of the forests or of the common pastures during part of the year, and sometimes even all their property if they left the estate. The government had to issue laws against the latter practice as well as against the unwholesome baronial habit of forcing tenants to sell them their whole produce cheaply so that, later in the year, the tenants had to buy back their own necessities at inflated prices.⁴ Most lords, however, enjoyed the more reasonable right of pre-emption at market or government prices. Mills and oil presses were usually in their hands, and if they allowed their vassals to take their grain and olives elsewhere for grinding and pressing they still insisted on the payment of a tithe.⁵

Worse than the feudal exactions in themselves were the frauds committed by the lords' agents, and their harshness and greed in collecting the rents for absentee barons and prelates.⁶ An English

---

¹ Consulta of the Council of Italy on the laws of inheritance in the Italian dominions, July 11th, 1598; Simancas MS. Secret. Prov. leg. 981. From this long and interesting document it appears that in Sicily (but not in Naples) most feudal estates were entailed, while in Milan females could not inherit at all and feudal estates could therefore not be joined by marriage.
² G. Verdirame, Le istituzione sociali e politiche de alcuni municipi della Sicilia Orientale nei secoli XVI, XVII e XVIII; Archivio Storico per la Sicilia Orientale, Anno I (Catania 1904), pp. 316 ff.
³ Ibid. pp. 110 ff.
⁴ Pragmatica of Charles V in 1535; Regni Siciliae Pragmaticarum Sanctionum, ed. R. Raymundettus, vol. I (Venice 1574), p. 224.
⁵ Documents printed by R. Starrabba, Suppliche e capitoli dell' Università di Monreale (an. 1516), in Archivio Storico Siciliano, new series, vol. XIII (Palermo 1887) pp. 447 ff.
⁶ Ibid. Complaints during the reign of Philip II were not substantially different from those of 1516.

traveller was struck by the miserable life of the Italian peasant in the fifteen 'nineties. His picture fits Sicily as much as the Italian mainland.

> 'The husbandmen and country people live poorely and basely, whome the Italians use and hire like oxen and asses for their Woorke, and at the yeares end turne them out of dores, not giving them Leases or accounting them servants belonging to the Family, as we use them. Thus oppressed and after harvest-tyme commonly turned out of service, they never grow rich nor study to advance their masters profitt further than themselves provide for it, and hate their masters for exactions... The landlords take no rent of them, but a proportion of Corne and all things they have, even of their Chickens and Eggs, in such hard measure, as they have not to eat or Cloth themselves in any convenient sort.'[1]

Not all extensions of feudal property, however, were made at the expense of the small holders. From the fifteenth century onwards there was a movement for the internal colonization of uncultivated land. The owner would enter into a contract with Sicilian peasants (or with Greeks and Albanians who had fled from the Turks) to settle and cultivate such land.[2] The terms offered were usually much more favourable than those enjoyed by the tenants of the old-established fiefs. Thus the Albanian inhabitants of San Michele took over two uncultivated fiefs from the baron of Ganzaria. They were to cultivate them and build at least thirty houses in two years. No gabelles were to be charged for five years, after which the dues customary in the district would be imposed. The settlers were to pay no more than ten per cent of their crops and of the value of their cattle – a rather lower rate than was usual – and the customary tax on wine and on the use of fallow land, all of which was at their disposal for the grazing of their animals. They were permitted to cut wood for their own use and had the right of pre-emption should the lord wish to sell his forest. Most unusual, perhaps, was the free right of the chase. No case involving penalties of more than two ounces[3] was to be tried in the baronial court, and if any member of the community was cited before a superior court, the lord was to provide for his defence. All baronial officials were to be residents of at least one year's standing. It is interesting to find that this

[1] F. Moryson's Itinerary, in Shakespeare's Europe, ed. C. Hughes (London 1903), p.150.
[2] The descendants of these Greek communities can still be found in Sicily and they still speak Greek among themselves.
[3] See Appendix II.

contract was endorsed by the viceroy and thus carried the government's guarantee.[1]

In contrast with this type of internal colonization of uncultivated land was the method of obtaining increased rents by farming out the tenants' common land to private persons, usually for intensive cultivation of olives, wine and fruit.[2] This process was called *infeudazione* and was practised more frequently by the communes than by the lords.[3] In theory, this abrogation of common rights in favour of the commune's patrimony was dependent on the unanimous consent of all inhabitants and on the approval of the Court of Royal Patrimony. But there seems to have been so little regard for the rule that in 1571 Philip II had to issue a proclamation forbidding the taking over of any more common land and ordering its restoration to communal use where illegal infeudation had been carried out.[4] Nevertheless, the government was often compelled to approve of infeudation as many communes had no other means of paying their taxes.[5] Permission in such cases was granted for not more than six years with the right of extension for another three. But, as always in Sicily, temporary expedients tended to become permanent. In the sixteenth and seventeenth centuries pasturage declined in favour of arable cultivation. The common was no longer as important to the villager as it had been and, with or without force, lords and communes added most of the country's commons to their own estates.[6]

The status of the tenant farmer was thus still further depressed until it approached that of the landless agricultural labourer. The workers preferred to drift into the towns and, during the sixteenth century, the population of Palermo, for instance, increased much

[1] R. Starrabba, Capitoli della terra di S. Michele, 1534 (probably a misprint for 1554 which was the date of the viceroy Juan de Vega's signature), in Arch. Stor. Sic. n.s. vol. IV (Palermo 1879). pp. 352.
[2] Cisneros mentions that the yield of Sicilian olive trees could have been much increased by grafting of the trees – a practice apparently common in Spain but unknown in Sicily. Letters and Papers . . . Sicily, MS. Add. 28 396, fo. 333.
[3] L. Genuardi, Terre Communi ed Usi Civici in Sicilia, Studi e. Documenti, in Documenti per servire . . . , ser. 2, vol. VII, pp. 44–129.
[4] Ibid. pp. 100 f.
[5] Ibid. pp. 101 f. 'Attenta la poca forma che la città di Castro Joanne (Castrogiovanni, now Enna) teneva et tenj in pagari le regii donativi et presertim la gabella de la farina . . . se donao ordine al magnifico blasco de Alagona tunc delegato in quella città, che havesse fatto . . . sopra ciò congregari lo consiglio generale per lo quali si conclusi che per la satisfactione de detti regii donativi se havessero di ingabellari seu infegare le communi di quella città per anni sei . . .'
[6] Ibid. pp. 107-129, there is a list of the commons held by a large number of Sicilian communes in 1593–94. The great majority of the commons was farmed out.

more rapidly than that of the rest of Sicily.¹ Contemporaries were seriously alarmed by the tendency and its effects on agricultural production,² for increased efficiency and internal colonization were insufficient to counter-balance the results of the scarcity of labour on the land.³ After a particularly bad harvest in 1577,⁴ Colonna wrote that wheat production was being ruined by the rack-renting of the lords and the exploitation of the peasants by the foreign merchants who controlled the corn trade. 'Everything is going so badly,' he concluded, 'that there do not exist in this kingdom any poorer people than those engaged in this occupation (i.e. of agriculture). Formerly this used to be quite different; and if this industry and the silk industry should be ruined there would be few kingdoms poorer than this...'⁵

It was calculated that the country needed about a million salma of wheat for its own consumption⁶ and another 200,000 for sowing.⁷ The margin remaining for export varied considerably and might be as high as 200,000 salma.⁸ During the twelve years from 1558

¹ Maggiore-Perni, La Popolazione..., pp. 168 ff. puts this increase down to a lower mortality rate in the city during plagues and famines. This may well have been a contributory factor, but I doubt whether it was the most important one.

² In a relation about the proposed extension of the city's boundaries to include the new mole (circa 1570): 'Aora si esta ciudad se amplia y habita de gente que ha de venir del reyno, çesará por aquella parte el arbitrio frumentario; y siendo la extraçion del trigo el principal miembro de las rentas reales, es inconveniente que esta gente se destraiga de su proprio officio... y oy es mas necessario que nunca por la falta que ay de gente y por otros instrumentos que para remediarlo se han publicado muchas leyes y prematicas y aun con todas ellas no se ha dado sufficiente remedio, de manera que cumple mas procurar por todas las vias possibles que se amplia este exercicio de trigo.' Simancas MS. Estado, leg. 1143, fo. 12. Also Olivares, Cosas del Govierno de Sicilia..., Papeles varios tocantes a Napoles, Sicilia, Milan etc. B.M. MS. Add. 14 009, fo. 396.

³ C. A. Garufi, Patti Agrari e Communi Feudali di nuova Fondazione in Sicilia, etc. pt. I. Archivio Storico Sicil. ser. 3, vol. I, p. 110. Garufi puts the number of communities founded between the end of the 15th cent. and 1583 at no more than 16, of which 10 by internal immigration and 6 by the settling of Greeks and Albanians. – Unfortunately, Garufi's figures are never entirely reliable if only because of his carelessness in arithmetic, of which there is a glaring example in this article. This type of carelessness is remarkably common among both older and more modern Sicilian historians. – It is, however, fairly certain that the number of new communities founded in the 16th cent. was very small. The mass of the new foundations occurred in the two following centuries.

⁴ Terranova to Philip II, April 9th, 1577, Simancas MS· Estado, leg. 1147.

⁵ Colonna to Philip II, June 25th, 1578, Simancas MS. Estado, leg. 1148.

⁶ At the rate of approx. one salma per person per year (thus for instance, in the Trattato di Sicilia, Naples, Bibl. Naz. MS. X. D. 46, fo. 5); cf. Appendix II.

⁷ Pedro Velázquez in 1576; Letters and Papers... Sicily, B.M. MS. Add. 28 396, fo. 41.

⁸ There was a lot of guessing, even by contemporaries, about average annual exports of corn, although all admitted that it was highly variable. Thus Velázquez, with an estimate of 40,000 for an average year, is rather low (ibid.). Scipio di Castro's figure of 400,000 salma export from a total harvest of 1,200,000 is much too optimistic (Avvertimenti al Sig. Marc. Antonio Colonna, quando andò Vicerè in Sicilia; Thesoro Politico, vol. II (Milan 1601) p. 471. For Castro cf. Appendix III).

to 1569 the average export of corn was 116,200 salma,[1] and during the fifteen years from 1576 to 1590 it was 123,900 salma.[2] There followed a year of famine and a number of very lean years, and only during the last years of the century did corn production again reach its former level.[3] It is clear, therefore, that during the reign of Philip II agricultural production increased but little and that in consequence the standard of living of the agricultural population remained as low as it had been earlier in the century.

While the relationship between lords and tenants was still maintained on the customary feudal basis, with the tenants paying the land-owner largely in kind or in personal services, both parties were becoming increasingly dependent on outside financial credit. To pay for sowing and for the upkeep of their animals in winter, the agricultural producers had to borrow from the banks or from the grain merchants.[4] The creditors would often buy up the whole crop and, if the harvest was bad, demand compensation based on the high, inflated prices of the scarce grain. Similar practices were common in the wine, olive, silk and cloth industries. In 1554, therefore, Juan de Vega[5] issued a number of orders (*pragmaticae*, or *prammatiche*) designed to limit this type of speculation: every year, on a certain day, a local council of all citizens elected five disinterested persons who were to fix prices according to the prospects and quality of the harvest.[6] The machinery for fixing and controlling prices was later elaborated and centralized by giving more power to the local *giurati*, the town councillors, and by the intervention of a government representative with the title of captain-at-arms (*capitan d'armi*). Yet the merchants continued to do well out of the credit system, and the cultivators continued to petition the viceroys for the reduction of their debts to the merchants. The viceroys sometimes acceded to these requests, but it was considered a very delicate measure; for if the merchants were not paid in time and could not meet their own obligations there would be a catastrophic collapse of the credit

---

[1] 'Relatione delli fromenti estratti del regno di Sicilia . . . nelli dodici anni seguenti . . . 'Sent by the Court of the Royal Patrimony to Philip II. Simancas MS. Estado, leg. 1133, fo. 133. Cf. G. Tricoli, La Deputazione, p. 12

[2] Trattato di Sicilia, Naples, Bibl. Naz. MS. X.D. 46, fo. 17, quoting a relation by Giovan Pietro Santillo, 'Detentore delli libri del Maestro Portulano.'

[3] Conde de Olivares, Cosas del Govierno . . . de Sicilia; Papeles Varios tocantes a Napoles, Sicilia, Milan etc. B.M. MS. Add. 14 009, fo. 393.

[4] P. Celestre, Idea del Govierno del Reyno de Sicilia; written in 1611; B.M. MS. Add. 24 130, fo. 18.

[5] Cf. Appendix I.

[6] Reg. Sic. Prag. Sanct., vol. I, pp. 192 ff. The preambles of these pragmaticas emphasized not only the economic harm resulting from the sharp practices of the merchants, but also the harm done to their consciences.

system upon which the whole economy of the island was based.[1]

Such economic disasters occurred with appalling frequency. During the emperor's reign there were no fewer than eight bank failures,[2] many of them due to the fraudulent practices of the bankers themselves.[3] As the result of a particularly bad spate of crashes, the government established the Tavola of Palermo in 1553. It was the third 'national' bank in Europe (after those of Venice and Genoa) and was founded nearly 150 years before the Bank of England. The Tavola had a stabilizing influence on the finances of the country and its business expanded rapidly. Nevertheless, the Sicilian credit system remained precarious, and the reign of the Prudent King witnessed another three bank crashes.[4] At the end of the reign only two private banks had survived in Palermo.[5]

Most of the country's financial business was in the hands of foreigners. A Genoese banker, Agostino Rivarola, could rise to be one of the principal (if unofficial) advisers to the viceroys and, despite a disastrous bankruptcy,[6] was sent by Alvadeliste as his special representative to Madrid.[7] The export of corn was carried on by merchants from the north, and in the silk trade the position was little better.[8] Next to agriculture the export of silk was the island's most important asset. Where the mountains and valleys above Messina are now given over to orange and lemon growing, they were formerly covered with thousands of mulberry trees. The Val de Demone,[9] the north-eastern province of Sicily, produced enough silk for Messina to export 2,000 bales a year at a total value of 2 million scudi.[10] In the early seventeenth century production rose to as much as 8,000 bales a year (of which 5,000 were exported) and, silk was so common that even the poor could afford to wear it.[11]

Compared with corn and silk all other Sicilian exports were of

[1] Celestre, Idea ..., B.M. MS. Add. 24 130, fo. 18.
[2] V. Cusumano, Storia dei Banchi della Sicilia, vol. I (Rome 1887), pp. 292 ff.
[3] Reg. Sec. Prag. Sanct., vol. I. pp. 45 ff.
[4] Only two are mentioned by Cusumano, p. 245. The third was the failure of the bank of Antonio Promotorio in 1580. The government intervened with great promptitude and was able to prevent the most serious losses. Colonna to Philip II, Nov. 4th, 1580, Simancas MS. Estado, leg. 1149.
[5] Trattato di Sicilia, Naples, Bibl. Naz. MS. X.D. 46, fo. 21.
[6] Relation of G. F. Rao to the king, 1585(?); Simancas MS. Estado, leg. 1155.
[7] *Consulta* of the Council of Italy, Sept. 7th, 1588, ibid. Secret. Prov. leg. 984.
[8] Cisneros..., Relacion . B.M. MS. Add. 28 396, fo. 333 '... (los extranjeros) tiran asi casi todas las facultades delos Sicilianos que, se bien son de agudissimos ingenios, no los emplean en cosas que le estan bien, y ansi se ve que los forasteros levantan en este reyno cada dia cosas muy principales y ricas de la substancia de los Naturales.'
[9] Supposed to be so called because of the demons living in and around Mount Etna.
[10] Trattato di Sicilia, Naples, MS. X.D. 46, fo. 19.
[11] G. Sandys, A Relation of a Journey begun An. Dom. 1610 (London 1627), p. 238

minor importance. The sugar trade, it is true, had an annual value of 120,000 scudi[1] and as much as 15,000 salma of salt was shipped each year from the pans of Trapani for consumption by the townships of the Po valley.[2] But the economic importance of these exports was comparatively slight, and that of the trade in pickled tunny and cheese from Palermo and of corals from Trapani was even slighter.[3] Sicily had virtually no merchant navy and her merchants abroad – mainly Messinese[4] – were dependent on Venetian and Genoese carriers. Nor were there industries to provide armament and ammunition for the Spanish galleys which refitted in the arsenals of the Sicilian ports; and when new fortifications were needed against the Turks, the viceroy had to write to his colleague in Milan for skilled engineers.[5] Messina boasted that its silk fair was inferior to none in Europe, and the lay-out of the shops and the decorations of the Strada della Marina, where the fair was held, presented a sight of which the citizens were rightly proud;[6] but even there many of the finest articles had been imported. In England the medieval wool industry developed from trading in the raw material to the manufacture and export of the finished article. No comparable advance took place in the Sicilian silks, and the Messinese ladies had to buy dresses made in Venetian workshops from silk produced in their own gardens.

Seriously under-industrialized, with most of its banks and credit controlled by foreigners, with the profits of its export trade enriching Genoese, Venetian and Catalan merchants, and with an agricultural organization which combined the disadvantages of the feudal economy with those of a modern credit system, Sicily remained a poor country and was never able to catch up on the lead which the North of Italy had gained in the later middle ages.

2. *The Organization of the Central Government*

The task of introducing the Renaissance principles of bureaucratic

[1] Trattato di Sicilia, Naples, Bibl. Naz. MS. X.D. 46, fo. 19.
[2] Terranova to Philip II, June 12th, 1574; Simancas MS. Secret. Prov. leg. 981. Ragazzoni gives double this figure in Albèri, Relazioni . . . , ser. 2, vol. v, p. 478.
[3] Ibid. Also Colonna to Philip II, June 24th, 1578, letter cit. '. . . pues los açucares, quesos y toninas no son cosa de sustancia . . .' Simancas MS. Estado, leg.1148. Terranova, letter cit., note [2] mentions an annual export of about 800 cantara of cheese (cf. Appendix II).
[4] Messina had the privilege of appointing all Sicilian consuls abroad. E. Laloy, La Révolte de Messine, l'Expédition de Sicile et la Politique Française en Italie, vol. I (Paris 1929), pp. 42 f.
[5] C. d'Aragona (i.e. Terranova), Corrispondenza particolare con Filippo II; ed. S. V. Bozzo: Documenti per servire alla storia di Sicilia, ser. I, vol. II (Palermo 1879), passim.
[6] G. Buonfiglio e Costanzo, Messina Città Nobilissima (Venice 1606), lib. VIII, p. 52.

government in the dominion proved to be much harder than the creation of a central machinery for the control of the whole empire. In Madrid Philip was able to work almost *in vacuo*. The Council of Italy was set up with the experience gained from the king's other supreme councils and with only a minimum consideration of existing vested interests. In Sicily, however, the king had to work within the setting of a definite political pattern, hemmed in on all sides by the powerful historic interests of the feudal classes who had for centuries dominated the public life of the island.

It was not the Prudent King's intention to effect an immediate and complete social revolution which would at one blow break the local supremacy of barons and communes, so hardly won during many decades of anarchy in the fourteenth century. Such a course of action would not only have plunged the country into immediate civil war (probably as deadly to Spanish supremacy as the War of the Vespers had been to Angevin rule), but it would also have been a reversal of all Spanish traditions, a policy wholly alien to Philip's own mode of thinking. Never afraid of war, if war it had to be, the Hapsburg ruler preferred to achieve his ends by legal and diplomatic means. A decision, unimportant in itself, provides a clue to his mentality. In 1588 the Council of Italy informed him that Palermo's privilege of holding an annual fair could not be revoked since its grant was dependent on the royal dignity and not on the person of the sovereign; but the regents went on to suggest that the confirmation of this *fuero*, or local privilege, should be used as a bargaining counter in an attempt to obtain money from the city. Philip disagreed. To his mind there was no question as to his power of revoking any privilege granted to his subjects. But if the regents could make political capital out of the confirmation – so much the better.[1]

Thus, without ever giving ground on positions previously won, the Spanish Monarchy could by-pass the immediate problem of power. Once an effective central machinery had been built up, the balance of forces would be weighted heavily in favour of the crown. The nobles and communes would lose, almost automatically, that independence which the king did not take from them directly.[2]

[1] Document printed in Riba, El Consejo ..., pp. 326 f.
[2] It is not suggested that this was a conscious and deliberate plan, worked out in all its implications. Philip and his advisers were faced with a concrete set of circumstances leaving them with several alternative lines of actions. Given the tradition of Spanish government, only one of these could possibly recommend itself to them as practicable for the objects they had in view, viz. the maintenance and increase of royal

Such policy Philip had inherited from his father, and his great-grandfather who had laid the foundations of conciliar government in Sicily. It was left to the Prudent King to systematize their work. The changes which the three rulers introduced in the government of the island in the course of more than a century were none of them as spectacular as the setting up of the Council of Italy; but in their total effect they constituted a revolution no less far-reaching in its political and social effects.[1]

The government of Sicily had been controlled by seven great feudal offices of state, most of which had become hereditary in certain families. But the restored monarchy of the fifteenth century could not allow its government to remain in the hands of men who owed their position not to royal favour, nor even to their own ability, but to their own independent power. The uneducated barons were, moreover, quite incapable of handling the ever-increasing amount of paper work and the legal technicalities of an expanding administration. By the end of the emperor's reign the seven feudal offices were little more than empty ceremonial garbs. The work of the Master Justiciary had devolved on his lieutenant, a lawyer who presided over the Great Court. The Grand Chamberlain's supervision of financial and economic administration had passed to the *maestri razionali* of the Court of the Royal Patrimony. With the absence of the king the duties of the Grand Steward had ceased entirely; and the viceroy, as captain-general of the kingdom, had taken over the duties of the Grand Constable and the Grand Admiral.[2] Only the *protonotaro* continued to fulfil ceremonial and clerical obligations connected with Parliament and the Holy Council, but he, too, had ceased to exert any appreciable influence over government policy.[3]

This administrative evolution did not take place without protracted opposition from the holders of the feudal offices. The two military officers, in particular, fought stubborn rearguard actions. But the Aragonese kings were careful to deprive their ancient ministers of functions by instalments, always leaving them in the full enjoyment of the social position their office conferred and

power. These objects were, in their mind, synonymous with their duty towards God in preserving the Hapsburg dominions from outside attack and in providing them with a just and efficient government.

[1] Many of these effects, however, did not become fully apparent until the seventeenth century.
[2] R. Gregorio, Opere Scelte (Palermo 1253), pp. 470 ff.
[3] Olivares, Cosas del Govierno, Papeles varios tocantes ..., B.M. MS. Add. 14 009, fo. 379.

successfully preventing the emergence of a united baronial opposition to any revolutionary move. And Parliament, the mouthpiece of the nobility, failed signally to arrest this piece-meal emasculation. In 1535 Charles V gave an evasive reply to a petition that the viceroy should consult the principal barons in military matters,[1] and when in 1585 the three houses finally asked that at least the office of the *protonotaro* should be restored to its former position of eminence, Philip II could afford to meet them with a blank refusal.[2]

In the reign of Charles V the work of government had become concentrated in the two supreme courts, or tribunals, as the Sicilians called them. The Great Court was the supreme judicial authority of the realm and took precedence over all other bodies. It was composed of the lieutenant of the Master Justiciary, four judges holding office for two years, and an *avvocato fiscale*, a kind of public prosecutor who was appointed for life. The Court of the Royal Patrimony or *Regia Camera* (it was called *magna curia dei maestri razionali* before 1485) supervised all matters of public finance and administration and exercised such control as the government enjoyed over the local administration of non-baronial towns and villages. In conformity with the customary lack of distinction between judicial and executive functions, it also acted as a court of law in matters arising from its own administration. Like the Great Court it had a president who was a lawyer and four councillors who were called *maestri razionali*, a *conservatore* who checked all accounts, and a number of minor officials. The treasurer, the *maestro secreto* who supervised the financial accounts of local authorities, and the *maestro portulano* who was in charge of the granaries (*caricatori*) were all members of this court.[3]

Both organizations were seriously understaffed. Duties which were left to the old feudal offices were not sufficiently distinguished from the work of the courts, and there was considerable confusion in the matter of appeals from the Great Court. As it was one of the maxims of Sicilian law that in a civil suit three similar judgments in the series of appeal courts were necessary for a final ruling,[4] litigants appealed from the Great Court to the viceroy. These appeals were then heard by two judges appointed for this purpose and these judges (according to a complaint by Parliament in 1558) were often young

[1] G. Capasso, Il Governo di Don Ferrante Gonzaga in Sicilia, Arch. stor. sic. n.s. vol. xxx-i, p. 419.
[2] Testa, Capitula ..., vol. II, p. 298.
[3] G. Capasso, Il Governo ..., Arch. stor. sic., n.s. vol. xxx-i, pp. 430 ff.
[4] La Mantia, Storia della legislazione, II. p. 62.

and inexperienced.[1] Already in 1535 Parliament had petitioned the emperor for an increase in the number of Great Court judges and for the establishment of a supreme court of appeal. Charles at that time had been content with a number of reforms in Sicilian law;[2] the request was renewed by Parliament in 1558 and Philip II in due course acceded.

The royal proclamation for the reform of the 'tribunals' was the result of years of negotiations and controversy. It is an indication of the preponderant position which the administration of law still occupied in sixteenth century government that the discussion centred mainly around the reform of judicial procedure and the composition of the law courts. Philip wanted to follow the precedent set in Naples of introducing Spanish councillors and judges, but Parliament stoutly refused to give up the most cherished of all Sicilian privileges, the exclusion of foreigners from public offices. Both Vega and Medinaceli argued that little would be gained by reorganization if Spaniards could not be introduced into the administrations and that it was better to leave matters as they stood. The Council of Italy accepted their view,[3] but less than two years later the king referred the question to the new viceroy, García de Toledo, and asked him to discuss with his advisers the problem of the length of tenure of judicial and administrative offices.[4]

When the marquis of Pescara published the reforms which had eventually been agreed upon,[5] it seemed as if Parliament had won a resounding victory. No Spaniard was allowed to fill any senior position previously reserved to Sicilian citizens, nor any of the newly-created offices. The surviving functions of the old feudal offices were abolished,[6] but the last holders could continue to enjoy their titles and salaries for life.[7] In the Great Court the number of judges was

[1] Testa, Capitula..., II. p. 233.
[2] Imperiales Pragmaticae Sanctiones etc., in Raymundettus, Reg. Sic. Prag. Sanct. II. Charles' reforms, though they did not touch the organization of the courts, went further than the mere tinkering with the problem which Capasso (following Gregorio) calls them (Arch. stor. sic. n.s. vol. xxx-I, p. 436). There was, for instance, pragmatica 14 (not quoted by Capasso) which laid down that officials and barons exercising the *mero e misto imperio* had to prosecute or set free any imprisoned person within seven days. While this may not always have been observed in practice, in law it was a kind of habeas corpus for baronial jurisdiction.
[3] *Consulta* of March 31st, 1563; Simancas MS. Secret. Prov. leg. 890.
[4] Philip II and Council of Italy to Toledo, Dec. 31st, 1564; ibid. leg. 1597, fo. 218.
[5] Raymundettus, Reg. Sic. Prag. Sanct., vol. II, pp. 1. ff.
[6] With the exception of those of the *protonotaro*.
[7] After their deaths the titles were continued with some small emoluments and appear to have been bestowed on, or sold to, deserving relatives of Sicilian ministers; e.g. *Consulta* of the Council of Italy on the provision of the office of Grand Steward, May 29th, 1581; Simancas MS. Secret. Prov. leg. 982.

increased to six, three for civil and three for criminal cases. The lieutenant of the Master Justiciary was honoured with the title of president, as was the deputy of the Grand Chamberlain who presided over the Court of the Royal Patrimony (or Patrimony, as it was usually called). The most important formal innovation was the establishment of the Court of the Holy Conscience, or Consistory. As court of appeal from the Great Court it was, in theory, the highest judicial authority in the kingdom. But to accord with the desires of such inveterate litigants as the Sicilians[1] yet another appeal in civil suits could be brought before the criminal judges of the Great Court,[2] and in 1577 the king further decreed that criminal appeals from the Great Court were not to be judged by the Holy Conscience at all, but by a special junta composed of the presidents of the three supreme 'tribunals', together with the viceroy and the *consultore*, his private adviser.[3]

The government at Madrid had given way on the question of the appointment of Spaniards, but it had gained an even more important point in the complete and irrevocable exclusion of the Sicilian nobles from all share in the central administration of their country.[4] Too late the barons awoke to the fact that they had been cut off from virtually all hope of political advancement, and belated attempts to reverse the decisions of 1569 were easily resisted by the government.[5] Except for the comparatively rare occasions when a Sicilian noble was appointed president of the kingdom in the absence of a viceroy, there was now no way in which he could directly influence the policy of the government. He might become the viceroy's private adviser,[6] but no longer could he claim office by virtue of his noble blood and social position. In 1594 Parliament once more asked the king to make use of Sicilian barons in his councils but no assent was forthcoming.[7]

---

[1] The fondness of the Sicilians for litigation was well known. In a memorandum to the king by the bishop of Patti, for instance, occurs the remark '. . . por ser los Sicilianos naturalmente inclinados a pleytar . . .' This passage is underlined and there is a marginal comment (by Philip II?) 'ojo, que conocidos los tengo, y quanta verdad es lo que aqui se dize.' Ibid. leg. 1598, fo. 324-5.
[2] Cisneros, Relacion, Letters and Papers . . . Sicily, B.M. MS. Add. 28 396, fo. 345.
[3] Philip II to Colonna, Aug. 26th, 1581, Simancas MS. Secret. Prov. leg. 1599, fo. 103.
[4] Pedro Velázquez, Memorial on the arming of Sicily, 1576; Letters and Papers . . . Sicily, B.M. MS. Add. 28 396, fo. 69.
[5] Philip II to Terranova, Sept. 3rd, 1575; Simancas MS. Secret. Prov. leg. 1598, fo. 236.
[6] e.g. the count of Landriano and Pescara; Letters from Italy, 1567-72, B.M. MS. Add. 28 401, fo. 53; the count of Vicari and Colonna, Correspondence . . . Naples and Sicily, vol. 1, B.M. MS. Add. 28 394, fo. 62.
[7] Testa, Capitula, II, p. 309.

The reform of the 'tribunals' was the turning point in the history of the crown's relations with the Sicilian nobility. The barons continued to struggle, and on one occasion went so far as to threaten civil disobedience,[1] but they were now on the defensive and without hope of regaining the initiative. A gradual change began to take place in their mode of life which was eventually to transform them into the court aristocracy of the eighteenth century *ancien régime*. Blood feuds could no longer be fought out in open war. In 1550 the Sanclemente and the Fardella of Trapani, and in 1555 the d'Aguaglia, the Asaro and the Bosco families of Piazza were induced by Juan de Vega to come to terms,[2] and in 1574 the Duke of Terranova arranged a similar contract of peace between the Celestre and Minafria of Licata.[3] These contracts between private persons read like peace treaties between sovereign princes, but with the essential difference that there was a supreme authority to enforce them. The military prowess of individual Sicilian nobles had once commanded the respect of all. Guglielmo Albamonte and Francesco Salomone took part in the famous contest of Barletta in 1503, when thirteen chosen knights successfully vindicated Italian honour against thirteen Frenchmen.[4] Pietro de Cardona, one of the leaders of the revolt against the viceroy Ugo de Moncada in 1516, fell fighting for Charles V at Bicocca.[5] Francesco Amodei was the captain of a galley which ran the Turkish blockade of Malta in 1565 and landed a much-needed contingent of soldiers on the island,[6] and Mariano di Giovanni and others distinguished themselves at Lepanto and in Parma's armies in the Netherlands. Yet, as a whole, the Sicilian nobility had ceased to be a military class. Vincenzo di Giovanni, diarist of the early seventeenth century and biographer of distinguished Palermitan nobles, has little to say of military exploits, but rather recounts victories in tournaments or actions against a rioting populace. There is, for instance, special mention of an Andreotto Lombardi who, unsuccessfully, tried to fire his pistol at the back of the leader of

---

[1] The 'revolt of the *braccio militare*' against Alvadeliste in 1591; cf. below, ch. 6, sect. 2.

[2] P. M. Rocca, Due Contratti di Pace tra Privati nel sec. XVI. Arch. stor. sic. n.s. XVIII, pp. 276 ff.

[3] G. Travali, Un Contratto di Pace tra Privati nel. sec. XVI. Ibid. vol. XIII, pp. 457 ff.

[4] F. Guicciardini, The History of Italy; transl. A. P. Goddard, vol. III (London 1753), pp. 160 ff.

[5] S. Salomone-Marino, De famosi uomini d'arme Siciliani fioriti nel sec. XVI; Arch. stor. sic. n.s. IV., pp. 293 ff.

[6] V. di Giovanni, Del Palermo Restaurato, Biblioteca Letteraria e Storica di Sicilia, ed. G. di Marzo, ser. 2, vol. II , p. 303.

one of these riots,[1] or of the author's father who, with a group of armed men, entered the house of some other popular leaders and strangled them while they were asleep. His admiring son thought this performance worthy of a Cicero.[2]

Where the youth of the nobility had formerly served in the field, they now became members of noble military academies. At least three of these were founded during the reign of Philip II.[3] Tournaments and games of chivalry became more sumptuous and more formalized. In the *staffermo* companies of knights, on horseback and clad in white armour, would charge two wooden figures representing Saracens;[4] in the *carosello* they would attack each other, armed only with fragile earthenware vessels filled with scent;[5] or they would stage the attempted capture and escape of queen Bianca. More and more did these games become a matter of form and make-believe, providing a distraction for the crowds and an escape from the increasing dullness of a rentier life for the nobility, now debarred from most of the higher offices of state, and losing both the opportunity and the taste for genuine warfare.[6] Only the violent quarrels which sprang up during these tournaments remained real.[7]

To compensate the nobles for their loss of political power and to flatter their self-esteem, the Spanish kings introduced new titles. Where formerly the Sicilian nobles had been content to be barons or counts, they now aspired to become marquises, dukes and princes. Soon, a certain income became sufficient justification to petition for another title.[8] In the Parliament of 1556 there was still only one duke, six marquises and nine counts.[9] Philip II created five princes and several dukes, and in the seventeenth century titles were given for the incomes from certain rights which the government had farmed

[1] Ibid. p. 308.
[2] 'Uno nuovo Marco Tullio,' ibid. p. 381.
[3] Viz. the Order of Santo Giacopo della Spata, in 1563 (Testa, Capitula, II, p. 240); the Accademia de' Cavalieri, in 1566 (G. E. di Blasi, Storia Cronologica de' Vicere, vol. II (Palermo 1790), p. 232); the Accademia della Stella of Messina, in 1595 (Capitoli dell'Illustrissima Accademia della Stella, B.M. MS. Add. 25 685).
[4] F. M. Emanuele e Gaetani, De giuochi bellici cavallereschi . . . unpublished; quoted in Bibl. Lett. e Stor. ser. 1. vol. I. p. 240 n.
[5] di Blasi, Storia, pt. 1. vol. II. p. 266.
[6] Duque de Medinaceli, Advertencias . . . á D. García de Toledo; in Colección de Documentos Inéditos para la Historia de España, vol. XXVIII, pp. 328 f; referring to the feudal service of the barons: '. . . es cosa de risa las armaduras que traen que parescen del tiempo del rey Artus.'
[7] F. Perino, Varie notizie di alcune cose notabile successe in . . . Palermo . . . B.M. MS. Add. 19 325, fo. 40.
[8] Letters and Papers . . . Sicily, B.M. MS. Add. 28 396, fo. 3; petitions of the barons of Rafadal and of Sortino for the title of marquis.
[9] A. Mongitore, Parlamenti Generali del Regno di Sicilia, vol. I (Palermo 1749), pp. 282 ff.

out, such as 'the barony of the grain', or 'the barony of the slaughter-house of Trapani'.[1] At the end of the eighteenth century the number of princes had risen to 142 and that of the marquises to 788.[2]

It was Spanish influence which, in the first place, had caused the abandonment of simplicity and the introduction of formality and ceremonial in Italy.[3] 'These ornaments, these ceremonies, these languors, these luxuries and these feastings were for the Spaniards nothing but the smiling mask of a martial personality, of a triumphant, overbearing and semi-barbarous society',[4] writes one of the finest modern historians of the period. But the Sicilians carried precedence and ceremony to such extremes as to appear ridiculous even to their Spanish preceptors.[5] They took from the Spaniards the outward signs of a life to which they were becoming increasingly incapable of giving content and which, at the same time, shut them off from original development. There were in Palermo literary, philosophical and musical academies, apart from the military ones,[6] yet Sicilian baroque civilization of the seventeenth century continued to lag behind and imitate that of Spain and the rest of Italy.[7] There was no outstanding Sicilian literary or artistic figure from the death of Antonello da Messina (1479) until Giovanni Meli (1740–1815).

The exclusion of the Sicilian nobility from the central government did not in itself solve the problem of the creation of an efficient administration. The fundamental difficulty of all governments of the time, and more especially of the Sicilian government, was the great dearth of capable and reasonably honest officials. There simply did not exist a sufficient number of adequately trained lawyers to fill satisfactorily the responsible position of a judge in the supreme court. The standard of legal training at Catania was notoriously low and there was no other law school in the country.[8] Yet Colonna

---

[1] D. Orlando, Il Feudalismo in Sicilia (Palermo 1847) pp. 72ff.
[2] E. Pontieri, Il tramanto del Baronaggio siciliano, Arch. stor. sic. n.s. LI, p. 110.
[3] B. Croce, La Spagna nella Vita Italiana durante la Rinascenza (Bari 1917), p.191.
[4] Ibid. p. 196.
[5] Medinaceli, in Documentos Inéditos, vol. XXXVIII, p. 361; '... todos los italianos usan epitetos y adjectivos, y estos desta isla mucho mas, y son communmente vanos y miran muchos en las cosas de fuerza y ostentacion....'
[6] di Giovanni, Del Palermo Restaurato, pp. 396 ff.
[7] Parts of Palermo, especially around the 'Quattro Canti', appear even now more Spanish than Italian.
[8] *Consulta* of the Council of Italy, March 26th, 1580: 'En el Reyno de Sicilia dize Marcantonio Colonna que ay muy grande falta de studios, y que la Universidad de Catania... esta muy deformada y tanto que muchos de los que se doctoran por ella son ignorantissimos porque haze ninguna difficultad de examen; y la manera de proceder de los lectores y de los demas de la Universidad es sin orden, y de mucha confusion, y viniendo en muchas occurencias de negocios a hechar de ver la mucha falta

had to fight mountains of prejudice, vested interest and jealousy to be able to raise the income of the university to as little as 2,000 scudi a year, a sum that was considered sufficient for the salaries of all university teachers in the four faculties and for all other expenses.[1] Bearing in mind the low quality of the Sicilian lawyers, and also wishing to discourage excessive litigation, the king and his advisers had reluctantly reached the conclusion that the judges of the Great Court and of the Holy Conscience should not receive fixed salaries but should be remunerated by fees from the litigants. It was hoped that this would urge the judges to greater speed in the dispatch of law-suits.[2] In the Great Court these fees amounted to about 2,000 scudi per annum[2] and were called 'candles'. From this name arose the witticism that he would always win his case who lit most candles for the judge to see the truth most clearly.[4]

The 'candles' system, however, did not produce the results anticipated. The judges came to neglect criminal cases in favour of civil suits from which they could extract greater profit, and the prisons were always overcrowded with poor wretches awaiting trial.[5] Colonna was able to provide a partial remedy for this evil by assigning the judges exclusively either to civil or to criminal duties;[6] yet the Great Court continued to attract far more cases from all over the country than the judges could reasonably handle, 'for their (hope of) gain made them think that they could manage everything,' as Colonna had to inform the king.[7] When they considered a law suit to be unprofitable they simply left it to their successors. Previous viceroys had tried to remedy this abuse by obliging the judges to deal with all their unfinished cases during the six months after their period of office when their conduct was examined by the 'sindicator'. Yet the harder the sindication pressed them, the more time they spent on their own defence. The viceroy did not suggest that the judges be paid fixed salaries, but proposed that provincial courts of

de letrados que ay en aquel Reyno...' Simancas MS. Secret. Prov. leg. 982.
Cf. also Federico Badoero, Relazione delle persone, Governo e Stati di Carlo V e di Filippo II nel 1557; Albèri, Relazioni, ser. 1. vol. III, p. 268. 'In Catania vi è uno studio di legge ma non è notabile per alcuna cosa.' The Venetian ambassador may be expected to voice a generally current opinion on such a subject.
[1] Colonna to Philip II, Aug. 7th, 1520; Simancas MS. Estado, leg. 1149.
[2] Philip II to Pescara, Sept. 17th, 1569, ibid. Secret. Prov. leg. 1597 fo. 382.
[3] Cisneros, Relacion..., Letters and Papers... Sicily, B.M. MS. Add. 28 396, fo. 342.
[4] Ranke, Die Osmanen, pp. 211 ff, quoting Scipio di Castro.
[5] Cisneros, Relacion, fo. 345.
[6] Fortunato, Avertimentos, Letters and Papers... Sicily B.M. MS. Add. 28 396, fo. 460.
[7] Colonna to Philip II, June 24th, 1587, Simancas MS. Estado leg. 1148.

appeal should be set up in the *valli* and that the Great Court should confine itself to the most important cases.¹ All his ministers, however, were opposed to such an innovation and nothing was done. Nor was it possible for the Holy Conscience to counterbalance these weaknesses of legal administration; for the 'candles' of its three judges did not amount to more than 700 scudi a year and the best lawyers were therefore attracted to the Great Court.²

The key position in the island's judicial system was occupied by the president of the Great Court. He was always one of the most distinguished lawyers of the kingdom; he took precedence in all the viceroy's councils and advised him on matters of state as well as of law. For nearly twenty years this office was held by the Spaniard Luca Cifuentes de Heredia who had acquired citizenship by marriage to a Sicilian. Though the president's salary was only a thousand scudi and therefore lower than the income of the judges, and though he had no vote in court, the eminence of his position and the fact that he held office for life made his influence supreme.³

The country was fortunate in having a series of learned and upright men to fill this high office. But the judicature was only one of the branches of sixteenth century government and no longer the most important. It proved as difficult to find capable and honest administrators as it was to find judges of integrity. As the range of governmental activities extended, so the work of the Court of the Patrimony increased, but without any corresponding increase in the number or efficiency of the councillors. Already in 1552 Vega had complained to the emperor that 'in this office of the Patrimony there are so few persons and there is such a lack of officials that some matters are lost and many others delayed because of this deficiency. And moreover it is necessary that I myself should perform the duties of the *conservatore* and the *maestro razionale* and supervisor of accounts, and I certify to Your Majesty', he concluded with characteristic exaggeration, 'that on the day I do not do this because I am indisposed or otherwise occupied, that on that day Your Majesty's estate will be worth less and a burden will have been laid on your conscience.'⁴

---

¹ A similar suggestion had been made earlier by the bishop of Patti; Philip II to Colonna, June 22nd, 1577, Simancas MS. Secret. Prov. leg. 1598, fo. 324–5. Patti thought that the provincial courts would be a good training ground for Great Court judges.
² Cisneros, Relacion, Letters and Papers . . . Sicily, B.M. MS. Add. 28 396, fo. 345.
³ Ibid. fo. 342. 'No tiene voto en el consejo pero es de tanta autoridad que adonde el ynclina todos los Juezes ynclinan . . .'
⁴ Vega to Charles V, Feb. 28th, 1552, Simancas MS. Estado leg. 1120, fo. 19.

Philip II was under no illusions that 'it was the Patrimony where the greatest confusion reigned.'[1] Yet so great was his preoccupation with the administration of justice that he failed to effect a reorganization of the Patrimony as far-reaching as the reform of the law courts. Unlike the judges of the Great Court the four *maestri razionali* of the Patrimony were permanent civil servants with fixed salaries. The two lawyers dealt with all legal matters arising out of government finance, while the two laymen, the councillors *di cappa corta*, handled the purely administrative matters.[2] The addition of two more *maestri razionali di cappa corta*[3] was totally insufficient to remedy the defects of an organization which resembled an agglomeration of government departments, rather than a court of law. In 1570 Pescara was forced by the continuing confusion in the council to divide its work into two main sections. Instead, however, of splitting the court itself into a number of departments, the only step he took was to have its activities recorded in separate books. The *libro d'assenti*, the book of expenditure, was subdivided into seven volumes for salaries, interest payment on debts, government mortgages, military expenditure and the like. In the *libro bilianciato*, subdivided into three volumes, all revenue was entered.[4]

The new system, naturally enough, did not produce the orderliness expected. In 1573 Terranova had to appoint four additional *razionali*, or assistants to the *maestri razionali*, to clear up accounts fifteen to twenty years in arrears.[5] It was hoped that this could be done in two years;[6] but in 1580 Colonna had to inform the king of the ineffectiveness of all attempts to bring order into the chaos of the court's financial work.[7] Following his suggestions the Council of Italy attempted the most thorough overhaul of the Patrimony up to date. The accounts department was to be completely separate; two additional *razionali* were appointed, their salaries were increased and a definite ladder of promotion was established, from the nine coadjutors to the *razionali* and eventually to the senior councillors, the *maestri razionali*. Of the latter always one lawyer and one

[1] Philip II to Pescara, Sept. 17th, 1569, Simancas MS. Secret. Prov. leg. 1597, fo. 383–5.
[2] Cisneros, Relacion, B.M. MS. Add. 28 396, fo. 347.
[3] Philip II to Pescara, Sept. 17th, 1569; Simancas MS. Secret. Prov. leg. 1597, fo. 383–5.
[4] Raymundettus, Reg. Sic. Prag. Sanct. II, pp. 66 ff.
[5] Ibid. vol. I. pp. 31 ff.
[6] Philip II to Terranova, Sept. 23rd, 1573, Simancas MS. Secret. Prov. leg. 1598, fo. 147–8.
[7] *Consulta* of the Council of Italy, April 24th, 1581, ibid. leg. 892.

layman were to control the administration of one of the island's three provinces.[1]

Excellent as this reform was from an organizatorial point of view, it left virtually untouched the fundamental problem of the court's personnel.[2] The minor officials were badly paid and tried to drag out their work for fear of being dismissed when it was finished.[3] The *maestri razionali* were very lax in supervising the work of their inferiors, especially in such dull matters as the revision of accounts. They were always able to plead the pressure of other duties, both more interesting and more profitable.[4] Locadello, one of Colonna's most trusted ministers, hardly ever went to his office and when he did so he occupied himself with his private affairs. Estévan de Monrreal, veteran Spanish official and self-styled authority on Sicilian affairs, had a similar reputation.[5] No wonder that Spanish soldiers hated the 'men of the long robe'. Diego Galán, Castilian adventurer and once captive in Turkey, recounts a typical incident. Passing through Sicily, after his escape from Constantinople, he appealed to the duke of Maqueda for help. The viceroy received him well 'and sent a note to the Patrimony of Palermo to give me ten scudi which are always given to Spaniards for their travelling expenses when they return from captivity; the gentlemen of the Patrimony kept me with good words for many days', says the indignant caballero 'until I was so angry that I left, esteeming better the loss of the money than the trouble and shame of asking for it, one of the greatest mortifications a man of honour can suffer.'[6]

The viceroys had clear instructions to prevent councillors from dealing with matters in which members of their families were involved;[7] but all penalties were useless and, from the highest to the lowest, they would try to use their position to advance the interests of relatives and clients.[8] *The avvocato fiscale*, Rao, and his *solicitatore fiscale*, Franchis, were accused of corruption. The regent León thereupon commented dryly that those who knew judged that the officials of the Great Court and of the Patrimony had defrauded the king 'of an infinity of money,' and 'that Rao and Franchis, by com-

[1] Philip II and Council of Italy to Colonna, ibid. leg. 1598, fo. 120–3.
[2] Philip II to Alvadeliste, April 2th, 1591, complained especially of the *razionali's* ignorance of Latin. Ibid. leg. 1600, fo. 14.
[3] Ibid.
[4] *Consulta* of April 24th, 1581; ibid. leg. 892.
[5] Idiáquez to Zayas, May 1st, 1581, ibid.
[6] D. Galán, Cautiverio y Trabajos, 1589 a 1600 (Madrid 1913), pp. 392. Galán's Sicilian companion had a similar experience.
[7] Instructions for Maqueda, Simancas MS. Secret. Prov. leg. 803, fo. 35.
[8] Philip II to Terranova, March 16th, 1573, ibid. leg. 1598, fo. 121–3.

parison with the other officials, are considered saints; for to procure a good match for one's daughter with the favour of the viceroy (in Rao's case), and to sell the office of treasurer at a high price (i.e. for the government), these cannot be considered crimes.'[1]

After only a few years Colonna's system was given up again. Until the end of the reign the government continued to devise new methods of increasing the efficiency of the Patrimony and of settling the outstanding financial accounts – but all without appreciable success.[2]

In spite of all its corruption and inefficiency the Patrimony began to extend its influence over the whole field of government, and it did so at the expense of the Great Court. This growing preponderance of the administrative over the judicial branch of the government was as inevitable as the parallel development in the Council of Italy. There were frequent clashes when the Patrimony trespassed on to the preserves of the Great Court and claimed to take cognizance of criminal cases arising out of its financial administration, while the rival body retaliated by refusing to give up those administrative cases which came its way.[3] In 1595 the viceroy Olivares wrote that, apart from its main work in finance and the supervision of local government, the Patrimony 'treats in particular of matters of justice, state, war and government, and in the last few years there have been no other advisers on matters of war than those of the Patrimony.'[4] The permanence of the position of the *maestri razionali*, as compared with the short period of office enjoyed by the judges of the Great Court and of the Holy Conscience, gave the Patrimony the final advantage over its rivals. In the seventeenth century there was no longer any doubt about its true position, even though it took second place in the rigid order of ceremonial precedence.[5]

At the apex of Sicily's governmental structure was the viceroy. Philip II took over from his father's reign not only one of the most efficient provincial governors of the century (whom he lost little

[1] León to the visitor Bravo (cf. below, ch. 7), Simancas MS. Estado, leg. 1155.
[2] Philip II to Alvadeliste, April 8th, 1591, ibid. Secret. Prov. leg. 1600. fo. 14–15.
[3] Fortunato, Avertimentos, Letters and Papers... Sicily, B.M. MS. Add. 28 396, fo. 495.
Despite these clashes there was a certain *esprit de corps* among the officials of all departments. They would always help the friends and relations of their colleagues in the hope that such favours would be repaid on a suitable occasion. Instructions for Maqueda, Simancas MS. Secret. Prov. leg. 803. fo. 34.
[4] Olivares, Cosas del Govierno, Papeles varios tocantes..., B.M. MS. Add. 14 009, fo. 377.
[5] Celestre, Idea..., B.M. MS. Add. 24 130, fo. 14.

time in dismissing),[1] but also an institution that was more highly developed than any other part of the machinery of imperial administration. This was natural enough. The conciliar type of government which the Spanish Monarchy tried to introduce in its dominions could not have as its head a grand justiciary, a powerful feudal baron who claimed his office by right of birth and social position. There had to be a governor who represented the king, and the king alone.[2] His functions had not, indeed, been fully defined at the time when Ferdinand I decided against permitting the Sicilians to have a separate king. Alfonso appointed three simultaneous viceroys on one occasion, and John II left Lope Ximénez de Urrea to govern the island for thirty years.[3] But already during the reign of the Catholic Kings appointments were limited to three years, with the possibility of renewal for further terms, and in 1489 the first Castilian viceroy took office,[4] much to the regret of the islanders.[5] The Sicilians could no longer aspire to the highest dignity in the country. Only in the temporary absence of the foreign viceroy might a Sicilian rule as president and, at times, the king found it convenient to continue a president in office for a number of years.

Both to compensate the Sicilians for the absence of their king and to impress on them the greatness of the monarchy, the viceroy had to appear with all the external attributes of his master. His first entry into Palermo or Messina was a triumphal procession, providing the crowds with one of those magnificent spectacles they loved so much and raising their hopes that the new governor might be an improvement on his predecessor.[6] Palermo and Messina vied with each other in organizing dazzling receptions until the costs became so excessive that they had to be limited by law to 500 scudi for each town.[7] Only Alvadeliste was imprudent

[1] For Juan de Vega cf. below, ch. 7.
[2] Philip II, Instructions for the duke of Maqueda: '... pues haveis de estar alli en mi nombre y representar mi persona ...' Simancas MS. Secret. Prov. leg. 803, fo. 49.
[3] Gregorio, Opere Scelte, pp. 694 f.
[4] G. B. Caruso, Memorie Istoriche di quanto è accaduto in Sicilia, pt. 3. vol. I (Palermo 1744), p. 90.
[5] Italian dislike of the Castilians made other Spaniards appear in a disproportionately favourable light; e.g. the following passage appears in a sixteenth century relation from Naples, on the occasion of a bread riot: '... se ricordi la memoria di quelli felici tempi de Rè Ferrante Cattolico, che ancora c'havesse bisogno de li grandi de Castiglia, non però mai mandò alcuno Vice Rè, nè in Napoli nè in Sicilia, ma si servi sempre di Valentiani, Aragonesi et Catalani ...'; Correspondence ... Naples and Sicily, vol. II, B.M. MS. Add. 28 395, fo. 146.
[6] Buonfiglio e Costanzo, Messina ..., Lib. v., pp. 46 f.
[7] In 1591 this was changed to 1,000 scudi, but only for the town where the viceroy first entered the kingdom. Giardina, L'Istituto del Vicerè di Sicilia (1415-1798), Arch. stor. sic. n.s. LI, p. 231. Also Letters and Papers ... Sicily, B.M. MS. Add. 28 396, fo. 66.

and tactless enough to ask his Sicilian ministers to meet him in Naples to receive his viceregal oath It was a blow to Sicilian susceptibilities for which the haughty Castilian grandee was never forgiven.[1] In the capital the viceroy and his lady were the centre of society. Fortunato recommended Olivares to follow Colonna's example of inviting members of the nobility to dine with him or to accompany him to mass[2] so as to compensate them on the social plane for what they had lost in political influence.

Don John of Austria was advised to pay special compliments to the Marchesa di Pescara who was not only the wife of the viceroy but the sister of the duke of Mantua.[3] Strict etiquette was the order of the day. This was so extreme that the master of ceremonies of Palermo had to suggest that in case of a chance meeting in the streets between the senate of the city and the viceroy, the senate should 'turn and flee'; otherwise the *pretore* would be bound to claim his place at the viceroy's side, which would be most impolite to whoever accompanied the viceroy.[4]

To enable the viceroy to live in a style suitable to his position he received a salary of six thousand scudi which was supplemented by certain extraordinary revenues from the export taxes on tunny and cheese. He also received the income of any office which happened to be vacant.[5] Some viceroys engaged in private business through confidential agents, but this was a dangerous practice and apt to give a handle to the viceroy's opponents.[6] At every session Parliament granted him 2,500 scudi and also made offers of much larger sums. These offers increased in value as time went on, but were never accepted as there was a tacit understanding between the parties that they were intended only to make a favourable impression in Madrid.[7] In 1609 the viceroy Villena broke this tradition by taking seriously an offer of 60,000 scudi. His action led to an undignified squabble with Parliament and eventually ended in his recall – without

[1] Caruso, Memorie, pt. 3, vol. I. p. 234.
[2] Fortunato, Avertimentos, Letters and Papers... Sicily, B.M. MS. Add. 28 396, fo. 407. The unbending Alvadeliste apparently did not follow this practice.
[3] Instruccion i advertencias... Papeles tocantes... España, B.M. MS. Eg. 367, fo. 27.
[4] B. di Bernardino di Bologna, Ceremonial dell'Illustrissimo Senato Palermitano, Documenti per servire..., ser. 4, vol. III (Palermo 1895–99), pp. 166 f.
[5] Giardina, L'Istituto..., Arch. stor. sic. n.s. vol. LI, pp. 225 ff.
[6] Cisneros, Relacion, Letters and Papers... Sicily, B.M. MS. Add. 28 396, fo. 329. Cisneros maintained that the viceroy must have a band (*capilla*). Colonna had a very good one which cost him 200 scudi a month. Ibid. fo. 340.
[7] Characteristically, the viceroys of Naples accepted similar offers and had no difficulty in obtaining royal permission for this purpose. Lettere Reali ai Vicerè, Palermo, Bibl. Com., MS. 3Qq. E.34, fo. 13.

the 60,000 scudi.¹ After this episode the king prohibited any further offers of this kind. The viceroys handed over all their sources of income to the treasury and in return were granted an income of five times the previous official figure.²

In theory, at least, the viceroy enjoyed complete control over the government of the country. No governor nor king in the whole world had such absolute power, wrote the Spanish *consultore*, Fernando de Matute, in the early years of the seventeenth century.³ He could convoke and dissolve Parliament, ask for new taxation, and publish pragmaticas with the advice of his Holy Council.⁴ No administrative action was lawful without his signature; he alone enjoyed the prerogative of mercy and his recommendations for advancement were usually accepted by the king. He treated directly with the Roman Curia on ecclesiastical matters and could prevent the publication of papal bulls in the kingdom.⁵ Finally, in his capacity of captain-general, he was in charge of defence and commanded all armed forces in the country.

Since, therefore, all functions of government depended on the viceroy personally, Granvelle, Castro, Fortunato and others with experience of Italian administration insisted that the viceroy should systematically divide his time between attendance at councils, public and private audiences, correspondence with other viceroys and with the Council of Italy, and in the preparation of memoranda for the king. In Colonna's routine, for instance, the mornings and afternoons of every day of the week were given up to conferences. Only Thursdays the viceroy kept free to write his long reports to the king. Perhaps his most arduous duty was the public audience he granted on Wednesday and Friday mornings to anyone who wanted to present a petition. Special favour was accorded to orphans, widows and poor monks whose claims the viceroy dealt with on the spot or handed over to the advocate of the poor or the president of the Great Court.⁶

The viceroy's personal attendance at his councils saved him from the isolation which was the fate of the king, working alone at his

¹ Giardina, Sul donativo straordinario del Parlamento di Sicilia al Marchese di Vigliena, Atti . . . , ser. 3, vol. XVIII, pp. 140–150.
² 'In view of the rise of prices' Maqueda's salary had been increased to 12,000 scudi; Simancas MS. Secret. Prov. leg. 1600, fo. 52.
³ F. de Matute, Descripcion de las cosas del govierno . . . de Sicilia, Madrid, R. Acad. de la Hist. MS. Estante 21, gr. 1 a, No. 3. fo. 1.
⁴ Cf. below, p. 104.
⁵ Cf. below, ch. 6.
⁶ Fortunato, Avertimentos . . . , Letters and Papers . . . Sicily, B.M. MS. Add. 28 396, fo. 413–15.

desk in the Escurial. Yet it also robbed him of Philip's detachment, of his ability to consider problems alone and at his leisure and with the advice of only his most trusted councillors. No matter was too small to be brought before the viceroy personally; the mass of cases which the Great Court was at pains to collect from all over the country drew him constantly into a labyrinth of minor problems on which he was expected to give a decision.[1] His instructions from the king and the Council of Italy charged him to take no action in judicial matters without consultation with his judges.[2] Yet no viceroy had been in the country for long before he found out how little he could rely on the advice of his legal experts. 'No other matter is so important for him who governs here than to watch out that he is not duped by the officials who are all natives of the country,' wrote Colonna after a year's experience of Sicily.[3] The officials, as much as the viceroy, were victims of the social atmosphere in which they lived. Ferrante Gonzaga, viceroy from 1535 to 1546, wrote that the whole country was divided into warring cliques; but by vigorous measures he had extirpated the feuds.[4] The boast was as empty as the similar claim of the modern Fascists to have eradicated the Mafia. The feuds remained like a poison dispersed through the body,[5] affecting all social classes and penetrating into all forms of public and private life. Vega said that if a Sicilian petitioned him for a just matter he would seize the opportunity to malign others. If the viceroy then cut him short and granted his request 'he would go away as discontented as if his suit had not been successful, only because he had not been allowed to slander and blacken others.'[6]

The judges of the Great Court and of the Holy Conscience could not escape from these feuds any more than any other Sicilian. False accusations abounded when the conduct of the judges was reviewed at the end of their two years of service. In consequence they tried desperately to obtain permanent appointments or a renewal of their term of office. To achieve this they would go to any length to please

[1] Matute gives an amusing illustration of this which also throws an interesting sidelight on the most famous of seventeenth century Spanish viceroys: '... Y yo vi que un gentilhombre se vino a quejar de que uno orinava debaxo de sus ventanas teniendo hermanas; fue preguntado el Reo por el Virrey si era casado, y respondiendo que si, juzgó el Virrey, Duque de Ossuna, que el actor fuesse, y orinasse debaxo delas vantanas del Reo.' Descripcion..., Madrid, R. Acad. de la Hist. MS. Est. 21 gr. 1a, No. 3.
[2] Instructions for the duke of Alcalà..., Instructions of Philip II etc. B.M. MS. Add. 28 701, fo. 89. Similar instructions were given to the Sicilian viceroys.
[3] Colonna to Philip II, June 24th, 1578, Simancas, MS. Estado, leg. 1148.
[4] F. Gonzaga, Relazione delle cose di Sicilia... 1546; Documenti per servire..., ser. 4, vol. IV, pp. 14 f.
[5] Michele Soriano, Relazione di Spagna, 1559; Albèri, Relazioni, ser. 1, vol. III, p. 353.
[6] Vega to Philip II; Papiers d'Etat..., vol. V, pp. 153 f.

and flatter the viceroy, not only giving judgments in accordance with his known wishes but even divining these from the very slightest indications. At the same time they were sufficiently subtle not to let him notice this.¹ The situation was the exact opposite of that prevailing in the Council of Italy where the councillors were afraid of giving any definite opinion at all.

Castro, who drew this picture of Sicilian judicial procedure, may well have exaggerated; for it was his business to warn the viceroys. Yet they were well advised to heed his warning. Vega was said to have covered his face with his handkerchief during meetings of the court, so as to prevent the judges from guessing his opinion.² Even this precaution did not prove sufficient. When his daughter married the duke of Bivona, he was instantly and inevitably accused of unduly favouring the duke's law suits.³ Colonna's enemies charged him with preventing by his partiality a free vote in council. During an audience he was often in such bad temper (it was asserted) as to cut short petitioners, saying that he had already heard them. It was considered wise to wait outside his room and inquire from those who had gone in before in what mood they had found the viceroy. If it was bad, it was best to come back another day.⁴

The unreliability of the Sicilian officials induced Spanish statesmen again and again to explore the possibilities of appointing foreigners. Pedro Velázquez and the regent Pedro de León were the most consistent advocates of such a policy.⁵ To León's mind the islanders' corruption was axiomatic. 'Carvajal was worse than the Sicilians; God forgive him,' was the crushing epitaph he wrote for a Spanish colleague in the Council of Italy.⁶ Apparently, nothing worse could be said about anyone. Yet all attempts to introduce Spanish ministers into the island foundered on the rock of Sicilian privilege. This might indeed be circumnavigated by appointing Spaniards who had married Sicilian wives.⁷ But they usually became involved (through those wives) in the Sicilian feuds and became parties to more law-

¹ Castro, Avvertimenti . . . , Thesoro Politico, II, pp. 474 ff. For Castro see Appendix III.
² Cisneros, Relacion, Letters and Papers . . . Sicily, B.M. MS. Add. 28 396, fo. 341.
³ Ibid. Also Vega to Philip II, Aug. 16th, 1556; Madrid, Bibl. Nacional, MS. 11055, fo. 81–82.
⁴ Cisneros, Relacion, fo. 341.
⁵ Velázquez, abstract of a memorandum on the defence of Sicily; Letters and Papers . . . , Sicily, B.M. M.S Add. 28 396, fo. 218; also Léon to Philip II, Nov. 1574, ibid. fo. 16.
⁶ León to Bravo, Aug. 20th, 1585, Simancas MS. Estado, leg. 1155.
⁷ e.g. Cifuentes, president of the Great Court 1571–90, and Navas de Puebla, president of the Holy Conscience, 1578–82.

suits than the Sicilians themselves.¹ The only policy left to the government was to concentrate all possible authority in those few offices which could legally be held by Spaniards. This applied to the *conservatore* of the Court of the Royal Patrimony and to the viceroy's *consultore*. Velázquez therefore suggested that they should be the pivots on which to hinge the government of the country.² Through the *conservatore's* hands passed all financial business of the Patrimony. It was said that his presence at the pay parades of the troops saved the king more than 30,000 scudi a year. 'I do not claim so much,' wrote the *conservatore* Estévan de Monrreal modestly; 'but ... I certify to Your Majesty that it is not less than 20,000 scudi.'³ The *consultore* was the viceroy's private legal adviser. He had the right to take part and vote in all courts and councils; he was next in rank to the presidents and reported directly to the viceroy, and he alone could decide questions of competence between the courts.⁴ Through these two officers the viceroy could therefore control finance and justice, the two most important branches of the civil administration. This system worked well as long as the viceroy and his two Spanish ministers were prepared to co-operate. But when the governor of the kingdom was himself an Italian, there was apt to be so much friction that *consultore* and *conservatore* could at best act as a brake rather than as controllers of the government. Colonna quarrelled violently both with his *consultore*, Taboada,⁵ and with his *conservatore*, Miguel Idiáquez,⁶ Both Toledo and Terranova were obliged to imprison Monrreal for intransigence.⁷ The Spanish ministers retaliated by accusing the viceroys of not taking their advice often enough.⁸ No mechanism could function smoothly on such creaking hinges.

Under these circumstances the viceroy came to rely increasingly on his six secretaries. Unlike all his other ministers, they were not

¹ Memorandum cit. Letters and Papers ... , II, B.M. MS. Add. 28 400, fo. 218.
² Velázquez, Memorandum, Letters and Papers ... Sicily, B.M. MS. Add. 28 396, fo. 218.
³ Monrreal to Philip II, Aug. 2nd, 1574, Simancas MS. Estado, leg. 1142, fo. 47.
⁴ G. Giardina, L'Istituto ... , Arch, stor. sic. n.s. II, p. 270.
⁵ *Consulta* of the Council of Italy, June 26th, 1581, Simancas MS. Secret. Prov. leg. 982.
⁶ Cisneros, Relacion ... , Letters and Papers ... Sicily, B.M. MS. Add. 28 396, fo. 346. Cisneros described Idiáquez as 'uno de los mejores, mas inteligentes y limpios hombres.'
⁷ Another *consulta* of the Council of Italy, June 26th, 1581, Simancas MS. Secret. Prov. leg. 982.
⁸ León to Philip II, Oct. 6th, 1575, Letters and Papers ... Sicily, B.M. MS. Add. 28 396, fo. 48.
Estévan de Monrreal, Memoria de cosas de grande Importancia en el Reyno de Sicilia, 1582; Correspondence ... Naples and Sicily, I. B.M. MS. Add. 28 394, fo. 208-19.

appointed by the crown but were members of his household and thus the only officials he could rely upon not to appeal to Madrid behind his back. Their duties were two-fold. In the first place, all incoming despatches passed through their office and were by them referred to the appropriate departments or councils. In the second place, it was the secretaries' duty to keep the viceroy informed on all important matters, so that he might be acquainted with the substance of a case before it was discussed in council. Vega used this method most effectively. Pescara and Terranova conferred with their secretaries every day, and Colonna was said to listen to their reports while still in bed or on his way to mass.[1] The viceroy signed every despatch himself, but this became such an intolerable burden that Colonna introduced a stamp for routine matters. This, too, was used by the secretaries. Alvadeliste's bad health compelled him to leave even more work to them and to the *consultore*.[2] The secretariat claimed to deal with minor appointments and money grants usually within the scope of the Royal Patrimony, with the result that the parties concerned had to pay double fees. There were complaints that the secretaries arrogated to themselves the right to issue export licences for certain commodities and that they kept the originals of royal letters, issuing only their own copies, so that ministers had constantly to ask for the viceroy's signature to cover themselves.[3]

Throughout Philip's reign the power of the viceregal secretariat was steadily increasing. Yet this development could not solve the two fundamental difficulties which faced the viceroy: the impossible task of personally supervising the details of the entire complex system of administration, and the lack of competent and reliable advisers. No Sicilian secretary had a vote in the councils, nor was his salary sufficient to attract to this office men of the calibre of an Antonio Pérez or a Mateo Vázquez who might relieve the viceroy of the burden of daily personal attendance at routine meetings of his councils as they relieved the king of it in Madrid. 'In this kingdom there is a great want of money . . .,' Terranova informed his master; 'but, assuredly, we have no smaller need of qualified and experienced persons who can help and advise him who governs in matters of state and war and on all occasions and during all necessities which arise every day.'[4]

[1] Fortunato, Avertimentos . . . , Letters and Papers, Sicily, B.M. MS. Add. 28 396, fo. 417–19.
[2] Ibid. fo. 418.
[3] Ibid. fo. 437–440.
[4] Terranova to Philip II, Jan. 18th, 1575, Simancas MS. Estado leg. 1144, fo. 7.

The viceroy's principal advisers, moreover, were as much overwhelmed by routine work as was their chief. It was essential that they should be relieved of some of their duties so as to be able to concentrate on the most urgent problems of defence, finance and diplomacy. Precedents were not lacking for such a development. In Spain itself the king's principal ministers met in the Council of State to discuss only the most weighty questions of imperial policy and of war.[1] Nearer at hand, in Naples, the viceroy's Collateral Council was similarly organized. In Sicily, however, no one seems to have thought of following these examples when the reform of the 'tribunals' was being discussed,[2] most probably, because the Sicilians were afraid that such a council of state would open the door to the appointment of Spanish councillors.[3]

The first important departure from the old system occurred not so much as a conscious attempt to improve the efficiency of the Sicilian government, than as the result of an act of personal favouritism. In 1576 Philip wrote to Terranova asking him to let the marquis de la Favara take part in council meetings.[4] The request put the president into a quandary. As a Sicilian aristocrat he was naturally averse to breaking Sicilian privilege; as a loyal vassal of the crown he was loath to disregard the king's personal recommendation. He compromised by admitting Favara to discussions on military problems but barring him from meetings dealing with all other questions.[5] Already a year later Colonna began to call regular meetings of his principal official and unofficial advisers to discuss questions of state and of war[6]. He suggested the institution of a Council of State on the Neapolitan model and continued to press this reform 'because of the multitude of business which the viceroy has to perform which can neither be suffered nor for which there is any remedy.'[7] The king approved his viceroy's action[8] but, as was his

[1] Merriman, The Rise..., vol. IV, pp. 412-13. Even in Spain, many of the functions which one would have expected the Council of State to perform lay in fact within the competence of the Council of Castile (ibid. pp. 415 ff.).
[2] In 1537 Gonzaga had, in fact, proposed a secret council of 3 or 4 members to advise the viceroy on all important questions; but nothing had come of it. Capasso, Il governo ..., Arch. stor. sic. n.s. XXXI (Palermo 1906) pp. 15 ff.
[3] Writing in 1611, Celestre mentioned that the viceroy's extraordinary councillors were mainly foreigners and that their influence was strongly attacked as constituting a breach of Sicilian privilege. Celestre, Idea..., B.M. MS. Add. 24 130, fo. 30.
[4] Letter of April 17th, 1576, Simancas MS. Estado leg. 1146, fo. 38. Lorenzo Téllez de Silva, marquis de la Favara, was a Spaniard and a relative of the king's favourite, Ruy Gómez de Silva.
[5] Terranova to Philip II, Sept. 30th, 1576, ibid. fo. 37.
[6] Colonna to Philip II, June 10th, 1577, ibid. leg. 1147.
[7] Colonna to Philip II, June 24th, 1578, ibid. Estado, leg. 1148.
[8] Philip II to Colonna, Feb. 6th, 1578, ibid. Secret. Prov. leg. 1598, fo. 344.

wont, put off indefinitely the decision on the fundamental issue.

The pressure of routine administration induced the viceroys not only to attempt the establishment of a new Council of State, but also to develop an existing organ of government, a body which enjoyed the advantage of having always been considered as the highest authority in the country. The Holy Council was a feudal survival: an extraordinary assembly of the senior members of the three supreme courts, together with the treasurer-general, the *maestro secreto* (who supervised the financial accounts of local authorities), and the viceroy's *consultore* and any senior military officers who might be required.[1] It was their duty to publish new laws and orders and to take decisions on important matters of policy. This body proved far too large and unwieldy and, as usually happens in such cases, an 'inner cabinet' began to take over all its most important functions. It was a development essentially similar to the evolution of the English cabinet from the unmanageable Privy Council. The viceroys came to prefer working only with the three presidents and the *consultore*. This junta acted at first only as the final court of appeal in the endless and complex hierarchy of the Sicilian courts.[2] Gradually its work came to include all important matters of government and increased to such an extent that it had to meet regularly every Thursday.[3] When a certain policy had been adopted, the presidents presented it to their respective courts where, in practice, it was always accepted. The full meetings of the Holy Council then did little more than register their approval of the decisions taken by the viceroy and his 'cabinet.'[4]

Towards the end of the century, therefore, the viceroys had begun to adapt their administrative heritage to its most essential requirements. Sicily had experienced the classical transformation of a feudal into a conciliar and bureaucratic system of government. It was a slow evolution whose origins reached back to the monarchial restoration of Martin I, and whose final and most decisive stage was the series of reforms in the first decade of the reign of the Prudent King. The re-organization of the courts was the conscious attempt of the Spanish Monarchy to give constitutional form to the new balance of power between the crown and the old feudal forces. It was the end of a phase, and because it was the end, the actors were

---

[1] Olivares, Cosas del Govierno..., Papeles varios tocantes..., B.M. MS. Add. 14 009, fo. 377; cf. also L. Genuardi, Parlamento Siciliano (Bologna 1924), pp. ccxixff.
[2] Cf. note 3, p. 87.
[3] Celestre, Idea..., B.M. MS. Add. 24 130, fo. 30.
[4] Ibid. fo. 10.

well aware of the parts they played in it. At the same time it initiated a new period: the transformation of a conciliar into cabinet government and the building up of an efficient civil service. Here the ground was less familiar; statesmen grappled with problems for which they had neither well-tried answers nor past experience. Traditional ways of thought among both Spaniards and Sicilians prevented the free growth of an administrative theory adequate to meet the demands of a changed situation. Vested interests, expressed in terms of the defence of the island's privileges,[1] wore down all attempts to carry out a fundamental overhaul of the government by the introduction of Spanish personnel. Lack of administrative talent and inadequacy of legal training in the Sicilian officials placed an intolerable strain on the viceroy and the senior ministers;[2] and the age-old feuds and almost venerable corruption in all classes of Sicilian society and Sicilian officialdom vitiated the efforts of the best intentioned governors. Yet if the Spanish Monarchy failed to establish that degree of bureaucratic control over Sicily which it enjoyed in Castile, it was able to construct a solid basis for the power of the crown, strong enough to enable Spanish rule to harness the resources of the island in the service of the empire and to survive both the rapid decline of the monarchy itself and two major revolts in the following century.

3. *The Central Control of Local Government*

While Aragonese and Hapsburg kings were building up a modernized civil service around the court and were progressively reducing the influence of the nobles over the government, the power of the barons remained unbroken on their private estates and in their own districts; and within their city-walls the communes cherished the traditions of self-government, characteristic no less of the ghibelline than of the guelfic towns of Italy. This local autonomy the Sicilian estates defended far more stubbornly than all their other political rights.

[1] Despite its virtual exclusion from a direct share in the central government the feudal nobility was still powerful enough to induce Olivares (viceroy from 1592 to 1595) to offer this piece of advice to his successors. 'With the barons you are everything – without them you are nothing.' Quoted by N. Palmieri, *Saggio Storico e Politico sulla Constituzione del Regno di Sicilia infino al 1816* (Losanna 1847) p. 69.

[2] Most Sicilian officials did not overwork themselves. Only in 1597, and then as a desperate remedy to clear up outstanding accounts, hours of work in the Patrimony were increased from five to six a day. *Consulta* of the Council of Italy, Oct. 24th, 1597. Simancas MS. Secret. Prov. leg. 987. Senior councillors took papers home to work after office hours – a custom which tended to increase the general confusion of Sicilian administration, ibid. leg. 1600, fo. 14.

Unlike the cities of northern Italy, the medieval towns of Sicily had developed under a strong royal authority. In the north the constitutions of the towns were concerned only with public law. In Sicily public law was the law of the whole kingdom and the communes were content to concentrate on private law.[1] The statutes and *consuetudines* of Messina (the town nearest to the other Italian towns in its tradition of striving for self-government as a city-state) deal almost exclusively with marriage and property law, and the competence and procedure of law courts.[2] Lacking *constitutiones* of public law, the towns valued all the more the privileges which they had obtained from the kings. Messina claimed privileges dating back as far as the Roman empire. On the basis of these privileges they developed their strong traditions of civic independence more successfully than the smaller towns subject to the great Italian city states of Florence and Venice.

In the course of the fifteenth and sixteenth centuries such democratic elements as had existed in the governments of the medieval communes were gradually displaced.[3] Just as the towns themselves based their status in the kingdom on privileges, so within the towns minorities extended their privileges and power, claiming exemption from taxes or the exclusive right to high offices. Even when there were no such claims, political power tended to accumulate in the hands of a few families who used the municipal revenues in their own interest.[4] Mineo, a small town in the Val di Noto, asked the viceroy to appoint three *sindaci*, one each from the nobles, bourgeoisie and artisans, to represent the town permanently at the Great Court. This was intended to equalize the town's status in the kingdom with that of the great communes which had this right of permanent representation at the government; but it was done at the expense of democratic rights; for formerly *sindaci* were elected by the civic council of all citizens.[5] In Caltagirone the nobles obtained a royal diploma excluding all others from election to the office of *giurato*, or town councillor,[6] and under Charles V they secured the

---

[1] R. Gregorio, Introduzione allo Studio del Diritto Pubblico Siciliano (Palermo 1794) pp. 188 ff.
[2] O. Hartwig, Die mittelalterlichen Stadtrechte Siziliens (Cassel und Göttingen 1867), pp. 57 ff.
[3] Gregorio, Opera Scelte, pp. 481 ff.
[4] Philip the Second's instructions to Medinaceli in 1557 to deal with this practice. Instructions of Philip II . . . , B.M. MS. Add. 28 701, fo. 43.
[5] G. Pardi, Carlo V e la communità di Mineo, Arch. stor. per la Sic. orient., II, pp. 76 f.
[6] Pardi, Un Commune . . . , Arch. stor. sic. n.s. XXVI, pp. 348 ff.

right to bar from the council all who did not have the unanimous approval of its members.¹ In Trapani the confusion and ineffectiveness of the administration, caused by the exemptions and privileges of certain families, grew to such an extent that the *giurati* threatened to resign in the middle of defence preparations against the Turks.² The most typical case was that of Messina. There the common people had been excluded from the government of the city long before the sixteenth century.³ The struggle between the nobles and the bourgeoisie, or *popolari*, continued ⁴ but the control of the administration came to be monopolized by a few noble families and by the silk and banking interests. When the great allied fleet of 250 sail and 80,000 men assembled in the port of Messina for the Lepanto campaign, Messinese shop keepers and silk merchants had the best year of the reign. Yet when the city constructed the magnificent Strada d'Austria in honour of Don John, the burden of the new *gabelles* imposed for this purpose fell mainly on the poor.⁵

It was in the interests of the defeated and oppressed classes that the crown could interfere most effectively in the administration of the communes. Such a policy of intervention accorded both with Philip's Christian conception of equal justice for all,⁶ and with his desire to curb the excessive independence of his vassals. In this spirit the king could limit the extraordinary annual expenditure of the Messinese senate to 3,000 scudi. Not one tari was to be spent over and above this sum without the viceroy's consent.⁷ Some years later Alvadeliste established a fund of 100,000 scudi to facilitate the provision of corn and to lighten the burden on the poorer citizens. As so often happened in Sicily, the intention proved better than the execution; for it was found that within a year the administrators of the fund had spent most of it irregularly; yet his action constituted a valuable precedent for further governmental interference.⁸

In Palermo and in most other towns the viceroys had early estab-

---
¹ Ibid. p. 358.
² V. Vitale, Trapani nelle Guerre di Carlo V in Africa, Arch. stor. sic. n.s.XXIX, p. 321.
³ C. Giardina, Capitoli e Privilegi di Messina (Palermo 1937) pp. 423 ff.
⁴ Instructions to Medinaceli; Instructions of Philip II . . . , B.M. MS. Add. 28 701, fo. 24.
⁵ G. Arenaprimo, Il Ritorno e la Dimora a Messina di Don Giovanni d'Austria; Arch. Stor. sic. n.s. XXVIII, pp. 73 ff.
⁶ Instructions to Medinaceli, B.M. MS. Add. 28 7011, fo. 36. The viceroy was to see to it 'que los mayores no opriman ni tiranizan los menores biviendo todos en la ygualded que la caridad y policia publica requiere.'
⁷ Reg. Sic. Prag. Sanct. vol. II, pp. 331 ff. Pragmatica of 1574.
⁸ Olivares, Cosas del Govierno . . . , Papeles varios tocantes . . . , B.M. MS. Add. 14 009, fo. 397.

lished the right to appoint the town councillors.¹ Co-operation between central and local administration could therefore develop smoothly without causing recurrent crises over privilege and in 1582 the viceroy Colonna and the senate of Palermo drew up jointly a whole series of orders defining the duties of all municipal officials and prescribing in great detail their functions and responsibilities. As in the case of Messina, this governmental intervention was justified on the grounds of procuring the fair and honest administration of the city and, in particular, lightening the burden of the poorer citizens who provided most of Palermo's revenue by paying indirect taxes on food stuffs.² So firm was the government's grip over the administration of the capital that a special officer, the *sindaco*, had to be appointed in order to represent the city's interests in its own senate.³

Messina, Catania and Syracuse, on the other hand, elected their own *giurati* by the peculiarly Sicilian mixture of indirect election of a small number of candidates from suitable citizens (a procedure called the *squittino*) and the election by lot (*bussolo*) of the officials from these candidates.⁴ These officials were naturally more eager to please their electors than the viceroy, and zealously upheld the city's privileges against the government, even those which were forgeries.⁵ In the fifteenth century Messina had obtained from Alfonso the right to have its law courts declare any royal act contrary to privilege. The authenticity of the city's claims was therefore quite irrelevant, and Messina soon boasted that she possessed more liberties than any other town subject to a prince.⁶ Viceroys who ignored these claims 'gained little reputation' as they caused tumults and riots and always had to give way in the end.⁷ For the city had powerful friends in Madrid, as García de Toledo found to his cost when he executed summary justice on a certain Ramondo Trimarchi, leader of a tumult against his soldiers.⁸

If Madrid failed to support the viceroy on this occasion, such an

---

¹ There were always four *giurati* in whose hands was the administration of the commune, except in Messina and Palermo where there were six.
² Capitoli et Ordinationi fatti dalli ... Signori Marc Antonio Colonna et altri Vicerè ... raccolti da D.Ido Lercaro (Palermo 1694) pp. 1–70
³ Ibid. cap. 68. p. 28.
⁴ Gregorio, Opere Scelte, p. 543.
⁵ Olivares, Cosas del Govierno ..., Papeles varios tocantes ..., B.M. MS. Add. 14 009, fo. 396.
⁶ Ranke, Die Osmanen ..., p. 209.
⁷ Fortunato, Avertimentos ..., Letters and Papers ..., Sicily, B.M. MS. Add. 28 396, fo. 411–413.
⁸ Castro, Avvertimenti ..., ibid. fo. 373. It was the beginning of the agitation against Toledo which effected his recall in 1567.

attitude was consistent with the general line of Spanish policy. It was not Philip's intention to provoke an open breach with the Sicilian communes, provided his objectives could be attained by other methods. It happened, for instance, that Alvadeliste proposed that the government should take over a certain number of fiefs held by three small towns, Caltagirone, Nicosia and Monte di San Giuliano. The Council of Italy thereupon suggested that they should be offered compensation; only if they failed to accept this a judicial commission should be set up to enquire into abuses in the fiefs. In Sicily one could always rely on there being abuses. Once they were proved the whole question could be left to the courts who would undoubtedly decide in favour of the government.[1] On this principle the central authority could impose at least an *ex post facto* check on the activities of municipal officials, and Olivares urged his successor never to neglect their annual sindications.[2]

The government was more successful in extending its hold over the law courts of the towns than over their general administration. In Messina the only direct representative of the king was the *straticò*, the president of the city's court of law. Nearly all Sicilian communes enjoyed the *mero e misto imperio*, the right of civil and criminal jurisdiction inside their territory. The Messinese, moreover, could claim to be tried by their own fellow citizens, wherever they resided. It was said that if there were only three Messinese in a town and two had a quarrel, they could be tried by the third.[3] The position of the *straticò* was therefore of the utmost importance, and he ranked fifth among Spanish ministers in Italy, preceded only by the viceroys of Naples and Sicily, the governor of Milan and the ambassador at Rome.[4]

Yet even in the judicial sphere the communes fought hard to maintain their independence. If the viceroy appointed the judges of the local courts[5] the towns insisted that only their own citizens were eligible,[6] even when this meant that most judges were laymen. In

[1] *Consulta* of Sept. 7th, 1588, Simancas MS. Secret. Prov. leg. 984.
[2] Olivares, Cosas del Govierno..., Papeles varios tocantes..., B.M. MS. Add. 14 009, fo. 396.
[3] Giardina, Capitoli..., p. 447.
[4] L. Bianchini, Della Storia economico-civile di Sicilia, vol. I (Napoli 1841) p. 78.
[5] Until 1578 they were appointed by the king. In that year differences of opinion arose in the Council of Italy and the appointments were referred to the viceroy and this custom persisted. Fortunato, Avertimentos..., Letters and Papers... Sicily, B.M. MS. Add. 28 396, fo. 427-8.
[6] In only 14 of the smaller towns did the government have the right of 'free' appointments. These towns were Giaci, Patti, Piazza, Taormina, Nicosia, Conillon (Corleone?), Polizzi, Sutera, Surgento (Girgenti?), Naro, Traina, Salemi, Sciacca and Cefalù. Olivares, Cosas del Govierno..., Paleles varios tocantes..., B.M. MS. Add. 14 009, fo. 381.

1597 the marquis of Geraci, then president of the kingdom, was rash enough to designate the marquis of Francaforte as *pretore*, or highest judicial officer of Palermo. The senate and the *sindaco* declined to accept him because he was not a citizen of Palermo, and were in consequence promptly imprisoned by the president. They appealed to the king, and Geraci thought it wise to release them. The senators, however, refused to leave prison until they, and the *pretore* they had themselves chosen in place of Francaforte, were fully re-instated.[1]

The central government found it as difficult to make headway against the local authority of the barons as against the privileges of the towns. Both individually and as a class the nobles were immensely wealthy.[2] In some seignorial towns some democratic customs had survived into the sixteenth century and a civic council of the whole population could discuss new laws or agreements with the lord.[3] But since the lord could prohibit all public meetings, such manifestations of the popular will were not likely to cause him much trouble.[4] Enjoying the *mero e misto imperio*, appointing the *giurati* and the captains of justice of the communes within his jurisdiction, and levying feudal dues at will on his vassals, the Sicilian baron ruled his estates with an authority far more absolute than that enjoyed by the king over the whole country.

Just as in the free cities, the government could at first interfere only when the nobles abused their powers. The *maestro giurato* toured the whole country twice a year to check the financial accounts of local governments and to institute the sindication of its officials.[5] Gradually the *giurati* came to be held responsible more to the central government than to their feudal lord and visitors for the sindication were sent direct from Palermo.[6] But throughout the reign the lords

[1] di Blasi, Storia..., vol. II, p.373; di Giovanni, del Palermo Restaurato, di Marzo, Bibl. Lett. e. Stor. 2nd ser. vol. II. pp. 256 f.
[2] In the fifteen 'eighties the combined income of the twenty-five greatest lords, the counts, marquises, dukes and princes, was more than 400,000 scudi or well over half the total revenue of the government (Cisneros, Relacion..., Letters and Papers..., B.M. MS. Add. 28 296, fo. 333–4). Of a total of 195 communes, listed in the census of 1583, one hundred and fifty three were baronial and only forty-two owed direct allegiance to the king. As the prosperity of the country gradually increased, the benefits were reaped by the nobles: in 1653 the number of baronial communes had risen to 242, while the royal communes had increased only by one, and a similar development continued in the eighteenth century (Maggiore-Perni, La popolazione..., p. 415 ff.)
[3] As for instance in Ferla; Verdirame, Le istituzione..., Arch, stor. per la Sic. orient., II, p. 53.
[4] Ranke, Die Osmanen..., pp. 210 f.
[5] Trattato di Sicilia, Naples, Bibl. Naz. MS. X.D. 46, fo. 7.
[6] This did not necessarily increase the efficiency of local government. The bishop of Patti reported in 1577 that the sindicators committed frauds and robberies and made pacts with the officials they were sent to judge. Philip II to Colonna, June 22nd, 1577. Simancas MS. Secret. Prov. leg. 1598, fo. 326.

successfully maintained their right of appointment. Every seignorial privilege was fiercely defended and even the most loyal Sicilian nobles would oppose the king on issues affecting the interests of their class. When in 1568 Philip rejected the barons' claim to receive free money grants from their vassals,[1] Terranova, as president of the kingdom, simply ignored the king's letter. Only a direct and very strongly worded order from the Council of Italy could, four years later, induce the recalcitrant governor to publish the king's command.[2]

With their sources of income thus curtailed the barons sought to compensate themselves by increasing the rents of their tenants. The new viceroy, Colonna, was a Roman aristocrat who had no personal interests in the question. He protested violently to Madrid that the nobles were ruining the country's agricultural production and that it was again the duke of Terranova and his friends who were blocking all reforms by maintaining that a forcible lowering of rents was tantamount to confiscation of their goods.[3] But a question in which royal jurisdiction was not directly concerned did not commend itself to Philip's legalistic mind as a suitable occasion for a trial of strength with the Sicilian nobility. The viceroy was to reform abuses such as the farming out of jurisdictional rights to the lords' foreign creditors, he wrote in reply to Colonna's remonstrances, but the nobles' interests had also to be considered, and Colonna was to proceed with the prudence and discretion needed to arrange these questions also to the satisfaction of the barons.[4]

It was economic necessity, rather than political consideration, which prompted the most important extensions of governmental interference with local administration and with the privileges of the nobility. Not all barons were as rich as the duke of Terranova whose estates yielded him an annual income of 40,000 scudi.[5] Many had failed to adapt themselves to the new money economy or were ruined by speculation. To prevent their estates from being broken up to the detriment of the cultivation of corn, the viceroys Olivares and Maqueda established a special commission[6] to administer the

---

[1] Philip II to Terranova, April 22nd, 1568, Lettere e Istruzioni Reali..., Palermo Biblioteca Communale, MS. 3Qq. C.33, fo. 92.
[2] Philip II (Council of Italy) to Terranova, Nov. 6th, 1571. Simancas MS. Secret. Prov. leg. 1598. fo. 53. The king's order was executed on April 19th, 1572.
[3] Colonna to Philip II, June 24th, 1578, Simancas MS. Estado leg. 1148.
[4] Philip II to Colonna, Oct. 24th, 1578, ibid.
[5] Cisneros, Relacion..., Letters and Papers..., Sicily, B.M. MS. Add. 28 396, fo. 333.
[6] It was called *Deputazione degli stati feudi e territori*.

property, to allow the creditors the current interest on their loans from the rents and to repay the capital of the loans as sufficient funds became available. The creditors could not touch the estate, but the owners had to live on the small pensions granted by the commission.[1]

The activities of this viceregal commission might be galling to the pride of those who had the misfortune to fall under its jurisdiction, but it affected only individuals. The viceroy's control of the corn-trade, however, touched the life of the whole country. This control developed inevitably from the government's determination to obtain financial advantage from the country's most important economic activity. In order to facilitate the levying of export taxes, the producers, or the merchants who bought from them, had to take all grain destined for export to granaries in a number of ports, known as *caricatori*. The viceroy then granted export licenses to foreign merchants,[2] and determined the duty. It was a task calling for the nicest judgment. If the duty was increased by only four tari per salma (as it was by Medinaceli in 1563) the buyers found it cheaper to import from Provence and Alexandria.[3] If the price was fixed too low, the producers could not make sufficient profits to pay their creditors who, in turn, would be unable to advance them money for the next winter's sowing, so that there would be a serious scarcity in the following year.[4]

Even more difficult was the determination of the amount of grain which could safely be exported. Quite apart from the question of revenue, the viceroy was often under heavy pressure from the government of Madrid to supply the Spanish navy at the expense of commercial exports.[5] Such supplies involved the loss of export taxes and the danger of shipping out of the country more than it could spare.[6] This danger was very real because of the unreliability of the viceroy's sources of information. It was the duty of the *maestro portulano* and his officials in the *caricatori* to estimate the amount of corn available. In order to please the viceroy they would present

[1] Olivares, Cosas del govierno..., B.M. MS. Add. 14 009, fo. 386. Celestre, Idea del govierno..., B.M. MS. Add. 24 130, fo. 13. Orlando, Il Feudalismo..., pp. 240 ff.
[2] The export licence for either one salma of wheat, or two of barley and vegetables, was called *tratta*.
[3] Castro, Avvertimenti..., Thesoro Politico, vol. II. pp. 473 f.; Caruso, Memorie.... pt. 3. vol. I. p. 180.
[4] Olivares, Cosas del Govierno..., B.M. MS. Add. 14 009 fo. 393; Celestre, Idea..., B.M. MS. Add. 24 130, fo. 18.
[5] Cf. below, ch. 5.
[6] Pescara to Philip II, Oct. 22nd, 1569; Letters from Italy, B.M. MS. Add. 24 401, fo. 97–98.

much too optimistic estimates.[1] Thus it happened in 1590 that Alvadeliste allowed the export of so much corn that the reserves left in the country were reduced far below the 1,000,000 salma needed for home consumption. The viceroy had been anxious to meet the heavy demands from Spain during the dark days after the defeat of the Armada and had, moreover, been seriously misled by his officials.[2] The result was the worst famine of the century; it lasted for several years, the producers not having even enough grain for seed. The peasants hoarded what little they had while speculation by unscrupulous merchants put the finishing touches to the catastrophe. A desperate scramble developed for the little corn that was still on the market. The seaports sent out their galleys and boats to capture passing grain ships bound for other destinations, and the viceroy was obliged to provide escorts for Neapolitan ships sailing through the Straits of Messina.[3] The senate of Palermo had to pay twenty scudi per salma of grain[4] (before the famine the price had been about $4\frac{1}{2}$ scudi[5]) and in Messina the price rose to as much as 40 scudi. The senates of the two cities sold bread below cost, at great loss to themselves, yet in Palermo alone twenty thousand people were said to have died.[6]

If a similar disaster was to be avoided in future, the government's control had to be extended beyond the *caricatori* and into the villages. Already forty years earlier Vega had led the way by appointing nine noble commissioners to supervise the marketing of corn in the country and by attempting to assess local needs before allowing exports,[7] but the practice seems to have lapsed. Moreover, information on the state of the harvest had to become far more accurate, and

[1] Olivares, Cosas del Govierno..., 'La materia frumentaria de las tratas tiene de suyo grandes difficultades y contradiciones por depender tanto de los successos de los temporales y de la facilidad de los revelos como por la passion y enteresse Universal aun de aquellos que los miran sin interesse, por lo que habla por lo que oyen a los que lo tienen y hasta el virey que viviendo siempre con desseo de abundancia le engañan todos le dan a entender siempre mejor el estado de las cosas del que en efetto es, y por que todo lo que se haze para bajar el prezzo del Trigo desanima a los agriculares y los que los anima lo encarece.' B.M. MS. Add. 14 009, fo. 393.
[2] Alvadeliste to Philip II, Feb. 6th, 1591, Simancas MS. Estado leg. 1157. On April 29th, 1590, the viceroy had assured the king that the island was well provided with all the grain it needed. Ibid.
[3] Alvadeliste to Philip II, March 9th, 1591, ibid.
[4] di Giovanni, Del Palermo..., Bibl. Lett. e Stor., 2nd ser. vol. I, pp. 246 f.
[5] Maggiore-Perni, La Popolazione..., p. 500
[6] Perino, Varie Notizie..., B.M. MS. Add. 19 325, fo. 71. 'Venivano li uomini e donne e fanciulle con l'erbe al bocca a guisa di capre, ed offerivano a chi gli dava pane non solamente quel che avevano, ma anco il loro honore le donne, e la loro virginità, si vedevano cascare morti con l'herbe sudette alla bocca li poveri Regnicoli...'
[7] Carlo d'Aragona (Terranova) to Charles V, Feb. 8th, 1551, Simancas MS. Est. leg. 1119, fo. 93.

Olivares now insisted on fortnightly reports. The *giurati* of both seignorial and domain towns were given power to fix prices[1] and to borrow money to buy corn, and the Patrimony sent confidential agents, with the title of captains-at-arms to supervise this operation.[2] In bad years Vega's practice of sending commissioners was revived. They were supplied with extensive powers of jurisdiction and could collect grain by force from hoarders and rich landowners to distribute it among poor labourers. Neither Olivares nor the jurists and civil servants who wrote about Sicilian constitutional practice looked upon these commissioners as anything but a last and desperate remedy. The viceroy suggested rather that the government should take over all private contracts for the sale of grain and cut out all middle-men.[3] For the commissioners were always liable to be infected by the Sicilian disease of corruption and personal bias. During the famine Alvadeliste's experience again served as a warning. He had appointed four special delegates (*vicarii*) in one province and they had done little more than quarrel with each other, they had defrauded the land-owners and had done, in general, more harm than good.[4]

The practice of appointing viceregal commissioners was not confined to the supervision of agriculture and the corn trade. They had been introduced at an early date for the purpose of strengthening the control of the central government over the provinces and of by-passing the privileges of barons and communes. They were endowed with far-reaching powers of jurisdiction. But their authority was always limited for special purposes, setting aside all local rights.[5] When an invasion threatened a *vicario*, or military captain-at-arms, was placed in charge of each of the three *valli* of Sicily and was endowed with powers resembling those of the viceroy himself. As long as members of the royal family had filled this position and as long as the greatest and most respected nobles were captains-at-arms, the system had worked reasonably well. But when these were not available and the viceroy had to fall back on lesser men, it was found that power rapidly corrupted those whose highest conception of honour was personal vengeance in private feuds.[6] They claimed ever

[1] Cf. above, p. 80.
[2] Celestre, Idea ... , B.M. MS. Add. 28 130, fo. 117–18.
[3] Olivares, Cosas del Govierno ... , B.M. MS. Add. 14 009, fo. 393.
[4] Fortunato, Avertimentos ... , Letters and Papers ... Sicily, B.M. MS. Add. 28 396, fo. 477–8.
[5] Castro, Avvertimenti, Thesoro Politico, vol. II, pp. 468 f. For the employment of captains-at-arms against bandits cf. below, pp. 117 f.
[6] The government at Madrid was well aware of this and instructed the viceroys to appoint captains-at-arms only in cases of the most urgent necessity. Instructions to

wider authority, displacing the ordinary local jurisdiction both in criminal and civil matters and ended by tyrannizing whole provinces.[1] Working, as was his habit, in favour of his own class, Terranova appointed nobles as captains-at-arms in their own districts. This made nonsense of the whole system of commissioners by increasing rather than decreasing the local supremacy of the barons.[2] Terranova himself and some of the other great magnates used their extraordinary authority as captains-at-arms to attract lawsuits from all over the country to their own courts.[3] It was largely due to Colonna that this dangerous development was arrested. The captains-at-arms were forbidden to stay more than three days in any one town and their jurisdiction was limited to those they had arrested in the country. Where formerly they had been appointed for life, their period of office was now reduced to two years, and with this limitation disappeared the basis for the extraordinary activities of Terranova and his friends.[4]

Nevertheless, complaints against the captains-at-arms continued, and Colonna himself had the mortification of seeing his enemies contrive to have his own brother, Pompeo, sindicated for his tenure of the office of *vicario*.[5] The old Sicilian problem, the impossibility of finding competent and honest officials, rendered futile every thought of using the system of viceregal commissioners to cut through the tangle of local jurisdictions, privileges, and vested interests. At best, the captains-at-arms could be employed as *ad hoc* agents to deal with a particular problem. At worst, the easy perversion of the office for private purposes represented a danger to the central government which was often greater than the evil it was designed to remedy.

During the whole of Philip's reign there was no attempt to launch a determined and systematic campaign for the extension of governmental control over local administration. Progress in this direction was haphazard and determined largely by immediate considerations of practical efficiency rather than by an overall plan. 'The best foundation of the security of the state is a contented nobility, which

Medinaceli, Instructions of Philip II . . . , B.M. MS. Add. 28 701, fo. 24. Instructions to Maqueda, Simancas MS. Secret. Prov. 803, fo. 36–37.
[1] Fortunato, Avertimentos, Letters and Papers . . . , Sicily, B.M. MS. Add. 28 396, fo. 479.
[2] Estévan de Monrreal to Philip II, Aug. 2nd, 1574. The *conservatore* mentions six specific cases. Simancas MS. Estado leg. 1142, fo. 47.
[3] Colonna to Philip II, June 24th, 1578, ibid. leg. 1148.
[4] Raymundettus, Reg. Sic. Prag. Sanct., vol. I, pp. 118 f. Cisneros, Relacion . . . , Letters and Papers . . . , Sicily, B.M. MS. Add. 28 396, fo. 343.
[5] Buonfiglio e Costanzo, Historia Siciliana, p. 658. Granvelle to the visitor, Bravo, June 26th, 1584. Simancas MS. Estado. leg. 1155.

does not want to improve its condition,' wrote Pedro Velázquez to his master in 1576,[1] and the *Rey Prudente* agreed with him. The reform of administrative organization, the slow increase in efficiency and the widening of the government's economic activities were, in the long run, bound to tell against the autonomous powers in the country. Yet only in the seventeenth century was the monarchy able to deal a substantial blow at the privileges of the baronage of Sicily by claiming for itself the right to appoint all officials in seignorial communes,[2] and the privileges of Messina could only be broken after a ruinous war which all but cost Spain the dominion over the whole island.[3]

4. *The Administration of Law*

The maintenance of justice together with the defence of the Catholic religion was, in Philip the Second's conception of kingship, the most important duty of a ruler. For it was God's will that the good should be rewarded and the evil punished, and to this end the law must be administered equally for great and small, for rich and poor, for natives and foreigners. In his instructions to his viceroys Philip stressed these points again and again: only thus could the state live in peace and the regent avoid burdening his conscience with sin.[4] There is no doubt that most of the viceroys agreed with the king and tried to carry out this task. 'Criminal justice is the *totum continens* of your charge.' Thus the most humane and likeable of the Prudent King's governors summed up his eight years' experience of Sicilian government for the benefit of his successor.[5]

The practical problems facing the viceroy in the just administration of the law were formidable. When García di Toledo arrived in Sicily,[6] he found Palermo a city of armed gangs and robbers. The nobles kept heavily-armed retainers; murder was an everyday occurrence while private feuds led frequently to pitched battles in the streets. The authorities dared not to interfere, for the assassins and robbers were under the protection of persons of great influence.[7]

It was comparatively easy for the new viceroy to restore order in

[1] Letters and Papers..., Sicily, B.M. MS. Add. 28 396, fo. 69.
[2] Antonio de Amico, Noticias del Gobierno del Reyno de Sicilia, 1632, Papers relating to Italian States, vol. II, B.M. MS. Add. 28 466, fo. 130.
[3] E. Laloy, La Révolte de Messine, l'Expédition de Sicile et la Politique Française en Italie (1674–1678) 3 vols. (Paris 1929–1931).
[4] Instructions to Medinaceli, B.M. MS. Add. 28 701, fo. 30, 35. Instructions to Maqueda, Simancas MS. Secret. Prov. leg. 803, fo. 26.
[5] Medinaceli, Advertencias..., Documentos Inéditos..., vol. XXVIII, p. 318.
[6] In February 1565. He did not immediately go to Palermo himself.
[7] di Giovanni, Del Palermo..., Bibl. Lett. e. stor. 2nd ser. vol. II, pp. 185 f.

Palermo by the imposition of a curfew and by the strict enforcement of the regulations against the carrying of arms of any kind.[1] Outside the big towns such measures were useless, and yet it was precisely in the country that brigandage was most widespread. When the central government became too strong for the nobles to maintain private armies, they resorted to agreements with independent bands of brigands or prevented the local authorities from proceeding against them.

In a country which though fertile was desperately poor, where little justice could be hoped for against powerful barons and everything must be feared from greedy officials, men found it easier to take to the mountains and live as bandits than to work for a miserable wage on another's estate. Farmers whose crops had been ruined by rainstorms and who could not afford to defend themselves in court against the claims of the treasury would prefer to let themselves be banished rather than linger in prison.[2] There were outlaws (*fuorosciti*) who acted the part of Robin Hood, robbing the rich to give to the poor, as did Vincenzo Agnello who was so much feared that the Viceroy's soldiers only pretended to pursue him.[3] However, most of the bandits' histories were as ignoble as that of Rizzo di Sapunara who worked hand in glove with certain members of the high nobility before he was forced to flee to Florence. He was extradited and died miserably with a poisoned apple between his teeth before he could give damaging evidence against his noble paymasters.[4]

The government launched periodic campaigns against the brigands by commissioning captains-at-arms to hunt them down and making laws against those who sheltered them.[5] Yet many officials did not dare to take action against bandits with influential backing, and many captains-at-arms made common cause with the hunted or used their office to take revenge on personal enemies.[6] The most successful method proved to be the promise of immunity from punishment to any *fuoroscito* who would betray his comrades.

All these repressive measures, though often successful for short

[1] Ibid. p. 186.
[2] Testa, Capitula ..., II, p. 241, 310.
[3] di Giovanni, Del Palermo ..., Bibl. Lett. e. Stor ..., 2nd ser., vol. II, pp. 168 ff.
[4] Perino, Varie Notizie ..., B.M. MS. Add. 19 325, fo. 51.
[5] Pragmaticas of Charles V in 1535, in Reg. Sic. Prag. Sanct., I, pp. 159 ff., and of Pescara in 1576, ibid. pp. 161 ff.
[6] Fortunato, Avertimentos ..., Letters and Papers ..., Sicily, B.M. MS. Add. 28 396, f. 456.
Medinaceli, Advertencias ..., Documentos Inéditos ..., vol. XXIII, pp. 323 ff. The general bad opinion of the captains-at-arms is reflected in the Instructions to the viceroys. Instructions to Maqueda, Simancas MS. Secret. Prov. leg. 803, fo. 36.

periods, did not touch the root of the problem – the reasons which drove men to banditry. The mass of the population had reason to distrust deeply the whole legal system. It was not because the nobles had legal privileges in the courts. The barons had long before lost the right to be tried by their peers, and only on very rare occasions were they able to escape the consequences of serious crimes by the payment of large sums of money. Olivares mentioned in his relation of the government of Sicily that he had allowed such a course on several occasions but that the king had disapproved of his action.[1] It was rather that, except in the most serious cases, the courts took no action against the nobles at all.[2] When Colonna, at the beginning of his period of office arrested the marquis de la Favara for having helped some prisoners to escape, 'it had seemed the most wonderful thing in the world, because in the past he (Favara) had been doing what he pleased which had made everyone terrified of him; for here the hand of justice lies only on the poor.'[3]

It was stated to be the duty of the Advocate and of the Procurator of the Poor 'to defend in civil as well as in criminal cases all poor persons, Sicilians and foreigners, who are imprisoned or otherwise charged by the state or by private persons,' and the salary of these officials was to be withheld unless they discharged their duties to the satisfaction of the Great Court.[4] Yet their salary was comparatively low, and the office enjoyed so little prestige that it was often left to indifferent lawyers who cared little for clients unable to pay fees.[5] It was not until the seventeenth century that Philip the Second's successors remedied these evils.[6]

As in all other countries at the time, criminal procedure was weighted heavily against the accused. The *avvocato fiscale*, the public

[1] Olivares, Cosas del Govierno..., Papeles varios tocantes..., B.M. MS. Add. 14 009, fo. 388. There were complaints that the *straticò* of Messina had commuted penalties (Philip II to Colonna, June 22nd, 1577, Simancas MS. Secret. Prov. leg. 1598, fo. 333). This right was strictly reserved to the viceroy, and Philip II insisted on being consulted in every case. *Consulta* of the Council of Italy on the Instructions to Marc Antonio Colonna, June 24th, 1577, Simancas MS. Secret. Prov. leg. 981.

[2] e.g. in 1577 the government hushed up the murder of a page by the baron of Miserendino; cf. below, ch. 7. Colonna to Philip II, Sept. 24th, 1582. Letters and Papers..., vol. II, B.M. MS. Add. 28 400, fo. 41.

[3] Memorandum on the government of Sicily; Letters and Papers..., Sicily, B.M. MS. Add. 28 396, fo. 198.

[4] Pragmatica of Terranova in 1572, Reg. Sic. Prag. Sanct., I, pp. 30 ff.

[5] Fortunato, Avertimentos..., Letters and Papers..., Sicily, B.M. MS. Add. 28 396, fo. 474.

[6] A. de Amico, Noticias, Papers relating to Italian States, vol. II, B.M. MS. Add. 28 466, fo. 121. Twice during Philip's reign, in 1563 and in 1571, the salary of the Advocate of the Poor was doubled, from 100 to 200 and 400 scudi respectively, but nothing was done to raise his status in an age where form was all-important. Simancas MS. Secret. Prov. leg. 1597, fo. 107; leg. 1598, fo. 62.

prosecutor, held office for life. This gave him an advantage over the judges and he was gradually able to usurp many of their powers. It was he, and not the judges, who examined witnesses and could, on their evidence, order the torturing of the accused – a terrible power in a country of false witnesses.¹ Fortunato, himself at one time *avvocato fiscale* of the Court of the Royal Patrimony, went so far as to claim that the insignificance of the judges and the great power of the prosecution were the reasons why there were so many criminals in the country.²

The people's justifiable distrust of the law,³ and the prevalence of false testimony, which was itself a symptom of this distrust,⁴ constituted a vicious circle, poisoning social relations, perpetuating feuds and making the fulfilment of the king's desire for the maintenance of justice well-nigh impossible. The fundamental reason for the attitude of the Sicilian peasant was, perhaps, his feeling that the whole legal system showed little concern for his own problems, but was an alien body of rules and regulations imposed by a ruling class for their own advantage. Such a feeling was neither conscious nor fully capable of expression. But the man who fired at a hare, missed it, and was yet imprisoned for five or six years because hares might be hunted only with dogs⁵ could not be expected to feel respect for the canons by which he was judged. The poor creditor who found his powerful baronial debtor accusing him of theft before an unsympathetic court with its strange and terrifying procedure⁶ felt himself closer to the hunted bandit than to the custodians of justice. It made little odds whether the rulers were Norman or French, Catalan or Castilian, Sicilian or Spanish – the country population remained psychologically outside the sphere of organized society, whatever their individual loyalty to their unknown king or their personal relations with their immediate feudal overlord.⁷

¹ Testa, Capitula..., II, p. 312; Fortunato, Avertimentos..., B.M. MS. Add. 28 396, fo. 471–2.
² Ibid., fo. 469.
³ All contemporary observers were agreed that, in practice, the law was heavily biased against the poor; they only differed in the conclusions they drew from this fact.
⁴ The government vainly imposed heavy penalties on perjury; e.g. pragmaticas of Charles V and of Medinaceli, Reg. Sic. Prag. Sanct. II, pp. 132, 139.
⁵ Fortunato, Avertimentos, Letters and Papers..., Sicily, B.M. MS. Add. 28 396, fo. 453–4.
⁶ Cisneros, Relacion, ibid. fo. 345.
⁷ In Professor Toynbee's terminology the Sicilian country population might be regarded as the 'internal proletariat' of that part of 'western society'. It seems that in southern Europe there was an even deeper political and psychological (though not necessarily economic) chasm between the peasantry and the more privileged classes than in northern and western Europe. Even now it still exists in the country districts of southern Italy. The problem, in its modern form, has been brilliantly illustrated by

The inevitable result was a degradation of moral standards which left no class of society unaffected. Not only was perjury for the defence in criminal cases not considered a sin,[1] but it became a habit to use any position of vantage to harm an enemy. Litigants appearing in court, or granted an audience before the viceroy, would take any opportunity for slander; nor would their accusations refer to minor transgressions, but always to murder, rebellion or heresy, 'and other matters which the devil himself could not think of,' as Medinaceli wrote despondently.[2] Vega, before him, had similar experiences[3] and his conclusions were even more cynical. 'In general they are like this in all matters,' he remarked, 'and he who commits most crimes is considered most honourable.'[4]

This was undoubtedly an exaggeration, and it may well have been deliberate, for Vega was trying to justify his policy of extreme severity against the nobility. Yet his opinion, over-emphasizing as it did national character as against social and political conditions, was echoed or quoted by nearly all subsequent writers on Sicily.[5] 'The worst people in the world,' was the current opinion about the Sicilians,[6] and at times they seem to have thought so themselves.[7]

Carlo Levi in his autobiographical 'Cristo si è fermato a Eboli' (Milano (?) 1947). The Author proposes a general theory of the conflict between a fundamentally pagan and anarchical country population and an alien, theocratic state – from the conquests of the divinely protected Aeneas to the Italian wars of the Roman Republic (perhaps the bitterest of all Roman wars), the bandit campaigns against the Bourbon police state, and the passive resistance to Mussolini's Fascists. Perhaps this is an artist's rather than a historian's theory; but the subject might well repay closer historical investigation.

[1] Medinaceli, Advertencias . . . , Documentos Inéditos, xxviii, pp. 346 ff.
[2] Ibid. p. 356.
The aristocratic equivalent for these accusations was the practice of bringing suits of illegitimacy against opponents in a civil action. At best one might win an otherwise hopeless case for an inheritance; at worst, it would still involve one's opponent in very costly litigation in the ecclesiastical courts. Such cases might even be transferred to Rome. In 1581 the Council of Italy ordered Colonna to issue a pragmatica against malicious suits of illegitimacy, defined quite simply as suits in which the petitioner could not obtain a favourable verdict. In such cases the principal suit would *ipso facto* be lost as well, and further severe penalties might be imposed. Simancas MS. Secret. Prov. leg. 1599, fo. 106.
[3] Cf. above, p. 99.
[4] Vega to Philip II, letter cit., Papiers d'Etat . . . , vol. v, p. 153.
[5] Both Scipio di Castro and Cabrera de Córdoba took over Vega's definition of the Sicilian character. Vega . . . 'son agudos, aunque no prudentes, sobre todo la gente del mundo apassionada en lo que dessean . . .' op. cit., p. 157; Castro: 'I Siciliani nell 'universale sono più astuti che prudenti, più acuti che sinceri . . . ,' Avvertimenti, Thesoro Politico, II. p. 346; Cabrera: 'Son los Sicilianos sagaces y sutiles, mas agudos que sinceros, amigos de novedades . . .', Filipe Segundo, I. p. 417.
[6] Instruction . . . al Señor D. Juan . . . , Papeles tocantes . . . , B.M. MS. Eg. 367, fo. 22. 'Los Sicilianos tienen opinion de las mas mala gente del Mundo . . . '.
[7] Cisneros, Relacion, Letters and Papers . . . Sicily, B.M. MS. Add. 82 396, fo. 333. 'Y en conclusion, los mismos Sicilianos confiesan que no ay cosa mala en esta ysla, sino la gente.'

While the viceroys did not abandon their purpose of maintaining justice and of showing compassion to the weak, they tended increasingly to seek the solution of all problems in the strictest severity. Pescara visited the prisons every month,[1] and Colonna criticized Vega for approving more of rigour than of equity;[2] yet it became the accepted maxim that the greatest mercy that could be shown to the Sicilians was to be harsh, as otherwise there would be no limit to their crimes.[3] This maxim gradually ceased to have the force of genuine opinion, and in the seventeenth century it was repeated, parrot-like, in nearly every relation on Sicily.[4]

The practical result of this view of the Sicilian character was greatly to increase the use of the *ex abrupto* procedure. This was one of nine different types of procedure in Sicilian law.[5] When employed, the accused could be put to the torture before being informed of the indictment against him. It had originally been applied only in extraordinary cases against great and notorious criminals, but during the reign of Philip II it came to be used freely against anyone suspected of certain crimes. In 1567 all who had the right of *mero e misto imperio* were empowered to proceed *ex abrupto* against highway robbers.[6] Abuses of this power were so common that in 1591 Alvadeliste had to insist that every accused should always be allowed to defend himself,[7] yet attempts by Parliament to limit or abolish the use of the *ex abrupto* procedure failed. Olivares claimed that its abolition would be the downfall of justice, because it was too easy in Sicily for a criminal to procure witnesses to exonerate him. The nobles, who had pressed the government for the abolition of the procedure, confessed to Olivares that they themselves could not live in peace and execute justice on their vassals if the use of the *ex abrupto*

---

[1] Fortunato, Avertimentos..., ibid. fo. 466–8.
[2] Colonna (?), Memorandum, ibid. fo. 192.
[3] Olivares, Cosas del Govierno..., Papeles varios tocantes..., B.M. MS. Add. 14 009, fo. 382. '... en Sicilia ... por lo mas ordinario conviene de usar de Rigor, y el hazerlo es la mayor misericordia que se puede usar porque lo que en esto se escusan los delitos, y se multiplican de lo contrario....'
The Conde de Castro, viceroy 1616–1622, in his marginal comments to Olivares' relation produced another plagiarism of Vega and Scipio di Castro: 'Es generalmente natural de los Sicilianos de mas astucia, mas agudos que sinceros, amigos de novedades, grandes pleytantes, cavilosos, aduladores, y la misma sumision en todo, haziendo por sus fines privados: però en las cosas publicas sumamente temerarios...' MS. Copy of 1685, Madrid, Real Acad. de la Hist., Est., 21 gr. l.a. No. 3. fo. 1.
[4] e.g. a relation of 1640, B.M. MS. Add. 14 009, fo. 406.
[5] La Mantía, Storia della legislazione (Palermo 1874) p. 211.
[6] Reg. Sic. Prag. Sanct. I. p. 155.
[7] Pragmaticarum Regni Siciliae Novissima Collectio, vol. I (Panormi 1636) p. 38.

were taken from them.[1]

Only two men broke through the conventional attitude towards the problem of justice. Argisto Giuffredi, a contemporary writer and poet, exhorted his son that if he became a magistrate he should never take a man's life which God Himself had given him, nor administer torture especially, as was so often the case, on mere hearsay evidence.[2] The other, Francesco Fortunato, was perhaps the only contemporary who saw clearly that crime was a social problem as well as a defect of character.[3] The republics of ancient times were wrong, he wrote, in holding that the judge should never see the criminal's face so as not to be moved to pity.[4] In Sicily the danger was rather selfishness and greed while pity was needed more than any other emotion.[5] 'I call on heaven as a witness', Fortunato exclaimed, ' that any prince who does not observe this . . . will neither maintain justice nor preserve his authority.' Such amnesties as had hitherto been conceded, were useless, because they had depended on the consent of the Great Court judges for each individual case. The judges had interpreted this as giving them the right to decide cases pending not only in their own but also in all other courts. In consequence, persons who claimed the amnesty preferred to make a private arrangement with the local captains-at-arms rather than face the delay, expense and uncertainty of going to the capital for their indulgence.

Fortunato suggested a form of amnesty in the shape of the sale of indulgences for fifteen to thirty tari, for all except the worst crimes. There was no Sicilian who would not take advantage of such an offer and it would, incidentally, provide a useful source of revenue for the government.[6] The whole *ex abrupto* procedure should be given

[1] Olivares, Cosas del Govierno, Papeles varios tocantes . . . , B.M. MS. Add. 14 009, fo. 383.
[2] A. Giuffredi, Avvertimenti Cristiani; ed. L. Natoli; Documenti per servire . . . , 4th ser. vol. IV, pp. 79 ff. Giuffredi may have been influenced in his attitude by his own prison experiences. His advice was, otherwise, that of the conventional petty bourgeois who did not disapprove of horrible punishments for convicted criminals, such as the cutting off of their hands, who advised his son to attach himself to a patron and never, under any circumstances, to oppose the government; and who, rather surprisingly, gave him hints on how best to be unfaithful to his wife.
[3] In specific cases, as when debtors defaulted after a bad harvest, this was realised by Parliament. Testa, Capitula . . . , vol. II, p. 310. When Parliament petitioned for an amnesty and a moratorium for debtors it was careful to point out that this should apply only to debts to the treasury, but not to debts to private persons.
[4] Fortunato, Avertimentos . . . , Letters and Papers . . . Sicily, B.M. MS. Add. 28 396, fo. 466.
[5] Juan de Vega had said the same (cf. below, pp. 174 f). Yet Vega had a greater reputation for severity than any other viceroy.
[6] Fortunato, Avertimentos, B.M. MS. Add. 28 396, fo. 453–5.

up, except for a very few, clearly specified crimes, and the use of torture (of which Fortunato disapproved, although not explicitly) should be strictly regulated, giving the accused a fair chance of defence.[1]

Few of Fortunato's suggestions for legal reform were adopted. Olivares, for whose benefit they had been written, held firmly to the traditional view of the Sicilian character and preferred conventional methods. The political results of the excessive use of the *ex abrupto* procedure (fully recognized already by Scipio di Castro)[2] had the opposite effect to that intended; instead of strengthening the authority of the viceroy they strengthened that of the Inquisition, his most serious rival. Yet such is the inertia of preconceived ideas, that the exploitation by the Inquisition of the fear of the *ex abrupto* procedure only strengthened the viceroys in their belief in 'rigour'.[3] All the king's conscientious attention to the problem of the just administration of the law, and all the viceroys' weary hours spent in public audience and in the supervision of the courts, could do little more than mitigate the worst injustices. They left intact a legal system based on an outlived social structure, determined by outworn ideas of social psychology, and administered by a body of corrupt officials.[4]

---

[1] Ibid. fo. 472–3.
[2] Castro, Avvertimenti . . . . Ibid. fo. 390.
[3] This question will be more fully discussed together with the relations between the viceroys and the Inquisition. See below, ch. 6, sect. 3.
[4] In the following century there appeared signs that, with the good intentions, there also grew up a profounder understanding. The *consultore* Fernando de Matute launched a full-scale attack on the whole *ex abrupto* procedure ('Descripcion . . . ,' probably written in 1616 for the count of Castro; Madrid, R. Acad. de la Hist. Est. 21 gr. 1 a. No. 3.) Matute had no illusions about the mentality of those who defended or excused the *ex abrupto*. 'It may be that the great difference in the habits and the state of mind of the people of this kingdom is the reason why their laws should be so tyrannical,' he wrote. 'St. Thomas (Aquinas) holds this view in his treatise De Regimine (Principum) in paragraph 130. This is the best quotation anyone could think of for putting his mind at rest about every tyrannical practice in the government of the kingdom of Sicily and it even suggests that one is driven to such practices by the desires of the people themselves (fo. 1).' (The reference seems to be to Lib. II, chapter 1,' . . . Quae aut in calidis sunt, intellectivae quidem sunt et artificiosae secundum animam, sine animositate autem propter quod subiectae quidem sunt and subiectae perseverant.')
It is pleasant to find so early a forerunner of Beccaria and Voltaire. After inveighing against the wicked practices of the *procuratori fiscali* (the public prosecutors) with a vehemence even greater than that of Fortunato, Matute makes his most interesting statement: that the judges often refused to convict and 'made a thousand dispensations' in order to mitigate the evils of the *ex abrupto* procedure and 'to close the door to so many false witnesses (fo. 30).' 'Rigour' was beginning to defeat its own ends, as it did in England before the great law reforms of the nineteenth century.

CHAPTER FIVE

Taxation and the Effects of Empire Finance on Sicily

ULTIMATELY the strength or weakness of Spanish dominion in Sicily depended on money. Only hard ducats [1] could pay for the *tercio* of Spanish infantry which safeguarded the country from invasion and the government from overthrow by turbulent barons; only ready cash could maintain the squadron of Sicilian galleys which kept the coast clear of pirates and secured the communications with the rest of the empire. Compared with military and naval expenses the charges of the civil administration were relatively insignificant. Even after the reform of the councils the government spent no more than 60,000 scudi a year on the salaries of all its officials, other than those concerned with military administration. In the budget of 1580/81 this sum represented less than six per cent of total expenditure.[2] In Madrid the viceroy was judged more by the success of his financial policy than by any other criterion; for on this depended the preservation of the kingdom within the Spanish Empire.

The government of Sicily had three main sources of revenue: Parliamentary grants, income from crown rights and crown property, and, finally, taxes which might be imposed without the consent of Parliament. The basis of the Parliamentary grants was the 'ordinary donative,' which had been fixed at 50,000 scudi a year in the fifteenth century.[3] As government expenditure increased Parliament voted extraordinary donatives; they were given for limited periods, but

[1] The rate of the scudo to the Venetian ducat varied in different parts of the empire. In Sicily the scudo was worth 12 tari and the ducat 13. In Milan the scudo was also less than the ducat, but in Naples the proportion was the other way round. Correspondence ... Naples and Sicily, vol. I, B.M. MS. Add. 28 394, fo. 78.

[2] 'Bilancio ... de Sicilia ... dal primo di Settembre ... 1580 infin'al primo di Settembre del 1581.' Madrid, Bibl. Nac. MS. 7633, fo. 34. For the budgets of 1588/89 and 1591/92 the figures are similar. 'Tanteo del Reino di Sicilia,' ibid. MS. 11004; 'Relatione ... dell'introito et essito ... di Sicilia' B.M. MS. Add. 28 396 fo. 482–6. These three are the only complete budgets I have been able to find. The first is the most detailed, and the only one which gives all military expenditure.

[3] C. Calisse, Storia del Parlamento in Sicilia (Torino 1887) pp. 171 ff. The name 'donative' was taken over from Aragon, as were many other Parliamentary terms; e.g. *braccio* the name of the houses of Parliament.

the viceroy could generally rely on obtaining extensions until the additional grants became permanent.¹ At the beginning of Philip's reign the government received 75,000 scudi over and above the ordinary donative.² After Medinaceli's disastrous expedition to Tripoli³ Sicily's strategic situation took a sudden and drastic turn for the worse. Every spring the country fearfully awaited the approach of the Turkish invasion fleet and Parliament hastened to grant another 100,000 scudi a year for defence.⁴ With this extraordinary donative the limit of Parliamentary taxation had very nearly been reached. Most viceroys were glad if they could obtain the prorogation of the 225,000 scudi, together with occasional special grants, and only towards the end of the reign could Parliamentary taxation be screwed up to its highest figure of 278,000 scudi.⁵ With the exception of the ordinary donative these sums were strictly appropriated. Sometimes the government was forced to use such moneys for purposes other than those specified by Parliament; but this happened rarely and, in general, only for defence.⁶

These taxes were borne in fixed proportions by the three Parliamentary estates. The clergy paid one sixth, and the nobility and the towns divided the remaining five-sixths equally between them. The baronial and the domain communes were then allotted their share which they raised almost entirely by indirect taxation. In order to ensure an equitable distribution of the tax-burden, Ferdinand the Catholic had taken a census of the whole population and of its property. Between 1501 and 1597 eight such censuses were taken, six of them in the reign of Philip II.⁷ They were not entirely

---

¹ Medinaceli, Advertencias..., Documentos Inéditos..., vol. xxviii, p. 309. '... ya Vuestra Serenitá (García de Toledo) sabe que siempre se prorogan semejantes servicios de manera que se perpetuan....'
² A. Mongitore, Parlamenti Generali del Regno di Sicilia etc. vol. ii (Palermo 1749) pp. 229 ff.
³ The destruction of the Spanish-Sicilian fleet at Gerba in 1560 'was by far the most significant victory of the Turks in the Mediterranean since the repulse of Charles V at Algiers.' R. B. Merriman, Suleiman the Magnificent (Cambridge Mass. 1944) p. 227.
⁴ Mongitore, Parlamenti Generali, vol. ii, pp. 324 ff, 334 ff.
⁵ Relacion de los Donativos... de 1594, Simancas MS. Estado. leg. 1157. In the course of the sixteenth century special donatives were made for the upkeep of watchtowers along the coast (3333 scudi p.a.), for the repair of roads and bridges (8000 p.a.) and for the maintenance of royal palaces (6667 p.a.).
⁶ Medinaceli, Advertencias..., Documentos Inéditos..., xxviii pp. 333 ff.
⁷ Maggiore-Perni, La popolazione..., p. 152. There were censuses in 1501, 1519, 1548, 1570, 1574, 1583, 1595 and 1597. From the budget of 1580/81: 'Le portione de tutti donativi toccante alle Universitá per repartita secondo valore delle Facoltà descritte di liquido in ciascheduna terra. Ma il donativo de macina fù repartito sopra l'anime numerati, havendosi havuto risguardo d'augmentar le portioni d'alcune terre nelle quali più che nelle altre concorre comertio...' (Bilancio..., Madrid, Bibl. Nac. MS. 7633, fo. 49.)

trustworthy: the cities of Palermo and Messina and the whole of the clergy were exempt by special privilege, and the rest of the population did their best to avoid enumeration or to make their property appear less than it actually was.[1] In consequence, the distribution of taxation remained haphazard, and many communes felt aggrieved at what they considered an unfair burden, with the result that Parliament asked for a new census far more often than was warranted by the shift of population and the redistribution of wealth.[2]

The easiest and most profitable source of Parliamentary revenue was indirect taxation on certain commodities of national importance. There was, firstly, the gabelle on the grinding of corn (*gabella della macina*) which was rated at 9 danari per tumolo[3] and which was calculated to produce 100,000 scudi a year.[4] Secondly, there was the tarino, a levy of one tari per ounce (i.e. one part in thirty) on furs, crude silk and other textiles, amounting to about 62,000 scudi a year.[5] Though this tax was imposed on the whole country, it fell most heavily on Messina with its virtual monopoly of the silk trade.

As in most countries at that time, these taxes were farmed out; and, conforming to the usual standards of Sicilian public morality, the tax-farmers seem to have made huge profits. In 1570 the government was forced to intervene and take the revolutionary step of appointing its own tax-collectors. Every care was taken to make the measure a success. Parliament voted the ample salary of 1,200 scudi for each of the three *percettori* (the new officials in charge of tax-collecting in the three provinces of the island)[6] and the Council of Italy issued the most detailed orders to safeguard the interests of both government and tax-payer.[7] So stringent were these regulations that the president had the greatest difficulty in finding anyone willing

[1] This latter point became more important after Vega's introduction of a Sicilian militia with quotas of recruits for each district.
[2] Maggiore-Perni, La popolazione..., pp. 136 ff.
[3] At the beginning of the 19th century 1 tumolo $=\frac{1}{2}$ English bushel; G. de Welz, Saggio su i mezzi da moltiplicare prontamente le Ricchezza della Sicilia (Paris 1822) p. 22 n.3.; but in the 16th century measurements were not uniform over the whole of Sicily.
[4] The average consumption of corn in the whole kingdom was estimated at 1,000,000 salma = 16,000,000 tumoli; 1 scudi = 1440 danari $\therefore \frac{16,000,000 \times 9}{1440} = 100,000$.
[5] C. d'Aragona, Corrispondenza Particolare; Documenti per servire..., 1st ser. vol. II, pp. 45 ff.
[6] Mongitore, Parlamenti Generali, vol. II, pp. 358 f. The institution of the *percettori* on the Neapolitan model had first been suggested by Toledo. Philip II to Terranova, April 11th, 1568, Simancas MS. Secret. Prov. leg. 1597, fo. 339.
[7] The draft for these regulations, dated 1571, is in Simancas MS. Estado leg. 1136, fo. 288–297.

to undertake this arduous task which involved a guarantee to pay the treasury the full sum on the appointed day, whether it had been collected or not.[1] Nevertheless the collectors were found to ignore their instructions and to oppress the peasants.[2] If the new system was an advance on the old methods,[3] it is at least highly doubtful whether at any time in the sixteenth century the Sicilian tax-payer did not have to contribute a substantially larger sum than his representatives in Parliament had granted the government.

As against the 'definite income' from donatives, there was the 'uncertain revenue' from domain land and crown rights. These latter comprised toll and other economic rights in certain cities (*secretie*); the income of vacant ecclesiastical benefices (*spoglie*); fines imposed by the courts (*fiscaglie*); the sale of offices; revenues from the mint of Messina; the *cruciata*, or sale of ecclesiastical indulgences for a crusade; and, finally, certain feudal dues called *decima e tari*.

The utmost confusion reigned in the collection of these taxes. As successive governments had imposed these contributions, special *ad hoc* bodies had been set up to administer their collection. These bodies had acquired an evil reputation for graft and tyrannical practices. Under the watchful eye of the local *giurati* and the general supervision of the *maestro secreto* the collectors of the *secretie* were indeed forced to maintain a reasonable standard of honesty. But the collectors of the *decima e tari* were no better than the *percettori*;[4] the commissioners of the *cruciata* claimed exemption from royal jurisdiction while steadily increasing their own, so that the tax-payers could never hope for redress against their exactions;[5] and the officials responsible for the ecclesiastical spoils would go to the house of a sick prelate and clear out his furniture, clothes and other possessions even before he was dead.[6] The king and his vice-

[1] Terranova to Philip II, Feb. 13th, 1573, ibid. leg. 1140, fo. 64. He enclosed the Latin instructions to the *percettori*.
[2] Colonna to Philip II, June 1578; Simancas MS. Estado, leg. 1148.
[3] Following Colonna's remonstrances, Philip did issue further orders to stop abuses; ibid. Philip II to Colonna, Oct. 24th, 1578. The introduction of the *percettori* is a further instance of the extension of governmental control over the country.
[4] Colonna to Philip II, June 24th, 1578, Letter cit. Simancas MS. Estado, leg. 1148.
[5] Philip's way of dealing with these abuses was characteristic of his political methods. On Feb. 13th, 1597 he informed the president, Geraci, that 'los ministros de la Cruzada solen pretender exempcion de la Jurisdicion Real; y porque no conviene que se les guarde ... Podeis usar con ellos de dissimulacion en lo que se offreciere sin permitterle cosas de momento sino algunas leves y de poca importancia ...' (underlined as in the original). Lettere Regie de secoli XVI e XVII, Palermo Bibl. Com. MS. 3 Qq. E.33.
[6] Philip II to Terranova, May 11th, 1576, Simancas MS. Secret. Prov. leg. 1598, fo. 265.

roys took action against individual abuses, but only a rationalized and honest civil service could have made the collection of taxes something better than legalized robbery. Yet such a civil service had to remain outside the range of possible developments in an age when the rights of tax commissioners were regarded as a matter of privilege, similar to any other feudal right, and when even the limited experiment of the *percettori* proved the hopelessness of the task of trying to find honest and capable officials in the corrupt atmosphere of sixteenth century Sicily.

More important than any other single item of 'uncertain income' was the export tax on corn. As we have seen,[1] this tax was imposed entirely at the discretion of the viceroy and had the great advantage of not being appropriated. Nor could the government mortgage it very easily for its value varied from as much as 400,000 or 500,000 scudi in good years, to practically nothing at all in a year of drought. This apparent disadvantage – the difficulty of using the export tax as a security for government loans – was to prove most useful when the viceroy had to send large sums of money to Spain. Whatever happened to all other sources of income, in the case of the export tax, at least, the future could not be mortgaged. It remained an unrestricted asset to be used freely in the interests of the court of Madrid.

These revenues were sufficient to cover all normal demands. Apart from the sums appropriated by Parliament for the building of roads and bridges and for the upkeep of royal palaces, the main items of expenditure were the salaries of government officials, pensions and charitable contributions paid by the crown, and the interest on government debts. What was left was spent on defence. The *tercio* of 3,000 Spanish infantry and the 300 light cavalry which together formed the permanent garrison of the kingdom, cost more than 200,000 scudi; fortress troops and artillery about 30,000, and the 16 galleys of the Sicilian navy accounted for another 130,000 scudi.[2] Over and above these expenses was the upkeep of the garrisons of Goletta and Tunis and the building of fortifications in Sicily itself.[3]

Demands on the Sicilian treasury, however, were rarely confined to these 'normal' expenses. In Philip's reign one could no longer

[1] Cf. above, pp. 112 ff.
[2] Figures mainly from the budget of 1588/89 which may be taken as giving average values for military expenditure. But the size both of the *tercio* and of the naval squadron varied a good deal. The upkeep of one galley was estimated variously, from 6,500 scudi per year upward, Tanteo del Reino de Sicilia; Madrid, Bibl. Nac. MS. 11004.
[3] A large proportion of this military and naval expenditure was covered by appropriated donatives.

talk of the Turks 'as if they were the antipodes', as Vega picturesquely put it.[1] When Ferrante Gonzaga took over the government of Sicily, at a time when the Turkish danger was for the first time becoming serious, he found that two centuries of external peace had left Sicily with hardly any fortifications.[2] Gonzaga could make no more than a beginning in the fortifications of the most important ports. After the successive efforts of Vega, Toledo and Terranova, the Venetian Resident Ragazzoni still commented on the poor state of the island's coastal defences.[3] More and more money had to be spent on towers and harbour fortifications; ever greater numbers of oarsmen had to be hired to man the Sicilian galleys, increased to the formidable number of 22 during the Lepanto campaign; thousands upon thousands of quintals of ships' biscuits had to be supplied to Spanish and Italian warships assembling at Messina for the relief of Malta. During Medinaceli's eight years of office[4] the country paid 738,000 scudi in taxes over and above the usual donatives 'which is no mean sum for such a small kingdom and one which is notoriously poor,' as the viceroy himself said.[5]

The greatest demands came during the presidency of Terranova when Sicily was the advance base for the operations of the Holy League against the Turks. Don John of Austria's requests for money and provisions seemed to have no limits; after two years the president wrote, in despair, that he could no longer meet them. The country had already contributed 1,200,000 scudi; if it suffered further blows some irreparable disaster might occur.[6] Eventually the king was compelled to send 75,000 scudi as a direct aid to the government of Sicily;[7] but before the end of his term of office Terranova had spent 1,600,000 scudi for naval provisions and for the defence of the island.[8]

[1] Vega to Philip II, Papiers d'Etat..., vol. v, pp. 165 f.
[2] Gonzaga, Relazione..., Documenti per servire..., ser. 4, vol. IV, pp. 5 ff.
[3] '... et l'imperfittione di dette fortezze è causata principalmente che non havendo essa Isola di Sicilia havuto guerra da 200 anni in qua, non ha havuto mai necessità nè occasioni di fortificationi...' Ragazzoni, Relazione..., Bodleian MS. Rawl. D. 616, fo. 189–90.
[4] 1557–1565.
[5] Medinaceli to Philip II (?); Papeles Curiosos Españoles Manuscritos, Bodleian MS. Rawl. D.582, fo. 27. This sum included special grants by Palermo and Messina, but probably not revenue from export taxes.
[6] Terranova to Philip II, together with accounts of Sicilian contributions for the years 1571 to 1573; Simancas MS. Estado, leg. 1141. Also many other letters to the same effect from 1571 onwards; especially on Dec. 14th, 1571; ibid. leg. 1136, fo. 105; and C. d'Aragona, Corrispondenza particolare, Documenti per servire..., ser. I, vol. II, pp. 77 ff., 145 ff. and passim.
[7] Terranova to Philip II, 27th March 1575, ibid. pp. 145 ff.
[8] Colonna to Philip II, June 10th, 1577, Simancas MS. Estado, leg. 1147.

The supplies furnished to the fleet involved the government in a double loss. Not only did the treasury have to buy wheat and pay for the manufacture of ships' biscuits, but it also lost up to five scudi in taxes for every salma that could otherwise have been exported commercially. Nor was it only the king's galleys that had to be supplied. The Turkish attack on her had cut Venice off from her usual sources of corn supply in the eastern Mediterranean. She therefore insisted on preferential supplies of corn, and after long negotiations[1] it was agreed that all allies of Spain should freely export corn from Sicily after the requirements of the island itself and of the Spanish navy had been met.[2] For such exports they were to pay a tax of not more than two scudi per salma. Soon, however, difficulties arose. Terranova claimed that the Venetians imported corn at the preferential rate not only for their war ships but also for their garrisons and for home consumption. To this they were not entitled, he maintained. He could not sell export licences to other merchants, for the Venetians would, at the last moment, demand the corn for themselves. The export trade was being ruined and the treasury suffered the loss of tens of thousands of scudi.[3] On their side the Venetians were as little satisfied. Their special Resident in Messina, Placido Ragazzoni, complained to the president; their ambassador in Madrid complained to the King; they mobilized the Pope on their behalf, and Pius V put pressure on the Spanish ambassador in Rome to add his representations to their own. They complained that the Sicilian government had failed to allow Venice the facilities she had been granted in the treaty of alliance and was showing undue preference to the ordinary commercial exporter.[4]

In Madrid they understood the situation well enough. The Venetians were claiming more than they were entitled to, and the financial situation of Sicily was extremely grave. Yet it was essential

[1] Pescara to Juan de Zúñiga, Spanish ambassador in Rome, who was conducting the negotiations, Aug. 8th, 1570, ibid. leg. 1133, fo. 91. i.a. '... uno de los punctos sobre que se ha debatido mucho, ha sido el de los tractos ... y assi conviendra de razon, que se insista, en que Venecianos se contenten ... con offrecerles en general todo buen acogimiento y la llaneza en el comercio, y que se procedera con ellos con toda equidad, y buena correspondencia de amistad ...'
[2] This *capitolo* of the treaty of alliance was sent by the Venetian ambassador in Madrid to Philip II in order to justify Venetian demands, Nov. 6th, 1571; Simancas MS. Secret. Prov. leg. 981.
[3] There were similar complaints from Terranova's predecessor, Landriano. The whole correspondence on this issue is to be found in Simancas MSS. Estado leg. 1134–1137, 1139, 1140; and Secret. Prov. leg. 981.
[4] Ragazzoni had to bribe liberally, and entertain lavishly, to obtain results. In the relation he presented to the senate, on Jan. 5th 1574, he claimed a considerable degree of success for his methods. Venice, Archivio di Stato, MS. Senato III (Secreta) F.24, folder Sicilia.

to keep the good will of the republic. The Pope 'with his holy zeal for the progress of his League would always be inclined to take the part of the Venetians, rather than ours,' so the ministers informed the king. It was better to give way than to provide the senate with a pretext for backing out of the alliance.[1]

In the end the sacrifice of Sicilian to imperial interests proved to have been vain. When Venice concluded a separate peace treaty with the Sultan, in 1573, there were still 11,000 salma to be exported at the preferential rate. Regretfully, the president had to allow this export, for the commercial export-tax had by that time dropped to little more than the two scudi which Ragazzoni had paid, and the government had spent this money and could not refund the tax.[2]

When the Turkish danger finally became more remote, the country had a chance to recover from her extraordinary efforts during the Lepanto campaign and the disastrous years following it. In 1581 Colonna boasted, in answer to attacks on him, 'that in the five years I have been here, I have not asked this kingdom for a single *real* of extraordinary taxes . . ., and having found the country plague-ridden[3] and the patrimony in disorder and without a penny, I have kept down ordinary and extraordinary expenses, have supplied all that His Majesty has asked of me, and have relieved this court of the greater part of its debts . . . and the money for all this was not sent to me from abroad, nor have I found a treasure hidden underground – a clear indication that it has all been due to good financial management, especially of the *trattas* (export taxes), the *decima e tari*, and other (taxes) from which more money has been obtained than ever before.'[4]

The claim was justified. While the average export of corn increased only slightly in the course of Philip's reign,[5] the export tax rose from an average of 2 scudi 1 tari and 1 grano per salma during the period of 1558 to 1569,[6] to 3 scudi 8 tari and 16 grani, for the years from

---

[1] *Consulta* of a special junta including the Cardinal (Espinoza?), Ruy Gómez, Velasco, Hernández de Lievana, the two regents for Sicily and the secretaries Antonio Pérez and Gabriel Zayas; Dec. 20th, 1571; Simancas MS. Secret. Prov. leg. 981.
[2] Terranova to Philip II, Aug. 2nd, 1573. Simancas MS. Estado, leg. 1139, fo. 110.
[3] The reference is to the bubonic plague of 1575–78. cf. G. F. Ingrassia, Informatione del Pestifero et Contagioso Morbo . . . nell 'Anno 1575 et 1576 dato allo . . . Rè Filippo (Palermo 1576); and Terranova's correspondence, C.d'Aragona, Corrispondenza Particolare, Documenti per servire . . . , ser. 1, vol. II. There is a modern account by F. Maggiore-Perni, Palermo e le sue grandi epedemie, (Palermo, 1894).
[4] Dec. 13th, 1581, Colonna to Juan de Idiáquez, Simancas MS. Estado, leg. 1151.
[5] Cf. above, p. 80.
[6] Relationi delli fromenti estratti dal regno di Sicilia . . . , Simancas MS. Estado, leg. 1135, fo. 133.

1576 to 1590.[1] The average revenue from these taxes was therefore about 176,000 scudi per year during the earlier, and about 325,000 scudi during the later period. These large sums, however, were no longer spent in Sicily, nor even on Mediterranean wars against the Turks. As we have seen, Philip's schemes for the domination of western Europe called for ever heavier contributions from all his dominions.[2] Colonna had boasted that 'he had supplied all His Majesty had asked him.' For his successors it was no longer a boasting matter. During the year of the Armada Sicily supplied more than half a million scudi, both in cash and provisions;[3] the upkeep of Gian Andrea Doria's 'royal galley' and of three Savoyard warships had been permanently charged to the Sicilian treasury and amounted to 82,000 scudi a year;[4] while the king's letters were filled with constant demands for more wheat, more ships' biscuits and more artillery. Worst of all, the danger of Turkish invasion, though no longer as acute as formerly, could by no means be ignored;[5] yet in 1588 Sicily had to send eleven of her sixteen galleys to Spain, and Italy was so much denuded of troops that little help could be expected in case of a sudden emergency.

It is impossible to calculate exactly the total contribution of Sicily to the Spanish monarchy after the end of the Turkish wars.[6] In the twenty years before the Prudent King's death, in 1598, it was not less than 2,600,000 scudi.[7] Apart from this sum hundreds of thousands of salma of wheat and large quantities of munitions had to be bought; their freight charges and insurance had to be met; galleys had to be provided to convoy the merchant ships to Spain;

[1] Trattato di Sicilia, Naples, Bibl. Naz., MS. X.D. 46, fo. 17.
[2] Cf. above, ch. 2, pp. 55 ff.
[3] Accounts sent by Alvadeliste to the Council of Italy, March 31st, 1589, Simancas MS. Secret. Prov. leg. 984. The exact figure was 533,459 scudi.
[4] Ibid.
[5] *Consulta* of the Council of Italy on a letter from Alvadeliste of Dec. 14th, 1588: '... porque siendo aquel Reyno la frente y primer encuentro del mas poderoso enemigo que Vuestra Ma¡estad tiene, y viendose cada año en el con sospechas de invasion de Armada (i.e. the Turkish fleet) quedaria a muy mal partido sin plaças fuertes ni gente que lo defiende y sin poder ser socorrido por tierra, de otras partes, faltando de las fuerças que podrian apresurar y facilitar el remedio ....'
[6] This coincided roughly with the invasion of Portugal, the first stage of Spanish imperialist policy in the west.
[7] This figure is calculated mainly from the correspondence of the viceroys with Philip II and the Council of Italy, Simancas MSS. Estado, leg. 1147–1158, Secret. Prov. leg. 981–4, 1597–1600. One can often not be absolutely certain that a particular figure may not be part of a previously mentioned total. The difficulty is increased by the fact that the correspondence for the last years of Alvadeliste and for the whole terms of Geraci and Olivares shows very considerable lacunae in the MSS collection of Simancas. (It is quite possible that the missing letters still exist in private collections in Spain.) I believe, however, that my figure of 2,600,000 is rather too low than too high. It represents an annual average of only 130,000 scudi.

fresh troops had to be paid for and shipped to Naples or Genoa for service in the Netherlands;[1] and tired veterans had to be rested and re-equipped in the island. Alvadeliste was soon forced to give up all his earlier attempts to redeem the mortgaged sources of revenue.[2] His urgent remonstrations about the state of the country's finances induced even the Council of Italy to plead for a reduction in Spanish demands.[3] 'It is most necessary and expedient for Your Majesty to order a halt to be called and not to burden the kingdom with new charges and obligations,' so ran a *consulta* of March 14th, 1589; 'so that it should not be reduced to the same or to a worse state than Milan or Naples.'[4] A most revealing comment on the condition of those two provinces. Philip sympathized with the views of his ministers, but his grandiose schemes forbade any thought of retrenchment. Towards the end of the century the average contibutions of Sicily rose to 300,000 scudi a year.[5]

Most of this extraordinary expenditure was paid for by the revenues from the export tax. But even the increased sums which could be obtained from the merchants by the higher rate of tax failed to meet the peak demands. Already in Gonzaga's time there was an annual deficit of 26,000 scudi.[6] From then on, and despite increasing revenue, budgetary deficits became more frequent and, at times, alarmingly high.[7] When the harvest failed, as it did in the year of plague, 1576/77, the deficit[8] was as much as 375,000 scudi;[9] but even in the comparatively normal year of 1580/81 it was nearly 225,000 scudi.[10] In the latter years of the reign it was often more and only rarely could the budget be balanced.

To cover these deficits, and to bridge the interval between the voting and the collection of donatives, the government had to

[1] Pay for the Spanish *tercio* was generally many months in arrear; but when troops were sent overseas they had to be paid as otherwise they would take the first opportunity of deserting; e.g. Colonna to Philip II, April 4th, 1578, Simancas MS. Estado, leg. 1148.
[2] Alvadeliste to Philip II, March 31st, 1589, Simancas MS. Secret. Prov. leg. 984.
[3] Cf. above, p. 56
[4] Simancas MS. Secret. Prov. leg. 984.
[5] *Consulta* of the Council of Italy, May 29th, 1600; ibid. leg. 1514, fo. 85–6.
[6] Gonzaga, Relazione ..., Documenti per servire ..., ser. 4. vol. IV, p. 20.
[7] It is not always possible to calculate the deficit, even for those years for which we have figures of revenue and expenditure. Often military expenditure or contributions to Spain were not listed and there appears a totally fictitious surplus, as in the budget of 1588/82. Tanteo del Reino de Sicilia, Madrid, Bibl. Nac. MS. 11004.
[8] The budgetary year was from September to September.
[9] 'Relatione sommaria ... del mancamento ... nel patrimonio regale di Sicilia ... ; Simancas MS. Estado, leg. 1147.
[10] Philip II and Council of Italy to Colonna, Sept. 3rd, 1581; ibid. Secret. Prov. leg. 1599, fo. 115–120.

borrow from private bankers or from the city of Palermo at an average rate of ten per cent. Terranova managed, on occasions, to borrow at seven per cent, but this was exceptional.[1] In March 1575 he complained to the king that he had to cajole and flatter the merchants into acceptance of a royal order of payment for 75,000 scudi and that even then they would advance the money for only two months and at an exorbitant rate of interest.[2] In his relation for his successor, Medinaceli wrote that government bills of debt changed hands at a discount of thirty to forty per cent, worse than in the case of a bankrupt merchant.[3] He himself attempted the drastic measure of reducing all rates of interest to six per cent. But in 1566 Parliament petitioned the king to restore the old rates of ten to fifteen per cent for all government creditors as they could not otherwise meet their own obligations. The king had no choice but to give way in order to prevent a complete collapse of the credit of the Sicilian government.[4] When Medinaceli replaced Vega as viceroy, government debts were 300,000 scudi.[5] In 1581 funded debt alone had risen to more than 925,000 scudi on which the treasury paid an interest of about 75,000 scudi. Certain specified revenues were earmarked for the payment of this interest, and the figure did not include short term loans at more than ten per cent.[6] At the end of the century the *soggiogationi* were 1,300,000 scudi, with another loan

[1] Aragona, Corrispondenza Particolare, Doc. per servire ..., 1st ser. vol. II, p. 60.
[2] Ibid. pp. 130 f.; cf. above p. 167.
[3] Medinaceli, Advertencias ..., Documentos Inéditos ..., XXVIII, pp. 350 f.
[4] Testa, Capitula ..., II, pp. 261 f. Vega once claimed that Sicilian government credit was so good that private citizens of Palermo lent him 22,000 scudi on his mere word (Letter to Charles V, July 2nd, 1551; Simancas MS. Estado, leg. 1119, fo. 142). One suspects, however, that his methods of obtaining this loan were those described in his famous letter to Philip II (Papiers d'Etat ..., vol. V, pp. 145 ff.) Vega would call a wealthy citizen before him, explain to him the danger of the impending Turkish invasion – 'already you can see the fires and hear the wailings of the people of Calabria whose fields are being burnt and whose wives and children are being carried off' – and ask him to lend him 500 or 600 or a thousand scudi for defence preparations for which he, Vega, would stand surety with his own property. The man would then say that his enemies had maligned him and that he had no money. The viceroy would reply that he would force him to pay four times as much and threaten him with prison. Thereupon the man would fall on his knees and tell the viceroy that he had misunderstood him and that, of course, he would pay; and to all he met in the street he would say that there was no man like the viceroy; and, as the Sicilians were a very curious people, this story would be quickly all over town and others would prefer to come voluntarily to offer loans.
[5] Medinaceli to Eraso, Secretary of Philip II, July 26th, 1564, Simancas MS. Estado, leg. 1128, fo. 85.
[6] 'Bilancio de patrimanio regio de Sicilia ..., Madrid Bibl. Nac. MS. 7633. This funded debt was called *soggiogationi* and was made up as follows: 175,000 scudi at 10%; 205,900 scudi at 9%; 2,765 scudi at 8½%; 130,000 scudi at 8%; 48,733 scudi at 7½%; 355,400 scudi at 7%; 3,250 scudi at 6%; 5,735 scudi at 5½%; and 1,100 scudi at 5%. Total capital involved; 927,873 scudi; total interest: 75,755 scudi.

of 600,000 for which the city of Palermo stood surety and on which the government paid 125,000 scudi interest.[1] Although the size of the funded debt frightened contemporaries, it was the short-term loans at a high rate of interest which were really ruinous.

Both Palermo and Madrid cast about for means of increasing revenue. Little relief could be expected from Parliament. Already in 1552 Vega had written to the emperor 'that the difficulty did not consist in not knowing how to ask for more (money); for while in other matters I may lack the prudence one would wish for – in this, necessity and the desire to fulfil my duties have made me an expert... They are ashamed of not conceding what is asked of them; but even... though they grant it, they do not give it, for they have not got it.'[2] Terranova voiced similar views[3] and Olivares stated, at the end of his term of office, that the country was so exhausted that one could not even start to think about increasing the donatives.[4]

Less opposition was to be expected from increasing extra-Parliamentary revenue. Various schemes were put forward from time to time[5] and in 1574, at the instance of the Council of Italy, Terranova sent a whole list of suggestions.[6] But taxes on playing cards or government monopolies of the manufacture of gun-powder were not likely to solve Sicily's financial problems. There were only two proposals which seemed at all likely to yield considerable sums: the sale of the right of *mero e misto imperio* to the barons and the sale of public offices. This latter expedient had been introduced by Gonzaga but Philip had not encouraged the practice. As a result there was great confusion: offices were sold openly by the government when the court at Madrid needed money badly; or surreptitiously by private persons who had, or pretended to have, influence. Only military and judicial offices were definitely excepted. Juan de Vega, who had a

---

[1] i.e. at a rate of 25%. *Consulta* of the Council of Italy, May 29th, 1600, Simancas MS. Secret. Prov. leg. 1514, fo. 85–6.
[2] Vega to Charles V, April 13th, 1552, Simancas MS. Estado, leg. 1120, fo. 31.
[3] Terranova to Phillip II, Nov. 17th, 1574; C.d'Aragona, Corrispondenza, Particolare, Documenti per servire..., ser. 1, vol. II, pp. 76 f.
[4] Olivares, Relacion sobre el Govierno de Sicilia, with notes by the Conde de Castro; Madrid, R.Acad. de la Hist. Est. 21. gr. 1. q. No. 3, fo. 3. This is another MS. copy of Olivares, Cosas del Govierno...
[5] Many of these schemes were quite phantastic. Thus Cutinario, regent of Naples, suggested that the obligation of three months' military service per year of the feudal nobility be converted into a money payment. Instead of 1,700 undisciplined cavalry one would get 43,000 scudi per year. Capitalized at 3% this would provide nearly 1,500,000 scudi. For this sum an annual rent of about 135,000 scudi might then be bought (Philip II to Colonna, May 22nd, 1577, Simancas MS. Secret. Prov. leg. 1598, fo. 310–11). Colonna, not unnaturally, rejected this piece of financial conjuring (ibid. fo. 363).
[6] June 12th, 1574, Terranova to Philip II; ibid. leg. 981.

distinct sense of humour despite his reputation for severity, tells how he would decide to give an office to a person who had not solicited it, because he had 'slightly less bad information about him than about the others.' This person would then refuse, and later Vega would find out that he had been trying to buy the office or had been pulling strings. 'They don't like it if they get it in any other way,' Vega concluded.[1] In practice, however, this source of income remained largely unexploited. Terranova had to agree that it would be easy to systematize[2] but queried the expediency of such a move.[3] His successor, Colonna, was not a Sicilian and had no such scruples. In his first three years he sold offices worth more than 50,000 scudi, as against a bare 1,500 in the previous ten years.[4] The office of *maestro notaro* of the Great Court, for instance, was valued at 22,000 scudi – an indication of the fees which its holder received as the court's secretary. The *maestro portulano* under whose control came export and import duties had to pay thirteen thousand scudi and the *protonotaro* nine thousand scudi for their posts. The total market value of all offices which were for sale in the central and in local government was calculated to amount to more than 300,000 scudi.[5]

Philip II was well aware of the damage to honest and efficient administration resulting from such a system. In 1561 he had written to Medinaceli that no permanent office should be sold, whatever the financial difficulties of the government.[6] Towards the end of his reign he tried once more to return to his old principles. The Council of Italy submitted a *consulta* on the appointment of the *maestro portulano*. The president,[7] they said, favoured a certain Pedro Espinola; he offered little but was considered very capable.[8] Philip's

[1] Vega to Philip II, Papiers d'Etat..., vol. v, p. 153.
[2] *Consulta* of the Council of Italy, Aug. 20th, 1574, Simancas MS. Secret. Prov. leg. 981.
[3] Terranova to Philip II, Febr. 17th, 1575; C. d'Aragona, Corrispondenza Particolare, Documenti per servire..., ser. 1. vol. II, pp. 126 f.
[4] Statement by the coadjutor of the Royal Patrimony, 1580; Correspondence... Naples and Sicily, II; B.M. MS. Add. 28 395, fo. 118–119.
[5] Arbitrio delle precci et valore d'alcuni officii vendibili del Regno di Sicilia; ibid. fo. 82–7.
[6] Philip II to Medinaceli, Nov. 20th, 1561. '... En lo que toca a los officios perpetuos ya se os ha declarado tantas vezes sobre lo nuestra voluntad que no ay para que repetirlo aqui mas de encargaros y mandaros expressamente que no embargante las estrechezas de lo de ay y necessidades que representeis, no toqueis en ellos ni deis lugar aque se vendan ni empeñen pues la experiencia delo passado muestra que la suma que dellos se saca no puede relevar cosa de momento, y queremos que estos queden libros para disponer dellos a nuestra Voluntad, no teniendo otra forma de gratificar muchos de nuestros criados...' Simancas MS. Secret. Prov. leg. 1597, fo. 42.
[7] Geraci.
[8] *Consulta* of Nov. 28th, 1597, Simancas MS. Secret. Prov. leg. 987.

answer came as a shock to the councillors: if the office was of such a confidential nature as they maintained, it would be better not to sell it but to make an appointment.[1] They reacted with the bitterness born of years of hopeless struggle against steadily increasing odds. 'And as to giving (the office) for two or three years to a trustworthy person...' they wrote, 'the Council considers it a very good idea that neither this nor any other office should be sold... But since Your Majesty's patrimony is reduced to such straits that we have had to search for taxes and invent new offices for sale (as Your Majesty well knows), we do not think that there should be any innovation in a matter which has been decided so long ago as the putting up for sale of this office of *maestro portulano*; and if there were, the same would apply to Naples where there are thirteen provincial *maestri portulani*...'[2] But the old king was not to be put off by this display of bad temper and irrefutable administrative logic. He insisted on having his way; and the Council had to write the new viceroy, Maqueda, to tell him of the decision and to ask his opinion.[3]

True to his aristocratic inclinations, Terranova had been much more enthusiastic about the sale of the *mero e misto imperio* than he had been about the sale of offices.[4] The right of jurisdiction over his barony was the most valued privilege a noble could possess. It had been granted to certain lords and communes as early as the thirteenth century. In the fourteenth and fifteenth centuries Aragonese kings had made further grants, but the right was by no means universal. In the following century Parliament repeatedly petitioned for permission for nobles to buy the *mero e misto imperio*; but both Ferdinand, in 1515, and Charles V, and 1520, gave evasive replies.[5] The emperor, however, continued to sell fiefs with jurisdictional powers attached, and gradually most of the local jurisdiction in the country came to be exercised by nobles or independent communes.[6] Philip II was far more careful than his father in extending the juris-

[1] Dec. 3rd, 1597; ibid.
[2] Dec. 10th, 1597; ibid.
[3] Ibid. In his instructions to Maqueda Philip wrote: 'Por las necessidades passadas han sido por mi Regia Corte vendidas y empeñadas no solo muchas de mis rentas reales, pero muchos officios qualificados principales y que requieren industria de personas y (de?) confiança, informaros eis dello muy particularmente y procurareis en virtud del pacto de retrovendendo que en todo caso se busque forma como se rediman, començando por los officios de mas importancia'; ibid. leg. 1803, fo. 42.
[4] Terranova do Philip II, June 12th, 1574; ibid. leg. 981, cf. above, p. 178.
[5] Orlando, Il Feudalismo..., p. 191.
[6] Gregorio, Opere Scelte, p. 549. 'Cosi tutta la procedura giudiziaria nei vassallaggi era in mano e in potestà de' baroni.' The 'tutta', however, is exaggerated; for the nobles would not have continued to petition for the *mero e misto* if they already had it all.

dictional power of the nobles. The lords claimed, with some justification, that only their courts could provide cheap and rapid justice, for most people could not afford the expense and delays of taking their cases to the capital.¹ The king, however, knew well the abuses which were liable to occur in this system, and instructed his viceroy to punish any misuse of seignorial jurisdiction.² He did not even answer Terranova's suggestion of raising money by the sale of jurisdictional rights, and when the nobles in the Parliament of 1585 repeated their request for the right to buy the *mero e misto imperio* at the rate of fifteen tari per hearth in their baronies,³ Philip replied with a curt *non placet*.⁴

Three years later the position had become completely reversed: Philip's viceroy, the dictatorial Count Alvadeliste, proposed the revocation of all baronial jurisdiction held at the king's pleasure.⁵ This time the Prudent King held back, unwilling to embroil himself with the powerful Sicilian nobility at the very height of the crisis in Western Europe.⁶ In the last years of his reign, however, his scruples returned, just as they had done over the sale of public offices. He seriously contemplated revoking or redeeming all grants of *mero e misto imperio*. Olivares, who reported this proposal in his relation on the government of Sicily, said that it was represented to the king that abuses were not universal and that Philip thereupon ordered revocation only in cases where barons oppressed their vassals.⁷ But it seems likely that Philip was equally influenced by the enormous cost of buying out those to whom the right of jurisdiction had been sold, and that simple revocation would have been met by determined opposition not only from the nobles but also the higher clergy and the communes.

After the death of the Prudent King, the financial position rapidly deteriorated further, and his successor was neither strong nor brave enough to do anything about it. Nothing more was heard of reversing

---

¹ Bianchini, Storia economica-civile . . . , vol. I, pp. 60 ff.
² Instructions to Medinaceli, B.M. MS. Add. 28 701, fo. 27. Instructions to Maqueda, Simancas MS. Secret. Prov. leg. 803, fo. 37. 'Por que el usar mal de los Barones del Reyno de los meros y mistos Imperios que tienen, causa non poco impedimento y disturbo a la buona administracion de la Justicia, sera bien y assi os lo encargo procedais por debidos terminos contra los que han abusado dello, castigando a los que hallaredes culpados para que con esto exemple cesen semejantes desordenes.'
³ In 1520 they had offered 12 tari.
⁴ Testa, Capitula . . . , vol. II, p. 298.
⁵ *Consulta* of the Council of Italy, Sept. 7th, 1588. Simancas MS. Secret. Prov. leg. 984.
⁶ Cf. above, p. 70, n.1.
⁷ Olivares, Cosas del Govierno . . . , Papeles varios tocantes . . . , B.M. MS. Add. 14 009, f. 389–90.

the disastrous policy of selling governmental offices. Already in the year 1600 the viceroy was ordered to resume the sale of the *mero e misto imperio* to individual nobles.[1] These sales, were, indeed, beset with regulations and restrictions; but the stage was set for the great victory of the barons in 1621, when they obtained as of right the ability to buy the jurisdictional powers over their fiefs.[2] Still the deficits increased, and all efforts to find financial relief were nullified by the increasing demands from Spain.[3] Only twenty years after the death of Philip II, the viceroy Castro could look upon the period of Olivares' term of office[4] as the golden age of Sicilian administration. 'It is now very different from what it used to be,' he wrote with some exaggeration. 'Donatives are twice what they were then, and yet there were more galleys and better ones; more Spanish infantry, more cavalry; and when the militia of the kingdom turned out for service it was paid, and paid punctually.'[5]

The financial demands of empire, as much as Sicilian opposition, were responsible for the failure of the Spanish Monarchy to carry through successfully and completely its plans for the modernization of Sicilian administration. In the first half of Philip's reign, Sicily's imperial obligations had served as a stimulus both to reform and the extension of royal power. After about 1580 the strain became too great. With the sale of offices much of the efficiency gained in the reorganization of the councils was thrown away again; and with the sale of the *mero e misto imperio* the crown had to give up all hope of breaking the local independence of the nobility by substituting royal for baronial jurisdiction. The Prudent King's work remained only half completed, and not until the Bourbon government in the eighteenth century was there another considerable extension of government control over the country.[6]

The adverse effects of empire finance on the country as a whole were not nearly as serious as they were on its administration. There are indications that in the reign of Philip II the wealth of Sicily was gradually increasing. Despite the two serious setbacks of the plague of 1575–1578 and of the famine of 1590–1591, the population of the

[1] *Consulta* of the Council of Italy, May 29th, 1600; Simancas MS. Secret. Prov. leg. 1514, fo. 85–6.
[2] Orlando, Il Feudalismo . . . , pp. 193 ff.
[3] The financial crisis of the early seventeenth century is discussed in detail by Professor Virgilio Titone of Palermo in his La Sicilia Spagnuola. Saggi, Storici (Palermo 1948) pp. 73 ff.
[4] 1592–95.
[5] Notes by Castro on Olivares, Relacion sobre el Govierno . . . , Madrid, R. Acad. de la Hist. MS. Est. 21. gr. 1 q. No. 3, fo. 2.
[6] Except for the abrogation of the privileges of Messina after the revolt of 1674–78.

country rose from about 1,010,000 in 1548 to 1,054,000 in 1599. The increase was slight – only about 4.4 per cent; but it was probably the first since Saracen times.[1] The census figures show an even more appreciable rise in the value both of real property and of movable goods.[2] Messina was able to build the new Strada d'Austria; Palermo drained her papyrus swamps by means of skilfully constructed subterranean canals;[3] successive viceroys laid out the Via Toledo[4] and the Via Maqueda, the two beautiful streets which still determine the topography of the Sicilian capital; the senate of the city was able to spend 80,000 scudi on a huge fountain;[5] and in 1566 was started the famous mole, one of the greatest engineering feats of the century.[6] All these are signs of the accumulation of capital and of a general spirit of economic optimism. And the trend continued. While in the seventeenth century public finances reached the nadir of their melancholy history, the nobles started to build their magnificent baroque palaces in the cities, and in the country the more enterprising founded new rural communities and brought greater areas of land under cultivation.[7]

This divergence in the development of government finance on the one hand, and the country's economic life on the other, may perhaps be explained by two historical facts, one positive and one negative. The positive fact was the rise in prices, and the negative fact was the absence in Sicily of a Spanish trading monopoly such as existed in the American colonies.

Even before the middle of the sixteenth century the effects of Spanish silver imports had begun to make themselves felt in Sicily, as they had done in other European countries. The value of money declined and commodity prices rose.[8] The following indices of food

[1] Provided Maggiore-Perni's figures may be trusted (La Popolazione . . . , pp. 155 ff)·
[2] Ibid. pp. 469 ff.
[3] Maggiore-Perni, Palermo . . . , p. 34.
[4] It was said to have cost 300,000 scudi. Colonna to Philip II, June 24th, 1578. Simancas MS. Estado leg. 1148.
[5] Ibid. It was made by the Florentine sculptors Camilliani and Naccherino and is now in the Piazza Pretoria, opposite the University
[6] Anonymous Spanish relation on Palermo; ibid. leg. 1143, fo. 12. The construction of the mole cost 27,000 scudi a year.
[7] Cf. V. Titone, Economia e Politica nella Sicilia del Sette e Ottocento (Palermo 1947).
[8] Unfortunately no systematic work has been done on Sicilian prices comparable with Hamilton's study of Spanish prices. Most (but not all) of the figures available in the archives of Palermo have been used by Maggiore-Perni, La Popolazione . . . , pp. 500 f. 563. I have been able to supplement and correct these, to some extent, from MSS. sources in Spain, principally the accounts for naval provisions. Since these provisions were bought by the Sicilian government in the open market, their cost may be taken as a reliable indication for the level of prices at the time of buying. There were considerable seasonal and regional differences. While these figures are far from complete, they provide, I think, a fairly correct indication of the trend in prices, at least for the most

UNDER PHILIP II OF SPAIN 141

prices, averaged over ten year periods, may perhaps be taken as giving an indication of the general movement of Sicilian prices in the sixteenth century:

1548–1557 = 100[1].

	1501	1548–57	1558–67	1568–77	1578–87	1588–97	1614
Corn	64	100	92	124	152	288	156
Flour	67	100		144	183		200
Bread	81	100		143	171		186
Biscuits	63	100		127	143	288	155
Pasta (Spaghetti etc.)	56	100		138	156	563	159
Meat	82	100		187	172	124	251
Wine	100	100		141	142	171	133
Oil		100		111	124		180
Cheese	58	100		212	203		300

These figures should now be compared with the indices for government revenue. If government income is assumed to have been the same in 1548 as in 1562 (less the extraordinary donative of 100,000 scudi in the latter year,[2]) the following indices are obtained:

1548 = 100

	1548	1562	1571	1578	1581	1589	1592	c. 1598
Revenue	100	119	140	104	154	181	152	149

From these two tables it is clear that prices rose at roughly the same rate as government revenue. The figures for total government income, however, do not provide a clear indication of the tax-burden imposed on the country. Since nearly the whole of the export trade was in the hands of foreign merchants, the export taxes were paid largely by them and not by the Sicilians, except in so far as they were reflected in lower prices to the producer.

The remainder of non-Parliamentary taxation was largely fixed dues, income from vacant ecclesiastical benefices, or impositions

important foodstuffs. Unfortunately I have not been able to find prices for textiles. The most important sources were the Simancas MSS. Estado, leg. 1136, fo. 137, 141; leg. 1137, fo. 12, 38; leg. 1139, fo. 33; leg. 1141, fo. 117, 152; leg. 1149; and many scattered figures from other documents.

[1] Prices in the decade of 1588–1597 were largely determined by the famine. They were at their highest in 1591–92, as is indicated by the index figure for *pasta*, for which only the price of 1592 was available.

[2] This is, admittedly, a guess; but it is not likely to be far out, as non-Parliamentary revenue did not vary very much in those years.

such as court-fines, none of which affected to a marked degree the general level of taxation. By far the most important variations in the tax-burden imposed on the whole population were, therefore, due to the extraordinary donatives granted to the government by the three estates.

Taking again 1548, with the Parliamentary grant of 125,000 scudi annually, as the base year and averaging over ten-year periods we have the following figures.

$1548 = 100$[1]

	1549–59	1560–69	1570–79	1580–89	1590–99
Parliamentary taxation	100	168	186	200	203

The rate of increase of Parliamentary revenue was, therefore, more rapid than the rate of increase of the total revenue of the government; and with it increased the tax-burden imposed on the population. The government spent most of its income on goods and services obtained in the open market. Since prices kept pace with this income, government purchasing power did not materially increase in the half century from 1550 to 1600. It is this fact which accounts for the inability of the Sicilian financial administration to stand up satisfactorily to the steadily increasing demands of imperial defence and of Spanish power politics. At the same time the incidence of taxation on the population of Sicily increased only very slowly. In the words of the Venetian ambassadors, Morosini, the Sicilians were only 'moderately burdened, and since they cannot hope to better their condition by changing masters they live perhaps with greater contentment and goodwill towards their king than all other vassals of His Majesty.'[2]

Perhaps even more important than the rise in prices was the failure of the Spaniards to develop a consistent economic policy for their empire in Europe. The Sicilian corn trade, indeed, was made to serve the ends of imperial politics; yet at no time was there an attempt to integrate the economic resources of the king's European dependencies in a consistent plan. It did not even prove possible to implement the relatively modest scheme of providing the city of Naples with Sicilian instead of Apulian corn, and selling the exports

---

[1] Figures for Parliamentary grants calculated from donatives listed by Mongitore, Parlamenti ..., vol. I, passim, and corrected, where possible, from available budgets, cf. note 2, p. 124.

[2] Relazione di Spagna, 1581; Albèri, Relazioni ..., ser. 1. vol. v, p. 315.

from Otranto and Gallipoli to Venice.[1] Sicily remained a producer of raw materials with an essentially colonial economy, and it was not to be expected that the Spaniards, with their history and background, would make any effort to adapt the economic habits of its populations to the needs of a world empire. Spain did not even try to take advantage of the island's inability to meet its own industrial requirements. Although Catalan merchants traded in Palermo and Messina, most of Sicily's imports were supplied by the north Italian towns. The king's subjects were even at a disadvantage against foreigners. The Genoese considered their trading privileges in Sicily as more valuable than those of the Catalans; for these latter depended on a royal act of grace subject to royal discretion, while their own position was based on the sworn patents of the king which might not be revoked without offence to a friendly power.[2]

Since Sicily was an old established kingdom enjoying traditional commercial relations with her neighbours, it never occurred to Spanish statesmen to treat her like the American colonies. The absence of a developed Spanish theory of empire in Europe saved Sicily from the trade monopoly which Spain imposed on the colonists in the New World. Failing a genuine co-ordination of economic resources, such a trade monopoly would have been the only way in which a Spanish economic imperialism could have manifested itself. Sicily was unable to emancipate herself from the financial tutelage of Genoese bankers and from her commercial and industrial dependence on Florentine and Venetian manufactures; but her citizens were, at least, able to sell the greater part of their wheat and silk to those who could supply them with finished goods.

While Spanish imperialism eventually ruined Spain, and came close to ruining the administration of Sicily, it only retarded, but did not fatally damage Sicilian economic development. The seventeenth century, which saw the decline of Spain, was a century, of slow but steady economic expansion in her oldest Italian dominion.

---

[1] This suggestion was first made by Philip II in a letter to the duke of Alcalá, the viceroy of Naples, March 24th, 1567. The matter was discussed at intervals and the king was still corresponding about it with the viceroy of Naples in 1581. No permanent arrangement seems to have ever been made, perhaps because the Venetians would not guarantee to buy Apulian corn. Lettere Reali ai Vicerè di Sicilia 1560–1590, Palermo, Bibl. Com., MS. 3Qq. E.34. fo. 102–3, 154, 218, 249, 319–20, 323.

[2] Genoa, Archivio di Stato, Lettere Consoli, No. 2647, Mazzo 14, Palermo, G. Centurione, Genoese consul in Palermo, to Doge; Aug. 28th, 1563.

CHAPTER SIX

The Sicilian Government and the Independent Political Organizations

AMID the multitude of conflicting social trends and political interests in Sicily, the Spanish Monarchy had been able to build up a central administration capable of performing at least the more urgent functions of government. At no time, however, did this central administration have undivided control over the whole country. Philip II claimed that in the exercise of his power he owed responsibility to none save God; yet, in practice, both his own government in Spain, and even more the viceregal governments in the dominions, were subject to severe limitations imposed on them by the existence of more or less independent forces. The barons and the communes acknowledged the supremacy of the viceroy; but locally their authority remained largely unimpaired, and the viceroy's writ ran only by their favour. Moreover, in its own national sphere, the government found itself faced with organizations demanding either a share in the control of the country or a great degree of independence from such control. These were the characteristics which the Church Hierarchy, the Sicilian Parliament and the Inquisition all had in common. None of these organizations owed direct allegiance to the viceroy, and this fact inevitably brought them into a position of rivalry with a civil government claiming to be the ultimate authority in the country.

1. *The Government and the 'Monarchia Sicula'*
Potentially the most dangerous of these rivals was the Church Hierarchy, for the ultimate basis of its authority was outside the king's dominions in Rome. But by the beginning of the sixteenth century the Papacy was already very much on the defensive in Sicily. As in Spain,[1] the king had the right of appointment to most ecclesiastical benefices and, in consequence, the Sicilian clergy looked for

---

[1] M. Philippson, *Philip II von Spanien und das Papsttum*; Historische Zeitschrift, vol. XXXIX (München 1878) pp. 277 f.

advancement to Madrid rather than to Rome. As so often happens when loyalties are divided, material power turned the scales. Choosing between 'the damage to their consciences' and the consequences of disobedience to the secular power, the clergy were more ready to obey the government than the Church.[1] Moreover, every papal bull or brief had to receive royal endorsement before it could be published in Sicily – a practice which the king enforced throughout his dominions[2] – and this assent, called the *exequatur*, could be withheld for part or the whole of the brief. Thus Medinaceli held up the publication of the decrees of the Council of Trent on the grounds that certain paragraphs in them were contrary to the king's ecclesiastical rights and privileges,[3] and Pescara was assured by Philip that in similar cases he could count on his fullest backing.[4]

In 1513 Luca Barberi, a jurist employed by the government of Sicily to search for documents supporting the feudal claims of the crown, found a copy of a letter purporting to be from Pope Urban II to Count Roger of Sicily.[5] According to this document Urban II had granted the count and his heirs the rights and privileges of an apostolic legate, in recognition for his services to the Church in fighting the Saracens. On this grant the Spanish kings based their claims to the supreme juridical authority, or *Monarchia*, over the Sicilian Church – an authority not unlike the supremacy of the English kings over the English Church.

Barberi's publication of the letter of Urban II did not affect the nature of the struggle between Church and State, but shifted its emphasis to the purely juristic and historical question of the authenticity of Pope Urban's grant and the validity of the claims based on it.[6] In Spain the monarchy enjoyed nearly as extensive rights over the Church as it claimed in Sicily.[7] 'There is no Pope in Spain,' said Figueroa, the president of the *Consejo Real*;[8] and on several occasions the struggle for the control of the Spanish Church came near to causing a breach between Spain and the Papacy.[9] In Sicily the fundamental question of power became to some extent obscured by

[1] Antonio Faraon, bishop of Cefalù, to Pescara, Febr. 10th, 1569. Cartas Reales y de Ministros del Reyno de Sicilia, Bodleian MS. Mendham 28, fo. 24.
[2] Philippson, Philip II . . . , H.Z. vol. xxxix, pp. 275 f.
[3] Prag. Reg. Sic. n.c. vol. III, pp. 64 ff.
[4] Philip II to Pescara, Sept. 11th, 1568; Simancas MS. Secret. Prov. leg. 1597, fo. 345.
[5] F. J. Sentis, Die Monarchia Sicula (Freiburg i. Br. 1896) p. 26.
[6] Ibid. pp. 112 f.
[7] Philippson; Philip II . . . , H.Z. xxxix, pp. 271 ff.
[8] L. v.Pastor, Geschichte der Päpste, vol. VIII (Freiburg i. Br. 1920) p. 279.
[9] Ibid. vol. IX, p. 267.

the fog of juristic and antiquarian controversy.[1]

While the apologists on both sides wrote learned dissertations, the basic position both of the Crown and of the Papacy remained clear enough. Philip wished for the Pope's approval for his claims and was always willing to consider remedies for the abuses in the administration of royal pre-eminence in religious matters.[2] But he was at no time willing to give up the *Monarchia*. This is quite clear from his instructions to the special envoys he sent to Rome in 1574 to discuss, among other matters, the problem of the *Monarchia*:

> 'In the matter of the *Monarchia* of Sicily, since it is of an importance for the good government of that kingdom well known to you, you are ... not to reply to anything which may be proposed to you on the part of His Holiness, but to refer it back, so that you can be instructed how to act. You may only assure His Holiness that, if there should be any abuses in the exercise (of the *Monarchia*) I shall be very glad to remedy them and that, if His Holiness would like to confirm and renew (the grant of the *Monarchia*), I shall receive it from his holy hands, even though – in the case of a privilege so old and a custom so inviolably observed in that kingdom – I neither can nor should have any scruples (in maintaining my rights) ....[3]

The position of the Papacy was equally uncompromising. The Popes were willing to grant the exercise of many of the jurisdictional rights claimed by the king,[4] but they could never admit in principle a claim which gave a layman greater ecclesiastical power than the head of the Church himself; and as the original letter of Urban II was never found, the question was incapable of legal settlement.

For the Sicilians the *Monarchia* represented the advantage of having the highest ecclesiastical authority in their own country. This advantage was admitted even by those who were otherwise

---

[1] The literature on the *Monarchia* both printed and unprinted, is immense, much of it exceedingly dull. As the question remained alive and led to periodic crises until the final revocation of the *Monarchia* by Pius IX, in 1867, all this literature is highly controversial. This applies even to Sentis' book, written at the end of the 19th century: while its facts are presented with a great degree of fairness and while its conclusions appear reasonable, it is definitely in the nature of an apologia for the papal point of view, designed especially as a refutation of G. B. Caruso, Discorso istorico-apologetico della Monarchia de Sicilia, ed. G. M. Mira (Palermo 1863). This is the best of the regalist books, written at the beginning of the 18th century, but not published until the 19th.

[2] Letter to Toledo, March 24th, 1567; Correspondence with the ambassador at Rome, vol. II, B.M. MS. Add. 28 404, fo. 207. Letter to Terranova, Dec. 82th, 1571, in Caruso, Discorso ... p. 283.

[3] Granvelle, Correspondence, vol. v. p. 112.

[4] Marquis of Alcañizes, Spanish ambassador in Rome, to Colonna; Caruso, Discorso ..., pp. 305 f.

willing to restrict the powers of the *Monarchia*.[1] The judicial functions of the *Monarchia* were exercised by ecclesiastical judges specially deputed for the purpose by the viceroy, and assisted by judges of the Great Court or the Court of the Holy Conscience.[2] Since the ecclesiastical judges often came from the lower ranks of the clergy and since few of the Sicilian clergy were trained lawyers, the influence of the secular lawyers was nearly always decisive.[3] This was an abuse recognized by all, yet as long as there were no clerical lawyers there was no remedy for it.[4] Not only did the judges of the *Monarchia* hear appeals from the courts of the metropolitans, but they took cognizance of cases in first and second instance by 'appeal for redress of grievance' by one of the parties. Alternatively they could themselves transfer cases from the episcopal courts to the *Monarchia*. There were no official rules of procedure and, owing to the influence of the secular judges, canon law was often neglected in favour of Sicilian secular law.[5] Even *ex-abrupto* methods were introduced. In this respect the *Monarchia* compared unfavourably with the Court of High Commission in London: for the absence of torture in its procedure was one the principal reasons for the great popularity of the English tribunal.[6] Otherwise the two contemporary institutions performed essentially similar functions. Through the *Monarchia* the Sicilian Church became nearly as independent from Rome as the English Church.

Having obtained the substance of power, the Prudent King was quite willing to make concessions, even on points of principle. He therefore suggested the ingenious compromise of allowing appeals to Rome if the verdicts of the three regular instances of ecclesiastical jurisdiction[7] were not in agreement. The Pope, however, should then undertake to remit such cases to an ecclesiastical court in Sicily, so that in fact no case could be taken out of the kingdom.[8] When the Pope failed to agree with this suggestion Philip proceeded on his own account to appoint his chaplain, Nicola Stizzia, as permanent judge of the *Monarchia Sicula*. Four years later, in 1583, Colonna issued twenty-three orders, the essence of which was to prevent

[1] Faraon to Pescara, cit.; Cartas Reales, Bodl. MS. Mendham 28, fo. 22–6.
[2] Pedro Allata to Philip II, June 27th, 1567, ibid. fo. 8.
[3] Sentis, Die Monarchia ..., p. 138.
[4] Juan de Torres Ossorio, judge of the *Monarchia*, Relacion del estado que oy tiene la Monarchia ... 1606; Papeles varios, B.M. MS. Add. 21 960, fo. 230.
[5] Sentis, Die Monarchia ..., pp. 137 ff.
[6] R. G. Usher, The Rise and Fall of the High Commission (Oxford 1913) pp. 116 ff.
[7] i.e. the courts of the bishop, of the metropolitan and of the *Monarchia*.
[8] Philip II to the Marquis de Alcañizes, Spanish ambassador in Rome; Simancas MS. Secret. Prov. leg. 1599, fo. 16.

appeals from going to the judge of the *Monarchia* before they had passed the canonical instances of the bishop's and archbishop's courts, and to insist on the administration of canon law.[1] If these measures silenced some of the critics in Sicily, they could never be accepted as legitimate acts of royal sovereignty in Rome, and, in consequence, no decision of the *Monarchia* was ever recognized by the Papacy.[2]

The provisons of 1583 were never fully observed; yet the *Monarchia* eventually became an effective instrument of royal power. The permanent judges had to swear to maintain its rights; the clergy could no longer appeal to Rome, and the viceroy could prevent unsolicited interference of the Curia by withholding the *exequatur* to papal briefs.[3] While the king thus exercised a right which the Papacy claimed to be a fundamental part of its ecclesiastical primacy, such procedure did not prove an unmixed blessing to the Sicilian viceroys. The Sicilian bishops were not so servile as to condone the way in which the *Monarchia* was administered.[4] They questioned whether its unusual powers in criminal jurisdiction were really necessary to 'bridle such fierce people as the priests.' Had not the Pope revoked the *Monarchia* and, if it was upheld by force, was the Pope no longer Pope, or was the king the Pope?[5] The most serious consideration was that not only the viceroy, but every count, baron and captain-at-arms appeared to be exercising ecclesiastical jurisdiction. A letter to the king in which these points were made ended with a solemn warning to heed the fate of those viceroys who had been foremost in supporting the *Monarchia*; Gonzaga had died in disgrace; nearly the whole of the house of Vega was extinct;[6] and Medinaceli's government had caused greater disasters to befall the Spanish Monarchy than that of any other viceroy.[7]

The bishops were unable to prevent the king from using the powers

---

[1] Printed in Caruso, Discorso..., pp. 313 ff.
[2] Sentis, Die Monarchia..., pp. 126 ff.
[3] Sentis, Die Monarchia..., pp. 129 f.
[4] Copia de Carta que los Prelados del Reyno de Sicilia escrivieron a Su Magestad por los agravios, que recibian de la Monarquia. No date; probably written during Colonna's government. Cartas Reales; Bodleian MS. Mendham 28, fo. 30–35.
[5] The accusation was unfounded, for the Pope had not formally revoked the *Monarchia*. Yet it is significant that this point should have been made in a letter to the king.
[6] Vega had boasted of his support of the *Monarchia* to the Princess-Regent, Dec. 13th, 1555: 'Lo digo a Vuestra Alteza, que uno de los servicios señalados que yo pretendo que he hecho a Su Magestad despues que estoy en Sicilia es haver rebivido esta Monarchia que se yva ya con el tiempo debilitando, y puestola en el estado que esta siendo una immunidad tan grande y preheminencia que Creo que ningun principe de la Cristianidad la tiene sino es el Rey de Sicilia...' Simancas MS. Estado, leg. 1123. fo. 111.
[7] i.e. the defeat of Gerba, 1560.

he claimed, but they could make use of the generally admitted abuses of the *Monarchia* as a reason for obstructing the grant of donatives in Parliament, and they could always be certain of being backed by the Curia.[1] With the full weight of the king's support behind it, the government of Sicily had won a great advantage over the Hierarchy. But a complete victory (such as might one day be hoped for against the barons and communes) could never be gained over a rival whose ultimate source of strength was beyond the reach of any civil government in a catholic country. After Colonna's reorganization the very instrument of the government's victory, the institution of the *Monarchia*, began to develop a will of its own – a characteristic not uncommon in the organs of Spanish government. Jurisdictional disputes arose, first with the Inquisition, and later with the viceroys themselves. A seventeenth century president, Gianettino Doria, suffered a painful defeat in one of these encounters.[2] Relations with the Papacy remained tense and, at times, flared up into violent quarrels, equally damaging to both sides. The issue was not finally put to rest until the formal abolition of the *Monarchia* by Pius IX in 1867.

2. *The Government and Parliament*

The re-establishment of royal power at the end of the fourteenth century was followed by the restoration of Parliament. Martin I and his successors were dependent on the co-operation of the Sicilian estates, and the most convenient form this co-operation could take was collaboration with Parliament. Sicily had known representative assemblies since Norman times,[3] and Swabian kings had summoned Parliament to obtain national consent for taxation and for important matters of policy and legislation. In 1282 a Parliament at Palermo had offered the crown of Sicily to Peter of Aragon.[4] The Aragonese Frederic II had introduced the custom that in all his kingdoms new taxes could be imposed only with the consent of the representatives of the towns[5] and that the king could neither declare war, nor conclude peace, without the knowledge and assent of his vassals.[6]

Throughout the fourteenth and fifteenth centuries Aragonese

---

[1] Castro, Avvertimenti..., Thesoro Politico, vol. II, p.460.
[2] Sentis, Die Monarchia..., pp. 129 ff.
[3] Mongitore, Parlamenti..., vol. I, pp. 22 f., says that the first Sicilian Parliament was called by Roger II at Palermo in 1130.
[4] Ibid. p. 39.
[5] L. Genuardi, Diritto Pubblico Spagnuolo in Sicilia; Rivista di Storia del Diritto Italiano, An. VI (Bologna 1933) pp. 72 ff.
[6] L. Genuardi, Parlamento Siciliano (Bologna 1924) pp. LXXIX f.

influence was strongly marked in the evolution of the form and ceremonial of the Sicilian Parliament. The combined upper chamber of clergy and nobility was abandoned in favour of an assembly of three houses, known as *bracci* after the Aragonese *brazos*[1] – perhaps the most important development in the early history of this Parliament. The pomp of the opening ceremony, the importance of precedence, the commissions of lawyers who drafted the acts of Parliament which were known as *capitoli*, the institution of the Deputation and finally the triennial meetings and the grant of a triennial donative, all these were practices taken over from the Cortes of Aragon.

By the sixteenth century Parliament had evolved into a form and was fulfilling functions which did not change materially until the Napoleonic Wars. It was summoned by the king or the viceroy for the primary purpose of granting donatives. With the loss of Sicilian independence the whole issue of external relations and decisions on war and peace became matters which affected the whole Spanish Empire, and the Sicilian Parliament, with its localized interests, could no longer have a decisive voice. The government, however, continued to make statements to Parliament on foreign policy and on the naval war against the Turks; the representatives continued to make suggestions on the details of the defence of the country; but Parliament took no share in the determination of policy. Even when the viceroys called extraordinary meetings (usually to obtain a special donative to meet some grave crisis such as a threatened invasion) they gave but a few details about the needs of the situation.

After the opening ceremony and the viceroy's address to the whole Parliament, the three houses assembled separately. As the clergy, or *braccio ecclesiastico*, originally sat with the nobility, they maintained much of their character of a feudal estate. Bishops and abbots were members of Parliament not because they represented the clergy but because they were the owners of feudal land.[2] In consequence they voted donatives only for themselves, and the rest of the clergy were, in theory, held to be liable to the taxes imposed on laymen.[3] In practice, however, the *braccio ecclesiastico* often spoke for the whole clergy and, in matters of secular taxation, upheld whatever protection the papal Curia still afforded; for all burdens

[1] Ibid. p. LXXXI.
[2] 'Archiepiscopi non vocantur ad parlamentum quia tales, sed quia feuda et castra tenent a rege.' Quoted in C. Calisse, Storia del Parlamento in Sicilia (Torino 1887) p. 84.
[3] Ibid. p. 85.

imposed on the clergy had to be formally approved by the Pope.[1] The real difficulty was not so much that the majority of the clergy were not formally represented in Parliament, as that the wealthy bishops and abbots could bear more easily the taxes they voted than the poor country priests whose only source of income was the contributions of their parishioners.[2] The theory of the feudal nature of the *braccio ecclesiastico* had further consequences in that laymen could represent abbeys and priories. In 1566 the *braccio* petitioned the viceroy to exclude laymen from its membership and to prevent the treasurer-general from voting on behalf of vacant benefices. But Toledo feared the resulting loss of government influence and advised the king to refuse the petition.[3] Of the three archbishops, six bishops and forty or fifty abbots and priors who constituted the *braccio*, most did not attend Parliament personally but were represented by a fellow member, by their own agent, or by a royal official. In the Parliament of 1556 only nine members of the house attended in person, and among these there was only one bishop.[4]

Personal attendance in the chamber of the nobility, the *braccio militare*, was no better.[5] Membership was confined to barons holding fiefs directly from the king and, as in the case of the clergy, it was the fiefs which were represented. Thus, nobles owning more than one had plural votes. As they acquired additional fiefs and as land rose in value, the number of votes and the membership of the *braccio* increased. From the beginning of Philip's reign until 1621 the number of Parliamentary barons rose from 72 to 146,[6] and in the eighteenth century the prince of Butera alone had accumulated as many as 41 votes.[7]

The third estate, or *braccio demaniale*, was composed of about forty towns and districts (*terre*) of the royal domain.[8] It was by far the wealthiest of the three estates, and in the census of 1582 its total property was estimated at 24 million scudi, as against the $13\frac{1}{2}$ million of the *braccio militare*. Since these two estates paid equal shares of

[1] Capasso, Il Governo..., Arch. stor. sic. n.s. vol. XXX-I, p. 410.
[2] C. d'Aragona, Corrispondenza Particolare, Documenti per servire..., ser. 1, vol. II, pp. 43 f.
[3] Toledo, Correspondence, Documentos inéditos..., vol. XXX, pp. 168 f.
[4] Mongitore, Parlamenti..., vol. I, pp. 280 f.
[5] In the same Parliament of 1556 only 17 of 72 lords took the trouble of making a personal appearance. Ibid. pp. 282 ff.
[6] Calisse, Storia..., pp. 91 f.
[7] E. Pontieri, Il Tramonto del Baronaggio; Arch. stor. sic. n.s. LI, p. 154.
[8] Mongitore, Parlamenti..., vol. I, pp. 284 f., gives a list of 36 towns, but it is not complete, Palermo, Syracuse, Giaci, and possibly others not being mentioned.

the donative the Deputation[1] in 1558 suggested that nine of the smaller towns should be rated with the *braccio militare*.[2] This would still have left a disproportion of three to four in the respective resources of the two estates, and the unfortunate nine towns would have had to pay more of the donative than they had done hitherto. This disadvantage, it was suggested, they would willingly suffer for the sake of helping a whole estate. No details have come down to us of the protests of the nine towns, but the viceroy rejected the suggestion.[3] It would have been extremely unwise to antagonize the towns for the dubious advantage of favouring an already overpowerful nobility. The barons did not themselves pay the taxes they voted, for their military service was considered a sufficient personal contribution. They passed their taxes on to their vassals[4] and, in consequence, were generally willing to vote the donatives which the government demanded. Opposition from the nobles (as we shall see) had to be expected on matters of privilege rather than of finance.

The members of Parliament sent by the towns (*procuratori* or *sindaci*) were usually elected by the *giurati* and a number of prominent citizens,[5] care being taken to select men who would be most directly affected by the payment of the donatives and who were least dependent on government favour.[6] Some towns sent several members – six in the case of Palermo – but they had only one vote between them. Normally they were accorded wide powers, but on occasion they had to refer back, or they were sent only as observers with no authority to vote at all.[7]

The reign of Philip II was not a period of revolutionary legislative changes. No religious struggles convulsed the island; no Reformation and Church Settlement had to receive the assent of the people's representatives; and no dynastic issue called for Parliamentary arbitration or confirmation as it had done in the thirteenth century. The ruling classes represented in Parliament were content with the social structure of their country and did not have to face the 'agrarian revolution' which troubled contemporary England. The most im-

[1] Cf. below p. 159.
[2] The nine towns were Syracuse, Vizzini, Giaci, Mazzara, Mineo, Sanfillipo, Lentini, Agosta and Carlentini.
[3] Ordinazioni e Regolamenti della Deputazione del Regno di Sicilia (Palermo 1782) pp. 216 f.
[4] Calisse, Storia . . . , p. 90.
[5] Genuardi, Parlamento . . . , p. CXVI.
[6] Ranke, Die Osmanen . . . , pp. 211 f.
[7] Genuardi, Parlamento . . . , pp. CXVIII f.

portant developments in sixteenth century Sicily took place in the organization of its government, and in this sphere Parliament played of necessity a subordinate role. The reform of the law courts, it is true, was first urged by the assembly; and the *sindaci* of Palermo, in particular, took a leading part in working out the details.[1] The great mass of Parliamentary legislation, however, was concerned with matters of detail and with the individual rights of barons, towns, or religious communities,[2] resembling in this respect the legislation of the English Parliament of the Hanoverians rather than the Tudors. This work, however, was neither useless nor entirely selfish. It was of the utmost importance to determine details of legal procedure[3] or the rate of interest on government loans;[4] it was necessary to induce the viceroy to concede amnesties and moratoria[5] and to prohibit the cutting down of olive trees;[6] and, above all, Parliament had to watch over the *capitoli* and privileges of the kingdom and prevent the appointment of foreigners to public offices and ecclesiastical benefices.[7]

The sessions of Parliament were held in camera, and no records of debates remain. It is clear, however, that every meeting of Parliament represented a major crisis for the viceroy, on the skill of handling which the success or failure of his government might well depend. Parliament sometimes reduced his request for a grant or refused it altogether – the most disastrous setback which could befall any viceroy. Or again the viceroy might find himself faced with changes in the method of taxation he had proposed and, worse still, the grant might be coupled with an attack on one of his favourites. Parliament's most dangerous gambit was to disguise its attack on the viceroy as a special service to the king. When their ambassador arrived in Madrid, ostensibly to offer the donative in person, he would have a splendid opportunity to level accusations against the viceroy. Moncada had been able to counter such a move by representing to Ferdinand that he himself could procure the acceptance of all *capitoli* which might be of advantage to the kingdom much better than a special ambassador.[8] But Medinaceli was unable to prevent the dispatch by

---

[1] C. d'Aragona, Corrispondenza ..., Documenti per servire ..., ser. 1. vol. II, p.57.
[2] Testa, Capitula ..., vol. II, pp. 235, 241, 269, 270, 278, 299 and passim.
[3] Ibid. pp. 251, 270, 280, 283, ff., 297, 304, 311 f., 319, 326.
[4] Ibid. pp. 261 ff.
[5] Ibid. pp. 241, 274, 289, 310.
[6] Ibid. p. 264.
[7] Ibid. pp. 234, 246 f., 251 f., 268, 287, 304.
[8] H. de Moncada to Ferdinand the Catholic, Oct. 23rd, 1511; Correspondence, Documentos Inéditos ..., vol. XXIV, p. 114.

Parliament to the court of the marquis de la Favara, and fell a victim to the charges brought against him by that influential and ambitious noble.[1]

The most persistent opposition was always offered by the *braccio ecclesiastico* and the *braccio demaniale*. For while the barons willingly voted taxes which hurt only their vassals, the clergy and the towns had to pay themselves. Many of the prelates were Spaniards. Appointed by the king and backed by the Curia over the question of the *Monarchia*, they could afford to scorn the viceroy's favour. Their lead, moreover, was often followed by the towns.[2] It was therefore essential for the viceroy to come to an agreement with the *pretore* of Palermo who represented that city. This was generally not too difficult, partly because the *pretore*, always a noble, inclined to agree with the attitude of the *braccio militare*, and partly because the viceroy could always play his trump card: the threat of removing the court to Messina, with all the loss of trade and prestige involved in such a move.[3]

Precisely because such a threat was usually effective, the viceroy had far greater difficulty in coming to terms with Messina. That ancient and wealthy city, boasting the possession of a personal letter from the Virgin Mary herself[4] and fortified by extensive privileges, had always denied Palermo's claim to be the capital of the kingdom. The Spaniards did not perhaps actively foster the rivalry between the two leading cities,[5] but were careful not to encourage its settlement.[6] Messina always regarded participation in a donative as a special favour to the king,[7] and as late as 1661 tried to refuse payment unless Parliament assembled within its walls.[8] The city's most bitter opposition was reserved for the 'gabelle of the tarì', an imposition of one tarì per pound on crude silk and other textiles. This

[1] Cf. below p. 180.
[2] Castro, Avvertimenti..., Thesoro Politico, vol. II, p. 460.
[3] In 1581 Palermo was so delighted with Colonna's impending return from a prolonged residence in the rival city that the general council of the capital granted the government 100,000 scudi for naval provisions. Gambacorta, president of the Patrimony, wrote to the viceroy, Oct. 27th, 1581 '... non sò se sia successo mai conchiudere conseglio con più contento e soddisfazione commune.' Simancas MS. Estado leg. 1151.
[4] A Latin translation of this letter was sent by the *giurati* to Philip II, Sept. 24th, 1575; ibid. leg. 1144, fo. 192. The *giurati* maintained they possessed the original, but it has never been found.
[5] Philip II to Medinaceli, July 30th, 1562; Simancas MS. Secret. Prov. leg. 1597, fo. 54.
[6] Badoero, Relazione... Filippo II...; Albèri, Relazioni ser. 1. vol. III, p. 167. Medinaceli considered these quarrels 'niñerias,' but thought they were useful to the Spaniards and should not be discouraged; Advertencias..., Documentos Inéditos..., vol. XXVIII, pp. 341 f.
[7] Colonna to Philip II, Dec. 17th, 1581; Simancas MS. Estado, leg. 1151.
[8] Calisse, Storia..., pp. 113 ff.

tax, first imposed by Toledo, yielded 100,000 scudi a year of which Messina alone was expected to contribute 60,000. From the beginning the *giurati* protested that the donative was contrary to Messinese privileges. Philip's reaction was typical: the Holy Council was ordered to decide whether the Great Court was competent to hear the appeal of the Treasury against the decision of the Messinese court. If such an appeal should prove to be contrary to the city's privileges and to the laws of the kingdom, the viceroy was given authority to abrogate these laws.[1] By simply declaring his own royal authority to be superior to perfectly valid laws, the king had over-topped the claim of the Messinese judges to decide the validity of their own privileges.[2]

The *giurati* then appealed to the Council of Italy,[3] and in 1569 that body pronounced its verdict: the gabelle was to be collected, but without prejudice to the city's rights.[4]

If the Council had avoided offending Messinese susceptibilities it had not managed to stifle the town's opposition which grew more determined as the time approached for the renewal of the donative, originally granted for ten years. In spite of Terranova's prohibition, Messina twice dispatched special ambassadors to Madrid.[5] The second envoy, the Neapolitan bishop of Massa, went directly to the king before the scandalized Council of Italy had been able to warn their master.[6] By 1578 the court at Madrid was becoming seriously alarmed at the attitude of the city, and Philip wrote to Colonna that he feared real trouble if the Turkish fleet should appear outside Messina.[7] The viceroy, however, was able to reassure him and, despite all protests, quietly continued to collect the gabelle.[8] At no time, in fact, was the town ready to offer armed resistance, for it would have found itself without any support in the country: the *braccio demaniale* was not inclined to support Messina against its own vote.

After ten more years of fruitless opposition Messina decided to offer the court of Madrid half a million scudi for the abolition of

[1] Philip II to Toledo, Dec. 31st, 1564; Lettere e Instruzioni Reali . . . , Palermo, Bibl. Com. MS. 3Qq. C.33, fo. 80–81.
[2] Cf. above, p. 108.
[3] Correspondence in Simancas MS. Secret. Prov. leg. 1597, fo. 239, 284, 289, 351.
[4] Council of Italy to Pescara, Sept. 17th, 1569; ibid. fo. 381.
[5] The baron de Cartaffi, in 1573; *consulta* of the C. of Italy, Jan. 12th, 1573, ibid. leg. 981; and the bishop of Massa, in 1574; *consulta* of Dec. 14th, 1574; ibid.
[6] Ibid. The Council advised the king to be firm about the re-imposition of the gabelle. Philip agreed, but added that the matter should be settled 'con buenas palabras.'
[7] April 16th, 1578; Simancas MS. Estado, leg. 1148. With customary Spanish understatement he wrote: '. . . conviene mucho estar con cuydado que no suceda algun inconveniente, come podria suceder facilmente se la armada del Turco asomasse por estas partes.'
[8] Philip II to Colonna, Oct. 24th, 1578; ibid.

the gabelle and for the confirmation of all her privileges.[1] The offer was too tempting to resist. In 1591 Philip accepted the proposal,[2] and for the rest of his reign there were no further difficulties with Messina over taxation.[3] But the anomalous position of a quasi-autonomous city in a centralized state remained, and in the seventeenth century the tension could be resolved only by a war, ruinous alike to Messina and Spanish prestige in Italy.

Less persistent, but at times more dangerous, was the opposition which the viceroy might expect from the barons. In the early years of the emperor's reign Monteleone had had to deal with the revolt of part of the nobility, led by the count of Camarate.[4] For nearly seventy years there was no further serious trouble until 1591 when Alvadeliste was suddenly faced with the rebellion of the whole *braccio militare*. It occurred at a moment when the government's popularity was lower than at any time since the overthrow of Ferdinand's hated viceroy, Hugo de Moncada.[5] The common people blamed the viceroy for the great famine,[6] and the barons had been enraged by his indiscriminate use of the *ex abrupto* procedure against them and by his persistent refusal to flatter their vanity.[7] To crown their resentment a royal order prevented titled persons from becoming familiars of the Inquisition. The nobles could, therefore, no longer escape from royal jurisdiction.[8] Incited by the Inquisitor, Lodovico Páramo, they refused payment of the donative until the king confirmed their rights and privileges, especially with regard to the *ex abrupto* procedure and the appointment of Sicilians as officers of the cavalry.[9] They proposed sending an ambassador to the king and giving back to the people the taxes which had already been collected. Taken completely by surprise, the viceroy was at first inclined to

[1] *Consulta* of the C. of Italy, Sept. 7th, 1588; ibid. Secret. Prov. leg. 984.
[2] G. B. Caruso, Memorie Istoriche de quanto è accaduto in Sicilia, pt. 3, vol. I (Palermo 1744) pp. 240 ff.
[3] The agreement of 1591 was a great victory for the silk interests inside the city. The 500,000 scudi for Madrid were borrowed from Genoese bankers, and for the repayment of this sum indirect taxes were imposed, as well as a new but lower gabelle on silk (ibid.). The silk trade had therefore succeeded in spreading part of the burden of the former silk tax over the rest of the community.
[4] In 1522. For an account of this event see La Lumia, Storie Siciliane, vol. III, pp. 183ff.
[5] In 1516. Cf. Buonfiglio e Costanzo, Historio Siciliana, pp. 404 ff.
[6] Cf. Appendix IV.
[7] On this particularly Fortunato's evidence; Avertimentos..., Letters and Papers ...Sicily; B.M. MS. Add. 28 396, fo. 407.
[8] Alvadeliste to Philip II, July 15th, 1591; Simancas MS., Estado, leg. 1157. Cf. below, section 3.
[9] The Inquisitor's complicity is clear from Alvadeliste's letter (note 2) and from a *consulta* of the C. of Italy, Oct. 16th, 1591; ibid. Secret. Prov. leg. 985. The viceroy accused him of being the leading spirit. Despite the Council's recommendations and Quiroga's promises to that effect, Páramo seems to have escaped serious punishment.

temporize. He issued a conciliatory statement accepting the demands of the *braccio* and promised to procure their acceptance by the king;[1] at the same time he concentrated the regiment of 300 light cavalry outside the capital.[2] He then made certain of the support of the clergy and the towns. The Holy Council pronounced, as expected, that the concurrence of two of the three *bracci* was sufficient for the grant of a donative. This was a severe shock for the nobles who had counted on the support of the whole Parliament. They retreated and proposed to submit the constitutional issue to the king and to hold up only the grant for the cavalry. But this retreat meant victory for Alvadeliste. It was resolved that the donative should be paid, despite the contrary vote of the *braccio militare*,[3] and the nobles, who had made no plans for resistance to armed force, had no choice but to comply. The viceroy had his revenge by imprisoning their leaders,[4] 'so that they should not pass from this to worse actions,' as he wrote to the king.[5]

As the Sicilian estates were never willing to carry their opposition to the length of armed resistance, Parliament found itself at a fundamental disadvantage against ruthless viceroys and a king who was as impervious to threats as Philip II. The distance of Sicily from Spain proved a grave weakness. Parliament attached conditions to its donatives, but the collections of taxes always began long before the king's signature gave the act legal force, and before it was known whether the petitions had been accepted. The sessions of the three houses were too short and too infrequent to make possible the development of a regular opposition with a clear policy, and the fact that there were three houses increased the difficulties of conjoint action. Thus the meetings of Parliament were never more than incidental battle grounds in the factional opposition to the viceroys.

Yet, in general, the viceroy was as much interested as Parliament in avoiding extreme situations. The probable result of a failure to secure a majority for his demands was his recall, rather than a head-on collision between the government in Madrid and the Parliament in Sicily. A skilful governor could usually obtain his majority by careful preparation. He could secure the support of an influential

---

[1] Di Blasi, Storia . . . , vol. II, pp. 348 f. Alvadeliste did not mention this temporizing in his letter of July 15th. But he gave only a brief account of the revolt and promised to tell the king more about it when he had returned to Spain.
[2] Letter of July 15th. This was the only regiment of professional cavalry in the kingdom. It was to have been sent abroad, but Alvadeliste delayed its embarkation.
[3] Mongitore, Parlamenti . . . , vol. I, pp. 416 ff.
[4] Caruso, Memorie . . . , pt. 3. vol. I, p. 240.
[5] Letter of July 15th, 1591, cit.

prelate if the latter was involved in a law-suit for which the favour of the court might be decisive.¹ There was always a noble faction willing to support the government, if only because their personal enemies were in opposition. Such nobles the viceroys could bind more closely to themselves by asking the king to grant them favours or by exhorting them personally.² The viceroys appointed the heads of the *bracci*, and negotiations with them and with other influential Parliamentarians took place before the session began.³ In debates they could rely not only on their own parties but also on those of their officials who took part. The treasurer-general voted on behalf of all vacant ecclesiastical benefices while other viceregal officials acted as *procuratori* for absent barons and for towns who had sent no representatives. These officials, unlike the independent members, had a definite policy. They knew on whom they could rely and had long experience of Parliamentary procedure.⁴ Viceroys even used the strategem of calling Parliament during the bad season so that prelates and barons would prefer to send representatives rather than attend themselves.⁵ The Parliament of 1594 complained that 'the majority of those who should come, and are invited, do not come nor send their own *procurator*, but present their votes to persons who by diligence and authority (i.e. their influential position) seek to accumulate many; so that it happens that one person has fifteen, twenty and even more votes (*procure*): and in this way the number of votes is reduced and concentrated in a few persons, and the real and free discussion of Parliament is suppressed.'⁶ Philip referred this complaint back to the viceroy; but as the latter preferred to deal with few persons who could be influenced, rather than with a whole assembly, the abuse of proxy voting continued. For similar reasons a Parliamentary request for voting by ballot had been rejected in 1562.⁷

[1] Castro, Avvertimenti . . . , Thesoro Politico, vol. II, p. 460.
[2] In 1574 Terranova asked the king to send some 'lettere credentiali dirette ad alcuni Prelati et titolati, acciochè sendo con tal favore aiutata la natural affectione di questo regno, et lo studio et de!egentia che in ciò de me sarà usata, possano più facilmente i buoni creati di Vostra Maestà riportare quel frutto che se desidera et spera in servitio di Vostra Maestà.' Documenti per servire . . . , 1st ser. vol. II, pp. 45 ff. There are many such royal letters to Sicilian magnates in Simancas, e.g. to the prince of Butera, Febr. 19, 1575, a letter which was intended to serve as a specimen for similar letters to other nobles and prelates. Simancas MS. Secret. Prov. leg. 1598, fo. 215.
[3] Calisse, Storia . . . , p. 133.
[4] Cf. Moncada's recommendation to the king of the work done in Parliament by the treasurer, his deputy and other officials. Documentos Inéditos . . . , vol. XXIV, pp. 103 ff.
[5] Castro, Avvertimenti . . . , Thesoro Politico, vol. II, p. 312.
[6] Testa, Capitula . . . , vol. II, p. 312.
[7] Calisse, Storia . . . , p. 139.

To offset the lack of continuity involved in the short and infrequent meetings, Parliament had in the first half of the fifteenth century followed the Aragonese example of setting up a special commission for the long periods between sessions.[1] It was the duty of this commission, 'the Deputation of the kingdom', to guard against the violation of *capitoli* and privileges and to see that appropriated donatives were not misspent. Membership, rules of procedure, competence and powers all remained vague for a long time and, at the beginning of the reign of Philip II, abuses and confusion in the Deputation had become notorious. Thanks largely to the efforts of Terranova an act was passed in 1567 reforming the Deputation and systematizing its work.[2] The viceroy appointed its twelve honorary members, four from each estate. A quorum of three had to meet regularly every week for the transaction of business. Except for the granting of donatives, the Deputation enjoyed the same powers as Parliament itself. It functioned in a dual role, both as committee of privileges and as a government department in charge of transport, coastal fortifications and the collection of taxes, supervising the work of the three *percettori*[3] and appointing its own commissioners for coastal towers and for roads and bridges.[4]

What distinguished the Deputation from all other councils of the kingdom was its responsibility, not to the viceroy, but to Parliament. Clearly, here was the basis of a potentially revolutionary constitutional development, if only the Deputation could preserve its independence from the government and extend its sphere of competence at the expense of other departments. The ever-suspicious Pedro Velázquez, in fact, warned the king that it was a dangerous centre of opposition, no less than the Deputations in Aragon and Catalonia. He recalled with approval how Medinaceli had snubbed the Deputation by declaring that it was not their business, but his, to defend the interests and prerogatives of the kingdom, and that he would brook no companion in this duty.[5] The king thereupon asked Terranova for a report, and the president had no difficulty in showing that by his right of appointment he kept complete control over the Deputation.[6] A few years later Colonna, questioned on the

[1] Calisse, Storia..., pp. 189 ff.
[2] Ibid. pp. 194 ff.
[3] Cf. above, p. 126.
[4] Ordinazioni e Regolamenti..., pp. 142 ff., 178 ff.
[5] Velázquez to Philip II, Febr. 5th, 1572; Letters and Papers..., Sicily, B.M. MS. Add. 28 396, fo. 26–28.
[6] C. d'Aragona, Corrispondenza Particolare, Letter of Jan. 25th, 1575; Documenti per servire..., ser. 1. vol. II, pp. 115 ff. Terranova had earlier persuaded Pescara to

same matter, pointed out that it was much better to have a Deputation which could be easily supervised than to provide an opportunity for others to meddle with the defence of privileges.[1]

The viceroys were always careful to have several of their senior officials in the Deputation. From 1570 onwards the president of the Great Court was always one of the four members for the *braccio demaniale* and so, at times, were the presidents of the other courts. Membership for the *braccio militare* was reserved for those noble families, such as the Aragona, the del Bosco or the Ventimiglia, whose loyalty was beyond suspicion.[2] Despite this predominance of governmental influence the Deputation continued to fulfil a useful function. It was not the policy of the Spanish and Sicilian governments to set aside the country's privileges, and when offences against these did occur the government was usually quite willing to act on the recommendations of the Deputation. When Villena in 1609 attempted to collect a tax without the consent of Parliament, the Deputation resisted this infringement of privilege with the stubbornness for which the Sicilians were famous.[3]

While the Deputation was successful in the limited sphere of Parliamentary privilege, it failed to build up a comprehensive control over the viceregal government akin to the influence developed by the English Parliament of the sixteenth and seventeenth centuries over the English executive. Representing those classes which benefited most by Spanish rule, Parliament could never become the mouthpiece of a nation-wide opposition. The assembly was most effective in the defence of sectional rights and in the prevention of as steep a rise in taxation as occurred in Naples. Yet by its very success in the defence of privilege, Parliament came to regard the defeat of a particular viceroy as its highest possible achievement. When the whole foundations of Spanish rule in Sicily came to be questioned in the seventeenth century, when a nation-wide opposition had come into existence, Parliament was simply ignored by both

restrict the authority of the Deputation to the control over the donatives for roads, bridges and coastal fortifications, and to relieve it from the supervision of the ordinary donatives.
  [1] Memorandum, Letters and Papers . . . , vol. II, B.M. MS. Add. 28 400, fo. 192–3. This memorandum was probably not written by Colonna himself, but it reflects his views in most points and was probably written at his orders by one of his officials.
  [2] Lists of members in Mongitore, Parlamenti . . . , vol. II, and in Ordinazioni e Regolamenti . . . .
  [3] Cf. above, p. 97. Cf. also Scipio di Castro's description of the Sicilian character '. . . sono dall 'altro conto d'incredibil ardire dove si tratti dal maneggio publico et all'hora procedono con modi tutti differenti dalle predetti (i.e. the timidity shown in their personal affairs).' Avvertimenti . . . , Thesoro Politico, II, p. 458.

sides. Without comprehending the possibilities of its own position, the assembly stood aside from the struggle for ultimate power.[1]

3. The Government and the Inquisition

Unlike both Church Hierarchy and Parliament, the Sicilian Inquisition derived its authority primarily from the Spanish Monarchy itself. It did, indeed, represent both Pope and King,[2] the spiritual and the temporal sovereignty, but in practice the two Sicilian Inquisitors were subordinate only to the Suprema, the Supreme Council of the Inquisition in Madrid. When Torquemada introduced the Inquisition in Sicily,[3] the new institution must have appeared to the viceroys of the time as useful an instrument of royal power as the *Monarchia* was to their successors. Through the *Monarchia* the king maintained his authority over the clergy; through the Inquisition he maintained it over the rest of the population. While the control exercised through the *Monarchia* was mainly juridical and disciplinary, the authority of the Inquisition was intended to preserve the religious beliefs of the people, equally necessary for their personal salvation and the preservation of loyalty within the whole system of the Catholic Spanish Empire.[4] In fact, however, the viceroys soon found the Inquisition to be their most consistent and successful rival, precisely because it claimed to represent the royal power just as the viceroys themselves. In its struggles with the Church Hierarchy and, to a lesser extent, with Parliament, the Sicilian Government had been backed by Madrid. In their conflict with the Inquisition the viceroys fought alone, for Madrid itself was divided on the issue.

Unlike the Neapolitans and Milanese in the sixteenth century, the Sicilians had not openly rebelled against the introduction of the Inquisition, though the Holy Office remained for a long time

[1] Cf. Koenigsberger, The Revolt..., *Cambr. Hist. Journal*, vol. VIII, No. 3, pp. 139 f.

[2] H. C. Lea, A History of the Inquisition in Spain, vol. I (New York 1906) p. 289. The history of the Inquisition of Sicily is one of the few subjects in the history of Sicily under Philip II which have been well treated by modern historians. Apart from Lea's chapter on Sicily in his The Inquisition in the Spanish Dependencies (New York 1908), there is a series of detailed and well-documented articles by C. A. Garufi, Contributo alla Storia dell'Inquisizione in Sicilia nei secoli XVI e XVII; in Arch. stor. sic. n.s. vols. XXXVIII–XLII. Neither author claims to have exhausted the whole of the vast MS material in the Simancas Archives; nor can I claim to have done so. Garufi, even more so than Lea, is strongly hostile to the Inquisition and his conclusions are, at times, based too much on the principle of *post hoc, ergo propter hoc*. This may be because Garufi really was a medievalist who was not very sure of the background of the period.

[3] In 1487. Lea, The Inquisition in the Spanish Dependencies, pp. 1 ff.

[4] The Inquisition did, in fact, help to suppress two popular risings, in 1560 and in 1585. Report of the Inquisitor Páramo, July 18th, 1590, quoted in Garufi, Contributo..., Arch. stor. sic. n.s. XLIII, p. 70.

highly unpopular. Confiscations from the condemned were insufficient to pay the salaries of its officials and as a result there was much peculation and petty oppression of the population. The fiscal and legal immunities of the Holy Office caused resentment which was not counterbalanced by a religious fanaticism among the people of Sicily comparable with that produced in Spain by the long struggle with the Moors.[1] When the Palermitans overthrew the viceroy Moncada in 1516, they also abolished the Inquisition and destroyed its records. It was re-established in 1519; but when Charles V visited Sicily in 1535 he had to accept severe restrictions on its powers in order to obtain an extraordinary grant of 250,000 scudi from Parliament.[2]

As soon as the political situation in Sicily permitted, the emperor restored the Holy Office to its full authority[3] and from that time it showed considerably more vigour than before. Between 1537 and 1572 nineteen *autos da fé* were celebrated with all the pageantry of a Sicilian religious occasion. Six hundred and sixty persons were condemned, twenty-two of them to the stake,[4] yet only some of these were heretics, the others being sorcerers, bigamists or Moriscos accused of backsliding. For a country with such a mixed population as Sicily and with its many ports, this number must be regarded as very small.

Unlike the *Monarchia*, the Sicilian Inquisition was entirely independent of the viceroy. The Inquisitors were appointed by the Suprema in Madrid with the king's approval.[5] Such control as the king exercised over the Sicilian Inquisitors came through the council and not through any civil authority. In Sicily the Inquisition comprised the two Inquisitors, their theological, legal and financial advisers and staffs, and a large number of unpaid servants, or familiars. In 1549 a royal decree placed the judges of the Inquisition outside the jurisdiction of the civil government,[6] and with this the Holy Office became a self-contained unit. All its officials and familiars enjoyed the privilege of having all their law cases, criminal as well as civil, tried in the Inquisition courts. If trial by the Holy Office held prospects of the utmost terror for the suspected heretic, it was far different for a member of the Inquisition brought before its courts

[1] Lea, The Inquisition..., pp. 11 ff.
[2] Ibid. pp. 21 ff.
[3] Cf. Letter of Charles V to Vega, 1551, quoted in Garufi, Contributo, Arch. stor. sic. n.s. vol. XL, pp. 310 ff.
[4] Ibid. vol. XXXVIII, p. 276.
[5] Lea, A History..., vol. I, p. 299.
[6] E. Rodocanachi, La réforme en Italie, vol. II (Paris 1921) pp. 173 ff.

on an ordinary criminal charge; for, unlike the secular courts, the Inquisition never made use of torture in any case which did not involve questions of faith.[1] The restoration of the Inquisition to its full powers coincided with the rapid increase in the use of the *ex abrupto* procedure by the government courts.[2] As a result the Inquisition courts acquired a popularity which they had not previously enjoyed, more especially as it was notorious that members of the Inquisition, even when convicted, were treated with great leniency.[3] Persons from all classes of society tried to become familiars and thus escape liability in proceedings which gave little chance to the accused.[4] The barons, who became familiars without performing any specific duties, could bring within the scope of their privileges all their servants and retainers, so that the number of persons enjoying the rights of familiars was greatly superior to that officially admitted by the Inquisitors. Thus in 1577 the Inquisitors acknowledged only 12,000 familiars while the viceroy claimed that there were as many as 24,000. Each figure may well have been correct. In every town the Inquisition had its representatives, often with no particular functions to fulfill, but immune from governmental jurisdiction and able to tyrannize their neighbours who had no redress against them.[5] To enhance its own power and prestige the Inquisition encouraged the nobility in particular to join and was thus able to build up a vast and independent organization much more powerful and dangerous than Parliament.

It was inevitable that this organization should come into conflict with the civil administration. The viceroys could not allow a limitation of their juridical power which placed a large section of the population entirely outside their control. There had been disputes over jurisdiction as early as Moncada's time,[6] but the real struggle started in 1543 when the president of the kingdom, the marquis of Terranova,[7] had two familiars of the Inquisition tortured in the course

---

[1] Castro, Avvertimenti..., Letters and Papers... Sicily; B.M. MS. Add. 28 396, fo. 390.
[2] Cf. above, pp. 121 f.
[3] Cisneros, Relacion..., Letters and Papers... Sicily, B.M. MS. Add. 28 396, fo. 342.
[4] Castro, Avvertimenti..., Ibid. fo. 390; also quoted by Garufi, Contributo, Arch. stor. sic. n.s. XL, pp. 447 f. In the Thesoro Politico Castro's very hostile chapter on the Inquisition was suppressed and only a short and neutral paragraph substituted. Garufi, however, misunderstood Castro's point; cf. Titone, La Sicilia Spagnuola, p. 54.
[5] Pescara to Cardinal Espinoza; Letters from Italy, 1567-72, B.M. MS. Add. 28 401, fo. 112-113.
[6] Moncada, Correspondence, Documentos Inéditos..., vol. XXIV, pp. 132 ff.
[7] Giovanni d'Aragona, Marquis of Terranova. Exactly the same happened to his son Carlo, duke of Terranova, in 1567. Papeles del Consejo..., II, MS. Eg. 1507, fo. 40-43.

of a criminal action, and was forced to do penance for this act of presumption.[1]

After this first victory of the Inquisition the struggle developed in a steady crescendo. The viceroys claimed that it was impossible to uphold justice and governmental authority while the familiars of the Inquisition could escape the just punishment of their crimes. Vega imprisoned the Inquisitor, bishop of Patti,[2] and quarrelled violently with Patti's successor.[3] Medinaceli, who was more favourably inclined towards the Holy Office than other viceroys, wrote that there was 'no horrible and enormous crime' in which a familiar of the Inquisition had no part and that the criminal was exempt from the only punishment which had any effect in Sicily, the torture of the cord.[4] The fear of the *ex abrupto* procedure and the intervention of the viceroys had broken up the solid front against the Inquisition which had existed in the reign of Charles V. Nobles who for any reason opposed the viceroys would attach themselves to the Inquisition, while those who had a quarrel with the Inquisitors would support the viceroy.[5] The struggle over jurisdiction thus became involved in the quarrels of the Sicilian factions and, to a lesser extent, in the rivalry between the Jesuits and the Dominicans of the Inquisition. There was thus practically an alliance, in opposition to the viceregal government,[6] between the tribunal and the most dangerous and influential classes, constituting a virtually autonomous state governed by its own laws and exempt from many of the Sicilian taxes.[7]

Both sides continually appealed to Madrid. Toledo said he would gladly go as far as the Indies, to say nothing of Madrid, to tell the king the truth about the Inquisition.[8] Pescara complained

[1] Prince Philip (II) to marquis of Terranova, Dec. 16th, 1543, ibid. fo. 36.
[2] Vega to the Regent (Princess of Portugal) Nov. 12th, 1555, Simancas MS. Estado, leg. 1123, fo. 102.
[3] Same to same, Sept. 25th, 1555, ibid. fo. 81.
[4] Medinaceli, Avvertencias..., Documentos Inéditos..., vol. xxvIII, pp. 338 ff.
[5] Castro, Avvertimenti..., Letters and Papers... Sicily, B.M. MS. Add. 29 396, fo. 489.
[6] Lea, The Inquisition..., pp. 25 ff.
[7] Comparison with the position of the French Huguenots would show only superficial resemblance. But it might be interesting to speculate how far the centuries under the militant theocracy of the Arabs (with freedom from taxes and other great privileges for the ruling Moslem minority) prepared the way for the Inquisition idea of the 'state within the state.' It may be more than a coincidence that the Spanish Inquisition was most highly organized and privileged in Spain and Sicily, the only two European countries which had experienced prolonged Arab domination. Both in Naples and Milan the Spanish monarchy had to give up its attempt to introduce the Inquisition, and in the Netherlands it precipitated the great revolt.
[8] Castro, Avvertimenti..., Letters and Papers... Sicily, B.M. MS. Add. 29 396, fo. 389.

bitterly of the lack of respect shown him by the Inquisitor Bezerra, of the latter's high-handed action against the Jesuits, and of his seditious co-operation with certain nobles who were working against the reform of the law courts.[1] On their side, the Inquisitors complained of interference with their rights and, in particular, of a decree of Juan de Vega which prohibited their issuing ecclesiastical censures against viceregal officials.[2] This prohibition they argued, made secular jurisdiction superior to their own.

The king was slow to interfere in this quarrel. Since both sides ultimately represented his own authority, the crown could not lose in this struggle. Yet during Colonna's government it assumed such dimensions as seriously to threaten the peace of the country. Pescara's and Terranova's protest had at least had the result of inducing the Suprema to sindicate the Sicilian Inquisitors. In place of the corrupt Bezerra and Gasco, Colonna was faced with two new Inquisitors, Juan de Rojas and Diego Haedo, whose personal integrity was beyond doubt and who were just as determined champions of the claims of the Holy Office as their predecessors.[3] The Inquisitors maintained that it was they who preserved the country from invasion and civil war, to which Colonna replied that he and his soldiers were quite sufficient for the country's defence. The Inquisitors were appalled by this attitude. Germany, the Netherlands and England had been lost not for lack of soldiers but for want of an effective Inquisition, and France was now in the throes of civil war for precisely the same reason.[4] To Philip this must have seemed an unanswerable argument. 'The Inquisitors of Spain', wrote Haedo, 'are feared and respected, not because they have greater apostolic authority than those of Italy, but only because of the favour and power given them by your Majesty with the temporal jurisdiction; from which it follows that if the one is taken away, the other (i.e. the authority of the Inquisitors) will be wanting.'[5] This was indeed the crux of the problem, yet it meant that in Sicily there would be two

---

[1] Letters of Pescara to Cardinal Spinoza, 1569–70; Letters from Italy, B.M. MS. Add. 28 401, fo. 75–183.
[2] Same to same, Nov. 15th, 1569; ibid. fo. 101. There is a copy of this pragmatica in 'Varios Escritos tocantes a la Monarchia de Sicilia, vol. II, Madrid, Bibl. Nac. MS. 2665, fo. 508.
[3] On this Colonna's own testimony: '... y que los inquisidores Haedo y Gorronero (Roja's successor) no hè visto yo que hayan passado nunca el termino de tener por fin lo de la jurisdicion, como yo tambien ....', Letter to Philip II, July 12th, 1583: Spanish State Papers, Home Correspondence, vol. XI, B.M. MS. Add. 28 344, fo. 138–44.
[4] Haedo to Philip II, March 1st, 1580, quoted in Garufi, Contributo, Arch. stor. sic n.s. vol. XLII, pp. 78 ff.
[5] Ibid. p. 83.

independent authorities representing the king and that the idea of the centralized state dispensing justice to all would be set aside.[1]

Philip attempted to solve the problem in characteristic manner. A conference (*junta*) was called between two members of the Suprema and two of the Council of Italy to decide the limits of inquisitorial jurisdiction. The Suprema was in a strong position. The Inquisitor-General, Quiroga, although no longer the king's principal adviser, was still able to command great influence;[2] the examples of France and the Netherlands were constantly before the king's eyes, and he was not averse from seeing a strong counter-balance to the authority of the governor in a distant dominion. The viceroy and captain-general of Sicily might be a danger to royal authority – voices were not lacking which suggested that Marc Antonio Colonna was planning to betray the island to the French or to the Turks, or even make himself king,[3] while the Inquisitors would always remain dependent on the Suprema and, ultimately, on the king himself. In consequence, the *Concordia* of Badajoz in 1580 was a substantial victory for the Inquisition. The Inquisitors were confirmed in their right of jurisdiction over all civil and criminal matters in which their familiars were involved, with the exception of feudal cases, orders concerning war or the plague, and crimes committed by holders of public offices in the fulfilment of their duties. Officials of the Inquisition were to observe the laws of the kingdom, but the Inquisitors had the right to proceed with ecclesiastical censures against all who impeded their jurisdiction. Conflicts were to be decided by two Inquisitors and two judges of the Great Court; if they could not agree the dispute was to be referred to the *junta* in Madrid.[4]

The *Concordia* of Badajoz did little to settle the dispute or to improve the relations between the viceroy and the Inquisition. The right of the Inquisitors to proceed against those who opposed their jurisdiction rendered the machinery for settling disputes valueless.[5] Judges of the Great Court were excommunicated when they took action against familiars according to their interpretation of the *Concordia*. The viceroy retaliated by inducing the judge of the

[1] Colonna to Philip II, April 10th, 1580, Correspondence..., vol. I, B.M. MS. Add. 28 394, fo. 129–131.
[2] e.g. Quiroga to Philip II, Sept. 12th, 1578, Papeles del Consejo..., I, B.M. MS. Eg. 1506, fo. 87.
[3] e.g. Haedo in the letter quoted, pp. 87 f; Monrreal in his 'Memoria', Correspondence..., vol. I, B.M. MS. Add. 28 394, fo. 213–14.
[4] Prag. Reg. Sic. Nov. Col. vol. I, pp. 69 ff.
[5] Garufi, Contributo..., Arch. stor. sic. n.s. vol. XLII, p. 98.

Monarchia or the archbishop of Palermo to absolve them. These absolutions the Inquisitors refused to recognize, claiming that their ecclesiastical authority was superior to that of the *Monarchia*.[1] The accusations against the viceroy which Haedo sent to Madrid became increasingly hysterical. Colonna, may have intercepted some letters.[2] He was certainly rash enough publicly to insult Haedo when the latter wanted to imprison one of the viceroy's servants.[3] On this occasion the Inquisitor preserved greater dignity than the enraged viceroy. In its *consulta* concerning this incident, the Suprema wrote to the king that Marc Antonio Colonna always avowed that in a matter of faith he would hand over his wife and children to the Inquisition but that in practice he never did anything to help them. The king again referred the dispute to the joint committee of the two Councils of the Inquisition and of Italy,[4] and this body, in the manner to which they were rapidly becoming accustomed, continued to remain in almost permanent session.

Neither Haedo's nor Colonna's successors were able to escape from the struggle. The count of Mussomele and the count of Racalmutto, both familiars of the Holy Office, had been involved in different murders. Alvadeliste maintained that assassination such as that committed by the counts and their servants was not covered by Inquisition privilege. The Inquisitors Peña and Gorronero, on the other hand, could not give up their extreme claims, however much they might be convinced of the guilt of the counts; for their alliance with the nobility rested on the protection which they could afford the latter against the viceroy. The dispute was therefore not only one of rival jurisdictions, but involved the whole question of the familiars on whom the physical power of the Inquisition in the country depended. To undermine the opposition in the viceregal courts the Inquisition had managed to place some of its members in high judicial offices.[5] Yet Alvadeliste showed even less respect for the Inquisitors than Colonna had done. The Suprema wrote that he had

[1] This point had arisen before the *Concordia* of Badajoz, but was not finally settled during the reign of Philip II. Consulta del Consejo, Papeles del Consejo . . . , I, B.M. Eg. 1506, fo. 72.
[2] Haedo to Philip II, March 1st, 1580, in Garufi, Contributo, Arch. stor. sic. n.s. vol. XLII, p. 89.
[3] Consulta of the Suprema to the king, March 20th, 1584; Papeles del Consejo . . . , I, B.M. MS. Eg. 1506, fo. 113–7.
[4] Ibid.
[5] Colonna to Philip II, May 18th, 1578; Simancas MS. Estado, leg. 1148; Philip II to Colonna and the Inquisitors, July 27th, 1581, Drafts of Letters of Philip II, vol. I, B.M. MS. Add. 28 357, fo. 451–2. Cf. also the hesitating attitude of the Great Court judges in the Racalmutto case. *Consulta* of the joint committee, 1586, Papeles del Consejo . . . , I, fo. 123.

publicly railed at the Inquisitors and had threatened that he would take away all their jurisdiction and then throw himself at the king's feet and explain how the Holy Office had usurped the royal prerogative. 'And although we have had encounters with the Italian viceroys', ended this *consulta*, 'never has the Inquisition been trampled under foot (*atropellado*) as now.'[1]

Up to this time the viceroys and Inquisitors had taken measures only against each other's agents.[2] But as the cases of the two counts dragged on and others were added to them, tempers became frayed. In March 1590 Alvadeliste sent his captain of the guard to the Inquisitors' palace where the count of Mussomele was held prisoner. What happened then is not quite clear, for the two sides sent contradictory reports to Madrid. There seems to have been an undignified scuffle in which the Inquisitors themselves were involved; the captain seized the count by force and transferred him to the viceregal prison. All this happened in full view of the crowds who undoubtedly enjoyed the spectacle. The Inquisitors now excommunicated the viceroy and laid an interdict on the city of Palermo. This action was clearly contrary to royal orders, according to which no ecclesiastical censures were to be issued against the viceroy without the king's permission. Haedo (who had been appointed archbishop of Palermo on his retirement from the Inquisition), the judge of the *Monarchia* and other influential persons now intervened with the Inquisitors, for there was no telling what the enraged viceroy might do. He had, in any case, taken no notice of the interdict. The Inquisitors thought it wise to revoke the censures, and both sides then sent extremely bitter reports to the king.[3]

In Madrid the joint committee had been arguing the legal points of the dispute for several years and had sent a number of *consultas* to the king. Each successive *consulta* had been more favourable to the claims of the Inquisitors,[4] a fact which was due largely to the influence of Quiroga who was president of the Council of Italy, as well as Inquisitor-General.[5] When finally the *junta* gave it as their opinion 'that it appeared that they (the viceroy and the Inquisitors) had shown some passion in this matter'[6] the king for once lost his temper and made a number of definite decisions. Mussomele was

[1] Papales del Consejo..., vol. I, B.M. MS. Eg. 1506, fo. 147-50.
[2] There was one exception: Vega's imprisonment of the bishop of Patti in 1555.
[3] *Consulta* of the joint committee, June 30th, 1590, ibid. fo. 169-72.
[4] Ibid. fo. 123-172.
[5] Cf. above, p. 71.
[6] *Consulta* of June 30th, 1590; Papeles del Consejo..., vol. I, B.M. MS. Eg. 1506 fo. 169-172.

to be tried by the Great Court and Racalmutto by the Inquisition. Assassination, which was instigated murder, was to be excluded from Inquisition privilege and, finally and most important of all, no titled person was to be a familiar.[1]

This was the first major defeat for the Inquisition in fifty years. The Inquisitors continued to press for a repeal, claiming that the Holy Office needed the protection and prestige conferred on it by baronial familiars, and that the Inquisition which used to be loved was now hated by the people. The old fortress of Castellammare, with all the Inquisition files, had been blown up and the house of the Inquisitors Páramo and Illánes had been burned to the ground. The fact that Páramo had been warned of this beforehand showed that it had not been an accident.[2] But, at least during the reign of Philip II, the Parliamentary nobility was not re-admitted to membership of the Holy Office.[3] Relations between Páramo and Olivares continued fully as bad as those between Peña and Alvadeliste. In 1592 the viceroy published a proclamation nullifying an inquisitorial order against persons who gave aid to bandits, as being an usurpation of the rights appertaining to the civil government.[4] The Suprema complained that Olivares went even further in his attacks on the Holy Office than Colonna and Alvadeliste had done. Further meetings of the *junta* followed, defining points of detail on the number of Inquisition familiars, the crimes for which no privilege could be claimed, and emphasizing the necessity for secular judges to seek immediate absolution if they had been excommunicated by the Inquisitors.[5]

Nevertheless, jurisdictional quarrels continued, and Gian Francesco Rao, president of the Great Court, acted as principal champion of the secular courts during the governments of Geraci and Maqueda.[6] Early in the reign of Philip III, there was one more serious crisis. A Spanish soldier, who was a familiar, had murdered two other soldiers. Both the Inquisition and the captain-general claimed jurisdiction over the murderer. The Inquisitors rejected the joint committee proposed by the Great Court and equally an offer of mediation by Archbishop Haedo of Palermo. On the 3rd August, 1602 they excommunicated the Great Court. On the 4th Haedo declared the

[1] Ibid.
[2] *Consulta* of the Suprema, Oct. 21st, 1593, ibid. fo. 212–14.
[3] Garufi, Contributo..., Arch. stor. sic. n.s. XLIII, pp. 68 f. suggested that the Inquisitors may have had a hand in the revolt of the *braccio militare* in 1591. This hypothesis has, in fact, proved to be correct. Cf. above, p. 156.
[4] Ibid. p. 85.
[5] Ibid. pp. 92 ff. Papeles del Consejo..., vol. I, B.M. MS. Eg. 1506, fo. 223–233.
[6] Ibid. pp. 104 ff.

excommunication null and void, gave the Inquisitors 24 hours in which to retract it, and then sent them his own notice of excommunication. The Inquisitors had barricaded themselves with 200 familiars in the Steri Palace and refused to submit. The duke of Feria, the viceroy, declared this action to be sedition and sent a company of Spanish soldiers to storm the palace. No other viceroy had ever gone as far as this. The soldiers broke into the court and found that the familiars had fled; but the Inquisitors had remained and dropped notices of excommunication on the soldiers from the windows. At this the soldiers refused to continue the attack and begged for absolution which the Inquisitors readily granted. The case was then referred to Madrid, and, as always happened, it dragged on without definite conclusion. But the incident had shown conclusively that the Inquisitors could not be made to yield to physical force.[1]

Nothing could show more clearly the confused and undeveloped state of Spanish ideas in imperial administration than this struggle between the civil government and the Inquisition in Sicily. Philip II and his advisers never doubted the necessity of having an Inquisition, both from a religious and from a political point of view. Yet it was in the very nature of the Holy Office to claim independence from any secular authority except the king himself; and this claim made nonsense of the principle of centralizing imperial administration through the viceroy and the Council of Italy. Undoubtedly the king was not sorry to have in the Inquisition a counterbalance to viceroys who were far away and liable to become too independent. Yet it is doubtful whether this consideration was uppermost in his mind. While the ultimate dependence of the Inquisitors on the Monarchy was beyond question, the Holy Office was too clumsy an instrument to fulfil effectively the functions of a constitutional or administrative check on viceregal government. The civil government of Sicily could be embarrassed by the development of a powerful organization virtually outside its jurisdiction; but it could not in this way be made less independent itself, nor linked more closely to the centre of the Hapsburg Monarchy. Philip's letters and instructions, moreover, leave no doubt that he conceived of the Inquisition first and foremost in terms of religion, of the defence of the Catholic faith. Neither the king nor anyone else made any conscious attempt to integrate the religious and political ideas currently accepted at the court of Spain to form a comprehensive theory of Imperial administration capable of producing consistent action.

[1] Ibid. pp. 104 ff.

CHAPTER SEVEN

The Viceroys and Madrid

WHEN Scipio di Castro wrote his account of the government of Sicily for the instruction of the prospective viceroy, Marc Antonio Colonna, he set the key for his study by beginning with the statement that the governorship of Sicily had been fatal to the reputation of its holders, from the viceroyalty of Juan la Nuza, in 1490, to the death of the marquis of Pescara, in 1571.[1] Cabrera de Córdoba[2] and later commentators[3] endorsed Castro's view, and the history of nearly all Sicilian viceroys of the sixteenth century bore out their contention. The government of Sicily had to cope with difficulties greater than those in any other Spanish dominion except the Netherlands. It was virtually impossible for the viceroys both to fulfil the demands of the court of Madrid and to satisfy the aspirations of the Sicilians. If they attempted to govern the country with a reasonable degree of efficiency, they could not fail to arouse the hostility of all those interested in the maintenance of Sicilian privilege and corruption. Their authority, so absolute in theory, was in practice limited on all sides: they had to follow the king's instructions and observe the immunities of the Sicilians; they could never disentangle their administration from the all-pervading feuds of the great families, nor were they able to control their ministers who were often ready to go over to the opposition and to appeal to the king over the heads of the viceroys.

While Philip II had no very clear conception of the true nature

---

[1] Castro, Avvertimenti..., Thesora Politico, vol. II. The former date should really be 1495.

[2] Cabrera, Filipe Segundo, vol. I, p. 280: '... (el) Duque de Alcalá ... daba en la administracion del estado (de Napoles) gran satisfaction, no el otro (Medinaceli) per ser fatal Sicilia contro sus vireyes desde el año mil y cuatro-cientos y noventa hasta el de ochenta dos.' Cabrera might well have taken the latter date as 1592 and included Colonna and Alvadeliste in the catalogue; but here, as in most of his references to Sicily, he was content to follow Castro.

[3] In the Spanish copy of Castro's Avvertimenti, in the Real Academia de la Historia in Madrid (Est. 21 gr. l.a. No. 3.) the title of the work is given as follows: 'Nota de las advertencias que dio Don Sipion de Castro al Señor Marco Colonna ... que por no haverse aprovechado de ellas padecio lo que arriba està dicho y se sabe' (i.e. Conlonna's recall and receipt of a note informing him of the king's displeasure which was supposed to have caused his death).

of his empire, his views on the obligations and duties of his viceroys were all the more precise. His secret instructions to the viceroy of Naples, the duke of Alcalá, leave no doubt on this point:

'The first thing which you must realize,' Philip wrote, 'is that the community was not made for the prince but rather that the prince was created for the sake of the community; and you will have to represent our person and act as we would act if we were present. Your principal object and intention must be to work for the community which is in your charge, so that it may live and rest in full security, peace, justice and quiet; to watch so that it may sleep without anxiety; and finally, to take heed that you are not accepting this office to be idle or to live at your pleasure, nor for any benefit of your own, but only, as I have said, for the peace and quiet and good of the community.'[1]

Sixteenth century rulers and statesmen were no political theorists.[2] Having firmly established the general principle that the aim of the ruler must be the good of the governed, the secret instructions went on to give practical advice on how to achieve this aim. First and foremost, the viceroy was himself to set an example of the kind of behaviour he expected the people to follow. A prince could not govern without being both loved and feared, loved by the just and

[1] Instructions..., B.M. MS. Add. 28 701, fo. 86.
[2] Philip's views were never unconventional; cf. the remark of Pedro Velázquez, a most prolific giver of good advice who could always be relied upon to reproduce the conventionalities of his day: 'The aim of a king is directed only towards the good of his vassals – the aim of a tyrant only towards his own personal good.' Velázquez to Philip II, Oct. 6th, 1575. Papers relating to Military Affairs; B.M. MS. Add. 28 366, fo. 81.

In the preamble of the famous Act of Abjuration of 1581, by which the Dutch renounced their allegiance to Philip II, it is stated that '... God did not create the people slaves to their prince, to obey his commands, whether right or wrong, but rather the prince for the sake of his subjects, to love and support them as a father his children, or a shepherd his flock...' quoted in C. V. Wedgwood, William the Silent (London, 1944), p. 224. The similarity between this passage and Philip the Second's instructions is sufficiently striking to suggest that the authors of the Act of Abjuration may have deliberately adopted the phraseology current at the court of Madrid. If it was the fashion in Spain to pay lip-service to the duties of a ruler in just such phrases, the revolutionary conclusions which the Netherlanders drew from these premises would have all the greater moral force. Such an interpretation does not necessarily preclude the influence of Duplessis-Mornay's *Vindiciae contra Tyrannos* on the political thought of the Netherlanders. But Duplessis-Mornay – if indeed he was the author of the *Vindiciae* – and the other Calvinist writers of the period had said nothing about the political obligations of a prince that was not a commonplace in Catholic political theory, and the framers of the Act of Abjuration cannot have been ignorant of this fact. Where they differed from Philip II was in making the fulfilment of the ruler's political obligations to his subjects the condition of the subjects' political obligation to the ruler. The attitude of the Sicilians, with their memories of the overthrow of Angevin rule and their insistence on the voluntary nature of their allegiance to the house of Aragon, was substantially similar to that of the Dutch. I am indebted to Dr G. N. Clark for drawing my attention to this point.

feared by the wicked. This was a sixteenth century commonplace,[1] but Philip was well aware of what it should mean in practice. A prince will be loved (the instructions continued) if the people see him perform virtuous actions and realize that it is his aim to help them. Yet as he cannot be fully loved unless he is known, and as he can be personally known only to a few, he will be judged by his works and actions. He must, therefore, make every effort to reconcile rival factions and on no account take part in their disputes. He must not give judgment in a law-suit without the advice of his judges, for he is no lawyer and cannot afford to make mistakes; nor should he punish any crime in anger, for anger will cloud his reason. Above all, he was to be most careful in the selection of his ministers; it was far better to give offices to unknown persons of ability than to have them bought by the great 'who intend to squeeze the blood out of the people.'[2]

Such was the advice formulated by the Council of Italy on the king's instructions and given to the viceroy about to take up his duties. In addition, each viceroy received more specific instructions dealing with the practical problems likely to arise and with suggestions for solving them.[3] These documents were all substantially similar.[4] New points were added only occasionally when the Council felt that a particularly urgent and new problem should be brought to the viceroy's notice. The instructions reveal how well-informed was the government in Madrid about the political and social conditions of the Spanish dominions and the difficulties of the governor. Special stress was laid on the impartial administration of justice and on the defence of the country. The viceroy must protect royal rights and *preeminencias* from all encroachments, but he must equally respect the privileges and *fueros* of the citizens. The orders given on

[1] Medinaceli to Philip II, 1561, '... es tan necessario para el que govierna que le tengan amor como temor.' Simancas MS. Estado, leg. 1126, fo. 140.
[2] Instruction ..., B.M. MS. Add. 28 701, fo. 87–90.
[3] In the seventeenth century this type of instructions was also called 'secret', as were the instructions for the count of Lemos which otherwise correspond to those for Medinaceli and Maqueda. Ibid. fo. 213–267.
[4] I have found two complete sets of instruction for Sicilian viceroys during the reign of Philip II: those for Medinaceli, at the beginning of the reign (B.M. MS. Add. 28 701, fo. 18–48), and those for Maqueda, at the very end (Simancas MS. Secret. Prov. leg. 803, fo. 26–50). Some chapters of the instructions for Pescara and Colonna are quoted in the viceregal correspondence at Simancas. These instructions do not achieve the clarity and orderly arrangement of the finest Venetian and Spanish relations, of which they may be regarded as counterparts. The 130 odd points are set down haphazardly; no one subject is exhausted in consecutive paragraphs, but each is referred to again and again after other topics have intervened. Matters of the highest political importance, such as diplomatic relations with the Papacy, are found side by side with detailed rules of procedure for paying the Spanish troops. Yet every point itself is clear and concise.

relations with the Church provide perhaps the best clue to Philip's ideas both of the rights and of the duties of his ministers. 'As our intention has always been to favour the cause of the Church,' so run the instructions, 'you are to honour, revere and serve our most holy Father . . . taking care to uphold and conserve the dignity and authority of the Church, not allowing that it should in any way be offended . . .' In the next paragraph the viceroy, a layman, is exhorted to see to it that the prelates live a godly and sober life.[1]

Philip's viceroy's did not find it difficult to accept these principles. Brought up to the same ideals of Catholic chivalry (watered down by the corrupting influence of secret diplomacy and court intrigue) their moral standards were not markedly different from those of the king. Differences arose rather over the problem of their precise relations with the government in Spain. At the beginning of Philip's reign Vega stated the extreme case for viceregal independence. The viceroy, being on the spot, was best qualified to know the conditions of the country he governed. He must have the complete trust of his sovereign; for if other ministers intervened and gave orders it was as if a dark body eclipsed the bright light of the sun and the moon.[2] For what were these ministers in Madrid? They were, in general, ambitious men of low birth who thought they could treat the viceroys of Sicily and Naples as if they were the mayors of Salamanca or of Avila: 'they do not know what it is to be a king, nor wherein lies the greatness and authority of monarchy, nor of the provinces of the world and the quality of their peoples; nor (do they know) of chivalry and honour, nor what manner of man a viceroy has to be, or a captain-general or any other minister of his status . . .'[3] A country such as Sicily – and Vega painted a dark picture of the character of the islanders – was in need of charity, piety and mercy more than any other. The door of justice must always remain open and all hope of success by foul means must be stifled. The people must be protected from the cruelty of the bandits and from the rapacity of the officials. They must be able to buy their food at reasonable prices; they must be protected from Corsair raids by im-

---

[1] Instructions for Medinaceli, fo. 19. Almost verbatim in the instructions for Maqueda, fo. 27.
[2] Vega to Philip II, Papiers d'Etat . . . , vol. v, pp. 144 f.
[3] Paruta e Palmerino (Diario . . . , Bibl. Lett. e Stor. 1st ser. vol. I, pp. 104 f.) report Colonna as saying to the Inquisitor Haedo: 'Il re dei pari miei conta con il digito, e di voi ne può carricare navi.' The precise expression may be apocryphal, but there is no doubt that Colonna was both capable of saying this and that in fact he did use words to this effect. Cf. Papeles del Consejo de la General Inquisicion, I, B.M. MS. Eg. 1506, fo. 113–117.

proved defences; hospitals, colleges and other pious institutions must be founded and supported, and order and dignity brought into the service of God. All this was the duty of the viceroy and for this he must have untrammelled authority. 'You might say to this,' Vega added, 'that then the viceroy will be the real king, and I and my council will be useless. But I say that it is easy to distinguish a good from a bad governor, for you will know them by their fruits; and if he is good, he must be left a free hand; and this is to be king of Sicily and of the world.'[1]

Vega's conception of the ends of government was substantially similar to Philip's. Where he differed was in his view of the status of the viceroy. In the isolation of his cabinet the Prudent King could never countenance such independence in a vassal as advocated by Vega. His crabbed and suspicious nature was offended in its royal dignity and in the knowledge of its own responsibility. Two considerations determined the king's attitude; on the one hand the authority of his representative must be publicly upheld, for any attack on him was an attack on the crown;[2] on the other hand he must never be able to escape from the control of Madrid. 'The power which I have bestowed on you in order that you may fulfil your task is as complete and free as you see,' Philip wrote in the instructions, 'for . . . you have to be there in my name . . . nevertheless I declare it to be my intention that you should observe and fulfil completely all the above (instructions) and that, moreover, you should use the said powers with the limitations and restrictions which will be specified below. . .'[3] There followed a list of governmental activities which the viceroy should never perform without reference to the king, including the prerogative of mercy for certain crimes, the appointment of all the more important officials, the provision of ecclesiastical benefices and the granting of military honours.[4]

To give effect to these limitations Philip made use of the system of viceregal correspondence which he had inherited from his predecessors.[5] His governors wrote to him every week, or even more

[1] Papiers d'Etat . . . , vol. v, p. 159.
[2] The viceroys, of course, always took care to admit no distinction between their own authority and that of the king. When the populace of Trapani attacked the office of the tax-collector with the cry 'Viva el Rey, y muera (la) tasa,' Colonna wrote to the king that this was lèse majesté, Oct. 6th, 1577; Simancas MS. Estado, leg. 1147.
[3] Instructions for Maqueda, ibid, Secret. Prov. leg. 803, fo. 49.
[4] According to the usual Spanish practice, these rules were quite often simply ignored; e.g. Philip's complaint in the instructions for Maqueda, ibid. fo. 49. Often enough the king was satisfied as long as their breach was not too flagrant.
[5] The system was already fully developed in Ferdinand's reign. Cf. Correspondence of Hugo de Moncada, Documentos Inéditos . . . , vol. xxiv.

frequently, detailing their activities and asking for instructions. Their dispatches varied considerably in method and style, from the ironical, exaggerated and polished relations of Vega, to the long-winded scripts of Medinaceli or Toledo's irritable and sometimes hysterical reports of the progress of the siege of Malta; from Colonna's painstaking, dignified and detailed descriptions, to the short notes of Alvadeliste, dry, concise and impatient.[1] These letters were read by the Council of Italy and then forwarded to the king, either in the original or in the form of an abstract of the main points.[2] Every viceregal act had to receive at least *ex post facto* confirmation from Madrid. In matters of real import no viceroy would risk taking action without precise orders. Toledo complained rather of the lack of instruction when it came to risking the Spanish fleet in the relief of Malta,[3] than of being excessively tied by orders from Spain. Colonna grumbled about interference by the Council of Italy[4] but was even more incensed by his inability to extract decisions on important points of policy from that body.[5]

We have seen[6] that the constitution of the Council of Italy and Philip's personal slowness were largely responsible for the indecision at Madrid and the consequent lack of control by the central government of the empire over the administration of the dominion. The most glaring instance was perhaps the case of the light cavalry. In 1578 Parliament petitioned that the donative for the 300 regular light horse be used to equip and maintain six galleys instead. The soldiers were very unpopular in the country, and the extra warships would help to keep the coasts clear of pirates.[7] The king asked the viceroy for a report, but took no decision. At every subsequent meeting of Parliament the petition was renewed, and every time the viceroys wrote to Spain urging a clear yes or no; for there was the danger that otherwise Parliament might refuse the grant altogether.[8]

[1] Only a small portion of this correspondence has been published, viz. most of Toledo's, together with the answers from Spain and elsewhere, in ibid. vols. XXIX and XXX; and Terranova's, without replies, Documenti per servire . . . , ser. 1, vol. II. Most of the rest, in MSS., is in Simancas and in the British Museum.
[2] This might be written on the back of the original.
[3] e.g. Toledo to Philip II, July 5th, 1565. Same to Eraso on the same date; Documentos Inéditos . . . , vol. XXIX, pp. 250, 260 ff.
[4] Colonna to Juan de Idiáquez, Dec. 13th, 1581; Simancas MS. Estado, leg. 1151.
[5] e.g. his attempt to obtain royal approval for moving back to Palermo after a period of residence in Messina. After several months of fruitless correspondence the viceroy went to Palermo without waiting for a decision. Letters to Philip II and Idiáquez. Sept.–Nov. 1581; ibid.
[6] Cf. above, ch. 2.
[7] Colonna to Philip II, Nov. 17th, 1578; Simancas MS. Estado, leg. 1148.
[8] Jan. 1st, 1580, Colonna wrote to Philip saying that he was being accused of not referring the petition to Madrid; ibid. leg. 1149. Granvelle to Bravo, May 26th, 1585;

But Philip continued to ask for memoranda and would not make up his mind. Not until 1593 was the light cavalry sent to Milan when a further and still vain attempt was made to commission the extra six galleys.[1]

But dependent as viceroys were on direct orders, the restrictions would have been less severe if they could have exercised effective control over the dominion's administration. This was far from being the case. The king appointed the principal members of the viceroy's government and, although he would usually follow the latter's suggestions, his assent was by no means certain. Toledo was not allowed to have the secretary Juan de Soto as his quarter master-general although he requested his appointment most urgently,[2] while Colonna demurred in vain at having Canales, a creature of Terranova, foisted on him by the secretary of the Council of Italy.[3] In consequence the king could rely on a measure of tension between the viceroy and his senior officials, a tension which proved very effective in limiting excessive independence.

As a result, imperial administration became not so much a matter of positive direction from the centre, as a system of checks and balances of semi-autonomous forces. The longer the viceroy remained in office, the more apparent became the contradictory tendencies of Philip's dual concept of authority and control. It was comparatively easy to defend the governor's authority from direct attacks. When the government in Madrid had to reprove a viceroy, it was careful not to do this publicly; Chinchón even advised against doing it through the Council of Italy.[4] When Don John of Austria demanded the right to give orders directly to Sicilian and Neapolitan officials, Quiroga was quick to point out the deleterious consequences to the viceroy's status.[5] But when the viceroy's ministers wrote to

---

ibid. leg. 1155. It is interesting to note that it was never suggested by the opponents of the petitions that the cavalry should be retained in order to keep the Sicilians in check.

[1] Olivares to Philip II, June 18th, 1593; ibid. leg. 1157. In Philip's defence it must be said that Parliament knew its mind no better than he did, and almost immediately started petitioning for the return of the cavalry. Seven years later Philip III acceded to their wish; ibid. leg. 1159.

[2] Documentos Inéditos . . . , vol. XXIX, pp. 115 ff, 171 ff.

[3] Colonna to Philip II, Feb. 10th, 1578; Correspondence . . . Naples and Sicily, vol. I, B.M. MS. Add. 28 394, fo. 5.

[4] Chinchón to Philip II, July 9th, 1578, concerning the viceroy of Naples, the marquis of Mondéjar: '. . . se entendiesse, que Vuestra Majestad tiene sus acciones por dignas de reprehensiones, pues se lo hace, y sabiendolo aquien otro que V. M. solo, no dexara de llegar a oydos del duque de Sesa y sus amigos, y hemulos del Marques, y dentro de pocos dias estaria la nueva en Napoles tan entendida como es ordinario en los caminos largos . . . ' ibid. fo. 59.

[5] Quiroga to Philip II, Oct. 23rd, 1574; Official Papers, Spanish, vol. II, B.M. MS. Add., 28 360, fo. 124.

the king behind their chief's back, the temptation to avail themselves of this extra check on their provincial governors proved too strong for the court in Spain. Despite solemn assurances to the contrary,[1] Madrid not only accepted but encouraged such information.[2] Once his suspicion was aroused, Philip would go to any length to obtain information, although he usually attempted to save his viceroy's face.[3] In 1581, for instance, the Council of Italy received an unsigned letter accusing Colonna of irregular financial transactions in the granting of export licences. He had been given a chance to state his case and the matter seemed clear except, so the councillors suggested, that he should be asked very politely which of the *razionali* of the Patrimony had advised him on this particular point. In this way his version could be checked unobtrusively. Philip agreed, but added that it would be better to ask for the names of those who had voted for the measure, and those who had voted against.[4]

Despite Philip's precautions, the court's avidity for criticism of the viceroys was well known in the dominions. The struggle of the personal opposition against the governor, begun in Sicily, would be transferred to Madrid.[5] There it merged with the rivalry of the Spanish parties who tried to push their own candidates for the viceregal office or who attempted to defend the viceroy whom the king had appointed at their instance. Nothing was stable at the court of Philip II, least of all the king's favour, and the viceroy's slightest indiscretion placed an effective weapon in the hands of his enemies. In the forty years of his reign Charles V had appointed only three viceroys.[6] His son, in forty-two years, appointed no less than seven, besides two presidents who held office for at least one full term. Juan de Vega, the viceroy in office at the time of Philip's accession

[1] e.g. Oct. 31st, 1580, Philip and the C. of Italy wrote to Colonna, showing great satisfaction with his conduct of affairs and added: '... y porque tenemos toda la satisfaccion que podeys dessear no ay para que hazer caso de las quexas de particulares quanto mas que no las ha havido (which was not true) y se alguno acudiere adalles (a darlas) se os advertira dellas.' Simancas MS. Secret. Prov. leg. 1599, fo. 51.

[2] e.g. Philip II (Secretary Vargas) to Monrreal, Feb. 19th, 1574. 'Vuestras cartas de 29 y 30 de septiembre se han recebido y porque cerca los cabos que contienen se scrive all Illustre Duque de Terranova nuestro Presidente y capitan general desse Reyno loque conviene sin declarar el autor dellos como vos lo haveis pedido, no havra que dezir en esta mas de teneros en servicio todo lo que advertis y encargaros lo comuniqueis siempre lo que a el tocare para que no se pierda tiempo en la provision de lo que conviene, y si algo nuevo degno de nuestra noticia no(s) lo podreis tambien avisar quando se offresciere el caso.' Ibid. leg. 1598, fo. 176.

[3] Philip's methods in this respect are well known from his treatment of the best of all his provincial governors, Alexander Farnese. Cf. L. van der Essen, Alexandre Farnèse, vol. v (Brussels 1937) pp. 273 ff.

[4] *Consulta* of Nov. 27th, 1581; Simancas MS. Secret. Prov. leg. 982.

[5] Ranke, Die Osmanen ..., pp. 215 ff.

[6] Viz. Monteleone, Gonzaga, and Vega; cf. Appendix I.

to the throne, had formerly been imperial ambassador in Rome.[1] A man of austere habits and with a biting wit, he had not been popular at the easy-going court of Paul III.[2] In Sicily his legendary efficiency and severity soon made him a host of enemies. He was accused of unduly favouring his son-in-law, the duke of Bivona, and resigned when the king failed to support him, complaining bitterly of the interfering lawyers in the council and of the king's faithlessness.[3] In vain he pleaded with Philip to trust his viceroys and not to listen to the calumnies which were always brought against them:[4] his successors fared no better.

Philip's first appointment made a striking contrast to his predecessor. Juan de la Cerda, duke of Medinaceli, had few qualifications for high office other than an ancient and distinguished Castilian title, a private income of 28,000 ducats,[5] and the friendship of Granvelle and Ruy Gómez.[6] Personally honest and likeable, he was popular in Sicily, not least because he showed none of Vega's ruthlessness in his dealings with the nobility. Yet his ineptitude for government[7] compelled him to rely too much on his selfish ministers, and his lack of personal authority made him a helpless onlooker in the quarrels and feuds of his most trusted servants. No fewer than five of these, (including his chamberlain and his secretary), were fighting bitter lawsuits with barons and communes, and the duke's

---

[1] He was no relation to the dramatist Lope de Vega.

[2] Buonfiglio e Costanzo, Historia Siciliana, p. 491. Marques del Saltillo, Juan de Vega, Embajador de Carlos V en Roma (1543–47), (Madrid 1946). Part of Vega's correspondence from Rome with Charles V is to be found in Bergenroth's transcripts from the Simancas archives, in the British Museum.

[3] Vega to Bernardino de Mendoza, Oct. 29th, 1556, in Saltillo, Vega, pp. 24 f. Vega to Philip II, Aug. 16th, 1556, Madrid, Bibl. Nac. MS. 11, 055, fo. 81–85.

[4] Ibid. fo. 84. Also Vega to Philip, letter cit. Papiers d'Etat . . . , vol. v, pp. 164 ff. Castro Avvertimenti, Letters and Papers . . . Sicily, B.M. MS. Add. 28 396, fo. 372, speaks of a sindication,' . . . cosa tanto sentita da Giovan di Vega, che non potendo dissimulare fu costretto a domandar licentia et scrisse all'Imperatore (should be Philip II) quella lettera, della quale vanno tante copie per il mondo, acciò se vegga il retratto d'un estremo risentimento, che fa un servitore, et d'una estrema patientia, che ebbe un padrone.' The letter referred to by Castro must be the one printed in the Papiers d'Etat . . . , vol. v. It speaks for Philip that he accepted this letter and made Vega president of the Council of Castile, perhaps the most important office in the Spanish government. Vega died on Dec. 20th, 1558.

[5] Stado de España; B.M. MS. Harleian 3315, fo. 72.

[6] Granvelle, Correspondence, vol. IV, p. XXII.

[7] Consulta of the Council of Italy, 1563; Simancas MS. Secret. Prov. leg. 980. 'Haviendose governado el duque de Medinaceli como Vuestra Majestad sabe, y sido en las de la justicia tan remisso, que estando el reyno de Sicilia limpio de foraxidos, se halla al presente lleno dellas . . . Pero mirada por otra parte la limpieza con que ha tractado las cosas del patrimonio y que si ha sido remisso proçede de defecto de natura . . . se deve tener cuenta de su persona antes de removerle de aquel cargo . . . .'

household seemed a veritable inferno.¹ A visitor was sent from Madrid to sindicate the administration, and the duke had to see his closest advisers dismissed or imprisoned, while accusations and counter-accusations raised passions to fever heat.² Isolated between the contending factions and betrayed by his own agent in Madrid, the viceroy was finally overthrown by his own party at court because he had incurred the enmity of the marquis of Favara, Ruy Gómez' brother-in-law.³ Cabrera sagely commented 'that a minister who serves far from the prince must keep on good terms with the prince's favourite, for his own best services are counterbalanced by the intrigues of his rivals; and in the same manner he must keep the regents of the Council well disposed by presents and favours given through courageous and intelligent agents.'⁴

Medinaceli's subsequent career was no more fortunate. After a brief spell as viceroy of Navarre, he was appointed as successor to the duke of Alva in the Netherlands – again through the influence of the Gómez party. In June of the year 1572 he arrived in Brussels, arousing great hopes by his princely and courteous bearing. Yet Alva, who still held the military command, refused to co-operate with the duke; in Madrid the Toledo party worked against him, and soon he became the pawn of the forceful and crafty personalities who dominated the political scene in the Netherlands. After a few months he asked to be recalled.⁵

The deterioration of the strategic position of Spain in the Mediterranean induced Philip II to make the next four viceregal appointments primarily on military grounds. Yet the influence of the parties remained supreme. This time it was the Toledo group which secured the double office of viceroy of Sicily and captain-general of the sea for one of its most competent members, García de Toledo.⁶ Having an unpleasant manner and with a capacity for making enemies unusual even in that heyday of personal feuds,⁷

[1] Castro, Avvertimenti, Letters and Papers..., Sicily, B.M. MS. Add. 28 396, fo. 394–5.
[2] e.g. the unjust imprisonment by the visitor of Augustin Gisulfo, head of the Patrimony. Simancas MS. Secret. Prov. leg. 980, passim.
[3] Castro, Avvertimenti; Letters and Papers... Sicily, B.M. MS. Add. 28 396, fo. 372–3.
[4] Cabrera, Filipe Segundo, vol. I, pp. 416 f.
[5] Granvelle, Correspondence, vol. IV, passim.
[6] For his early career cf. Enciclopedia Universal Illustrada, vol. LXII (Bilbao y Madrid 1923) p. 492. García was a cousin of the duke of Alva and son of Charles the Fifth's great viceroy of Naples, Pedro de Toledo.
[7] Juan de Zúñiga to his brother, Luis de Requesens, Aug. 21st, 1568. Documentos Inéditos..., vol. XCVII, pp. 435 f. Also Toledo to the secretary Eraso, April 15th, 1565, ibid. vol. XXIX, p. 98 ff and passim. – A near-contemporary chronicler writes of

he was left in charge only long enough to save Malta and to organize the defence of Sicily against another possible attack of the Turks.

From the very beginning the new viceroy was in difficulties. His appointment of a captain-general of the sea had deeply offended Juan de Mendoza, himself a candidate for this post, and with him the whole Mendoza clan and their allies in the Gómez party.[1] Toledo's first action in Sicily had been to clear up the corruption in the navy where incompetent officers were running up large private bills which they charged to the government. After only three months he wrote to Spain that a great outcry was being raised and that he was already very unpopular.[2] For some time the king assured him of his full confidence, and immediately after he had raised the siege of Malta, the world was full of his praises.[3] But within a few weeks all this was forgotten. A bitter campaign against the viceroy was initiated by Jean de la Valette: the Grand Master of Malta knew that Toledo distrusted him as a Frenchman and was dissatisfied with the degree of co-operation he had received from Sicily.[4] In October 1565 Requesens reported that Rome was still honouring the king for his action against the Infidel, but that Don García was never mentioned.[5] At the beginning of the year 1566 his best friend at court, the secretary Eraso, was temporarily in disgrace[6] and the elimination of his influence was sufficient to weight the scales in favour of Toledo's enemies. The king's letters to him suddenly became much cooler in tone, and in a quarrel between the viceroy and his colleague in Naples Philip decided in favour of the latter.[7] Toledo sent the *protonotaro* Alfonso Ruyz, to Madrid, but was then himself obliged to follow in an unsuccessful attempt to exonerate himself from the charges brought against him.[8]

After Toledo's recall no further Spaniards with sufficient military

him that his first act in Sicily was to have a delinquent quartered by 4 galleys, rowing in different directions. To a plea for pardon for another criminal he is supposed to have replied: 'Che grazia! non sono io venuto in questo regno per grazia ma per giustizia. Chi vuole grazia vada a Sua Maestá'. V. di Giovanni, Del Palermo Restaurato, Bibl. Lett. e Stor. di Sic. ser. 2, vol. II, p. 184 f.

[1] Paolo Tiepolo in 1560; Calendar of State Papers, Venetian, vol. VII (London 1890), p. 218. Toledo's actual appointment was in 1564. Tiepolo's remark of 1560 therefore shows for how long the intrigues about these offices went on and how old and deep-seated was the resentment against Toledo.

[2] Toledo to Eraso, April 15th, 1565, Documentos Inéditos . . . , vol. XXIX, pp. 98 ff.

[3] Ibid. pp. 164, 513, 537.

[4] Toledo to Eraso, Oct. 19th, 1565, ibid. pp. 542 ff. Same to Philip II, Febr. 8th, 1566, ibid. vol. XXX, pp. 125 ff.

[5] Requèsens to Gonzalo Pérez, Oct. 22nd, 1565, ibid. vol. XXIX, pp. 557 f.

[6] Eraso to Toledo, May 12th, 1566, ibid. vol. XXX, pp. 239 ff.

[7] Philip II to Toledo, Febr. 17th, 1567, Simancas MS. Estado, leg. 1132, fo. 37.

[8] Buonfiglio e Costanzo, Historia Siciliana, p. 567.

experience were available[1] and for the next three appointments the king had to turn to Italians. Once more a candidate of the Gómez party was chosen.[2] Francesco Ferdinando Avalos de Aquino, marquis of Pescara, had been general of the cavalry of Milan and had a fine reputation as a soldier. Don John of Austria was particularly instructed to consult him on all military matters.[3] As the son of the victor of Pavia and as the first Italian viceroy of Sicily since Ferrante Gonzaga, Pescara was acutely aware of his responsibilities. The most disinterested of the Prudent King's viceroys, he studiously kept clear of all personal entanglements, yet could not prevent his ministers from perpetrating the indiscretions which he himself eschewed. His views on religious matters and his attempts to find a compromise on the question of the *Monarchia* made him unpopular in Madrid, while in Sicily the Spanish officials could never forgive him for being an Italian. His *conservatore*, Pedro Velázquez, went to Spain and successfully turned the court against the marquis. Only an early death preserved him from public disgrace.[4] Even his personal honour did not remain unstained; for it was rumoured that his last illness and premature death were due to over-indulgence with his mistress.[5]

Perhaps to make certain of the island's co-operation during the war of the League against the Turks, Philip decided to appoint a Sicilian as president of the kingdom. No other act could have shown more clearly the king's belief in the fundamental loyalty of the Sicilian nobility. Carlo d'Aragona e Tagliavia, duke of Terranova, was related to the royal house of Aragon and, like his father before him, had already served for a short time as president.[6] The new

[1] According to the Venetian ambassador, Sigismondo Cavalli, Spain had at that time only three generals with personal experience of leading an army: the dukes of Alva and Sessa and the marquis of Pescara. Albèri, *Relazioni*, 1st ser. vol. v, p. 178.
[2] Cabrera, *Filipe Segundo*, I, pp. 566 ff.
[3] 'Instrucción i advertencias que embio Julio Claro al Señor Don Juan de Austria ...' in Papeles tocantes a la Historia de España 1522–1696. BM.. MS. Egerton 367, fo. 86.
[4] Cabrera, *Filipe Segundo*, vol. I, pp. 556 f. The fullest account is in the Madrid copy of Castro's *Avvertimenti*, R.Acad. de la Hist. MS. Est. 21 gr. l.a. No. 3, fo. 7–9. The B.M. MS. copy of Castro does not give as many details on Pescara, neither can these be gathered from the official correspondence at Simancas and in the B.M., except for the viceroy's quarrel with the Inquisition. But relations between the viceroy and the government at Madrid usually remained at least officially correct until the viceroy's recall, and even this often took the form of voluntary resignation. But it is also possible to read between the lines, and when we have letters by either the government or the viceroy to third parties, Castro's version is always found to be substantially correct (e.g. in the case of Vega and Toledo). Moreover, Cabrera, who knew the court well, had no hesitation in accepting Castro's account.
[5] Di Giovanni, *Del Palermo* ..., Bibl. Lett. e Stor., ser. 2, vol. II. p. 199.
[6] From 1566 to 1568. Cf. Appendix I.

governor was altogether a more subtle politician than his predecessor and made no attempt to disguise his Sicilian family connections, but rather relied on their support and, at times, pursued his pro-noble policy even in defiance of Madrid.[1] He did his best to content his Spanish ministers and in this was successful at least in the case of Luca de Cifuentes, the president of the Great Court, who became his principal adviser. His agent, Juan Bayarte, spent large sums in Madrid, and in consequence Terranova could rely on the support of the secretary Gaitan and of an influential party in the Council of Italy.[2] Yet even he could not escape the opposition of the Spanish nobles and ministers. His *consultore*, Pedro de León, complained to the king and to the Inquisitor-General, Quiroga, that Terranova did not consult him in the appointment of important officers of state.[3] Pedro Velázquez went further and accused the president of nepotism, of embezzling the taxes on the export of corn and of incompetence in military matters to which last he attributed the loss of Goletta.[4] Lorenzo Téllez de Silva, marquis de la Favara (cousin and successor of the Favara who had brought about Medinaceli's downfall) painted a frightening picture of the loss of prestige which the Spaniards had suffered under Terranova's government, warning the king of the likelihood of another Sicilian Vespers.[5] The president protested violently to the court,[6] but the barrage continued, Favara writing dramatically that he and his friends were only waiting for the day when they would wake up with their throats cut.[7] In 1576 León was appointed regent in the Council of Italy, and thereafter the combined pressure of Quiroga and himself became too strong for the Terranova party. In 1577 the president was recalled to Spain, although with full honours.[8]

The *Gran Siciliano*, as Terranova was later to be called, had demonstrated that by skilful use of influence and by judicious bribes

[1] Cf. above, p. 111.
[2] Memorandum, Letters and Papers, vol. II, B.M. MS. Add. 28 400 fo. 198.
[3] Letters and Papers ... Sicily, B.M. MS. Add. 28 396, fo. 16, 43, 45, 48.
[4] Ibid. fo. 218–36.
[5] Ibid. fo. 280–284.
[6] Terranova to Philip II, Dec. 10th, 1574; Aragona Corrispondenza Particolare, Documenti per servire ..., ser. 1, vol. II, pp. 88 ff.
[7] (Sic), Favara to Philip II, Jan. 30th, 1577; Letters and Papers ... Sicily, B.M. MS. Add. 28 396, fo. 76.
[8] *Consulta* of Quiroga to Philip II, Aug. 24th, 1576; Papeles del Consejo ..., vol. I, B.M. MS. Eg. 1506, fo. 39–40. Council of Italy to Philip II, April 1st, 1577: '... ha parescido que se adviertа a Vuestra Majestad de lo bien que el Duque de Terranova ha servido en este cargo el tiempo, que ha estado en el, y quan apta es su persona para ser empleado en otros de semejante qualidad ... y quan justo sera que correspondiendo a esto V.M. le honrre y haga le merced que su persona y servicio merescen.' Simancas MS. Secret. Prov. leg. 981.

it was possible for a good administrator both to govern Sicily effectively and to safeguard his personal position at least over a number of years. Lacking the mercurial ambitions of a Colonna, the overbearing genius of a Granvelle or the frightening brilliance of a Parma, the Sicilian statesman was one of the few ministers whom Philip was always prepared to trust. Terranova successively occupied the positions of viceroy of Catalonia, governor of Milan, and Spanish representative at the abortive congress of Cologne, and was finally rewarded for his services by the elevation to the Order of the Golden Fleece and the grandeeship of Spain.

It soon appeared, however, that Terranova's career was exceptional. The duke's successor, lacking his unusual diplomatic abilities and the advantages of his family connections in the island, found himself faced with impossible odds. Marc Antonio Colonna, viceroy from 1577 to 1584, had the advantage of a military reputation scarcely inferior to that of Don John of Austria and the duke of Alva. His father had been the last member of that great Roman family to attempt to play an independent part in the politics of Italy. Marc Antonio, disavowing a policy for which the basis of material power no longer existed, was all his life a loyal imperialist, eager to rise in the service of the king of Spain.[1] Here was a viceroy who had more than held his own in the tortuous intrigues of Roman and Neapolitan politics, and who was determined to administer Sicily with an efficiency unknown in the island since the days of Vega.[2] He had taken the precaution of appointing a permanent agent in Madrid[3] and, after Granvelle's arrival in Spain, he had a powerful and disinterested supporter in the person of the king's principal adviser.[4]

All the more bitter was the opposition he aroused from all those

[1] Colonna to Philip II, June 10th, 1577 (6 weeks after his arrival in Sicily): '... Yo no soy de los que dizen que Vuestra Majestad los ha sacado de su casa y que nunca pretendieron cargos; mas soy de los que mas han desseado emplearse en su Real servicio y esto sabe Dios que nadie lo ha podido dessear con mas recto y honrrado fin, ni mas fuera de passiones e interesses particulares...,' Simancas MS. Estado, leg. 1147. For Colonna's earlier career cf. Enciclopedia Italiana, vol. x (Milano, Roma 1931) p. 854.

[2] For his abilities as governor cf. the testimony of Granvelle:'... haverme parescido Marco Antonio, por lo que he visto despues que aqui estoi (i.e. as president of the Council of Italy), ser un valiente governador, y que ha hecho en lo de la hazienda, y por reformar la Justicia, muy buenas cosas, y yo le tiene en esto, por uno de los bastantes que pueda tener su magestad en qualquiere govierno, y es diligentissimo etc.' Letters and Papers... Sicily B.M. MS. Add. 28 396, fo. 138.

[3] Colonna to Philip II, Dec. 4th, 1577, Simancas MS. Estado, leg. 1147.

[4] This is clear from Granvelle's letters to the visitor Bravo, in 1584, at a time when Colonna's reputations had already suffered considerably. There is no evidence at all for the popular theory of Granvelle's hostility to the viceroy (e.g. in Di Giovanni, pp. 232 ff). Simancas MS. Estado, leg. 1154.

Sicilians with a vested interest in the traditional corruption, and from those Spaniards jealous of the success of another Italian. Soon it became apparent that Colonna had no intention of continuing his predecessor's pro-noble policy;[1] that he would not concede one iota of his viceregal rights to the Inquisition, and that he would treat his own officials with unheard-of high-handedness.[2] Admired on one side and hated on the other, the viceroy became the centre of intrigues and faction fights which soon reached a new level in bitterness and ferocity.

Within a few months of his arrival in Sicily, Colonna had already incurred the enmity of the commander of the *tercio*, Diego Enriquez. This Spanish-Sicilian noble claimed that his private finances did not allow him to review the Sicilian militia, and then calmly turned round and accused the viceroy of having prevented him from carrying out his duty.[3] Among the Castilian grandees Colonna's appointment had never been popular. The admiral of Castile, the duke of Medina de Riosecco, led the anti-Colonna party at Philip's court because of a quarrel over an appointment to the semi-autonomous county of Modica where the duke enjoyed special rights. He was soon joined by the duke of Sessa and the whole powerful Córdova family, estranged from the viceroy because of an alleged slight to Geronimo de Córdova, a captain in the Sicilian *tercio*.[4] The viceroy was accused of preferring Italians to Spaniards, of allowing his favourites to accumulate vast fortunes, even of writing poor Spanish and sending badly drafted dispatches.[5] He attempted to procure the abbacy of Parco for his son and with this piece of diplomatic tactlessness made an enemy of the king's private secretary, Mateo Vázquez, who was himself negotiating for this rich benefice.[6]

---

[1] Colonna to Philip II, June 24th, 1578, ibid. leg. 1148; cf. above, p. 132. In another letter of the same date he wrote: '... y lo que conviene mucho a lo que governa este Reyno es tener contenta la gente comun porque los nobles sin ellos no son nada.' Ibid. This was not a policy to recommend itself to Terranova and his friends.

[2] e.g. *Consulta* of the Council of Italy on the imprisonment of the *consultore* Taboada, June 26th, 1581, ibid. Secret. Prov. leg. 982.

[3] Enriquez to Colonna, June 13th, 1578; Correspondence... Naples and Sicily, vol. II, B.M. MS. Add. 28 395, fo. 53. Colonna to Vázquez, July 10th 1578; ibid. vol. I Add. 28 394, fo. 63. Colonna and Enriquez were reconciled later, for the viceroy wrote a very flattering letter about his maestro di campo's abilities to the king, Jan. 1st, 1581, Simancas MS. Estado, leg. 1150.

[4] Colonna to Philip II, Jan. 16th, 1578; ibid. leg. 1148.

[5] Correspondence... Naples and Sicily, vol. I, B.M. MS. Add. 28 394, fo. 42, 60–64. The last charge had some justification but Colonna was no worse in this respect than most of his contemporaries.

[6] Colonna to Philip II, Febr. 10th, 1578;ibid. fo. 5. On 20th Aug. 1577, Colonna had suggested that Vázquez be given another vacant abbacy. Simancas MS. Estado. leg. 1147.

The first major crisis occurred in 1579. The marquis of Giuliana had died suddenly after a meal and his wife, sister of the duke of Terranova, was suspected of having poisoned him. Colonna ordered a judicial inquiry and immediately the case became a feud involving the leading Sicilian families. The marquesa wrote pitiful letters to the king, and Terranova's agents in Madrid presented formidable allegations of judicial persecution by the viceroy.[1] Colonna pleaded his own case no less vigorously, and the Council of Italy gave judgment against the marquesa[2] although, in deference to the duke of Terranova, no sentence seems to have been carried out.[3]

But the opposition attack grew constantly stronger and more vicious. In addition to his struggle with the Sicilian Inquisition,[4] Colonna became involved with his two most important Spanish ministers, the *conservatore* Estévan de Monrreal and the *consultore* Taboada, both of whom he had failed to treat with the respect they demanded. Accusations against the viceroy began to reach Madrid with increasing frequency, and Colonna retaliated by intercepting letters and imprisoning his critics. Monrreal, who was one of the victims, prepared a long and vicious memorandum summarizing all the main points of an attack on Colonna by an opposition which now included such old rivals as Favara and the Aragona (Terranova) family.[5] Colonna was depicted as a man of the worst personal morals, avaricious, cruel and licentious to an extent that no woman was safe from him. His un-Christian behaviour was, it was alleged, only too clearly demonstrated in his attitude towards the Inquisition. Some chance remarks to members of the nobility were interpreted as treasonable intentions (and the viceroy's tactlessness and impatience with all opposition may well have lent colour to such

[1] Letters and Papers..., vol. I, B.M. MS. Add. 28 399, fo. 232–241; vol. II, Add. 28 400, fo. 88–90; Correspondence... Naples and Sicily, B.M. MS. Add. 28 394, fo. 157–9.
[2] Letters and Papers..., vol. II, B.M. MS. Add. 28 400, fo. 91–2, 251.
[3] Ibid. vol. I, Add. 28 399, fo. 261. Also *consulta* of the Council of Italy of Oct. 9th and Nov. 23rd, 1579. Simancas MS. Secret. Prov. leg. 981.
[4] See above, ch. 6, sect. 3.
[5] 'Memoria de cosas de grande Importancia al Servicio de Su Magestad en el Reyno de Sicilia.' The marginal notes may be by Taboada or one of Colonna's enemies in Madrid. Correspondence... Naples and Sicily, vol. I, B.M. MS. Add. 28 394, fo. 208–19.
Relations between Colonna and Terranova had been excellent at first, for Colonna had a high opinion of the duke's record and experience, and he used to consult him on all important matters of government in the months after his taking over in Sicily. (Colonna to Philip II, April 25th, 1577; Terranova to Philip, Oct. 31st, 1577; Simancas MS. Estado, leg. 1147). Distrust started when Colonna was accused of not making sufficient provision for Terranova's safety on the latter's journey to Spain. He lost his ships and only by swimming ashore he escaped Turkish captivity. Ibid. leg. 1148 .

charges), and finally he was again accused of preferring Italian to Spanish officials.

The anti-Colonna party in Madrid had now become sufficiently powerful to induce the king to send a visitor to Sicily in order to sindicate the whole administration. The instructions of this official, the lawyer Gregorio Bravo de Sotomayor, called for the investigation and punishment of abuses committed by all Sicilian officials, with the single exception of the viceroy himself.[1] In theory, the visitor was to co-operate with the viceroy; but as his powers were derived directly from the king, the juridical control he exercised was in fact entirely independent of all other authority. Expected to show results in the form of dismissals and punitive sentences, the visitor inevitably found himself in the camp of the opposition. Bravo was too intelligent not to realize this and had to be reassured by Granvelle that it was both legitimate and necessary 'to make use of scoundrels in order to discover the sins of other scoundrels.'[2] Otherwise, however, Bravo fully justified the view, commonly held by aristocrats like Vega and Colonna, that 'men of the long robe' should not be trusted with the exercise of authority, for power went to their head. Colonna claimed that he attempted to co-operate with Bravo – his officials were, after all, not appointed by himself. But the visitor rejected all overtures, and so the viceroy threw up his hands in disgust and left him free to do as he pleased.[3]

Nevertheless, clashes were unavoidable. Bravo set up a household as sumptuous as the viceroy's court, spent vast sums of public money in salaries for his underlings, and completely disregarded all local privileges. Finally his indiscretions called down upon him the wrath of Granvelle. 'Does your Honour want to imitate the Inquisitors?' wrote the indignant cardinal, 'for not all of what they do is approved of here . . . and no viceroy anywhere will stand for it.'[4] The visitation of a province was a regular part of Spanish imperial administration. Neither the king nor Granvelle had conceived of Bravo's activities

---

[1] I. Carini, Gli Archivi e le Biblioteche di Spagna, vol. 1 (Palermo 1884) pp. 354 f. A viceroy of Mexico and Peru (Montesclaros) once likened such a visitation 'to the whirlwinds often seen in the public squares and streets, which serve no other purpose save to stir up dust, straw and other trash and scatter them about the heads of people.' Quoted in L. E. Fisher, Viceregal Administration in the Spanish-American Colonies (Berkeley, California, 1926) pp. 34 f.
[2] Granvelle to Bravo, June 26th, 1584; Simancas MS. Estado, leg. 1155.
[3] Colonna to Idiáquez, April 24th, 1584; ibid. leg. 1154. Colonna showed, at times, considerable tactical shrewdness. Thus he asked Bravo in full council to investigate the conduct of his old enemy, the *consultore* Taboada. Relation of Rao and Franchis, 1585; ibid. leg. 1155.
[4] Granvelle to Bravo, April 24th, 1584; ibid.

as an attack on Colonna's authority. Yet the Sicilians could not be expected to make the subtle distinction between the viceroy and his administration,[1] and when Pompeo Colonna, Marc Antonio's brother was cited before Bravo's court, the whole of Sicily regarded this as a triumph for the opposition.[2] Thus while the Inquisition had set up state within the state, the visitation came near to setting up an alternative government, composed of the viceroy's enemies.[3]

Colonna's downfall was not, however, the direct result of the visitation. Philip and his first minister would not have willingly detracted further from the viceroy's authority by giving the impression that he was being dismissed because of a quarrel with the visitor.[4] The end came as the result of one of those feuds of jealousy, murder and revenge so common in the Italy of the sixteenth century. All the bitter passions aroused in prolonged political rivalries were finally concentrated in a personal struggle, that engulfed the viceroy in a Websterian tragedy.

Colonna first came into contact with the Corbera family immediately after his arrival in Sicily. Galceran Corbera, son of the baron of Miserendino, had married the beautiful and wealthy Eufrosina Zaragossa. He was young, adventurous, empty-headed; and, being weak, he fell completely under the influence of his father. The latter was, by all accounts, a mean and cruel man, whose extravagance, moreover, had plunged him into heavy debts. When his daughter-in-law refused to pay his creditors, the baron, together with his equally impecunious kinsman Ottavio Bonetta, persuaded young Galceran that his wife had deceived him with a page. They seized and tortured this young unfortunate page, and when he could

[1] Colonna wrote to Idiáquez, letter cit., 'que no solo por esta ciudad, pero por todo el Reyno se dixesse que me processava . . . ;' (referring to the visitor). Ibid. leg. 1154.
[2] Granvelle wrote to Bravo, June 26th, 1584, that Colonna's family were complaining of Pompeo's sindication. 'No me paresce que entienden que cosa es visita, pues no es para hazer processo formado sobre que se haya de condenar, como en juyzio ordinario, sino es para informar la mente de Su Majestad . . . .' Ibid. leg. 1155. Colonna's enemies were as quick to exploit the visit as his friends were to resent it, and the above passage shows nothing so much as Granvelle's naivety about Sicilian politics. – Pompeo Colonna died before his case could be heard.
[3] Such, at least, was the opinion of Rao and Franchis, *avvocato* and *procuratore fiscale*, respectively, and supporters of Colonna. Memorandum to the king; no date; probably 1585. Ibid. It is typical that this memorandum was promptly forwarded to Bravo.
[4] Cf. the *consulta* of the Council of Italy on the occasion of the visit of the marquis of Oriolo in the time of Medinaceli, 1563; 'Advertiendo tambien a Vuestra Majestad que aunque convendria que este remoçion no se dilatasse mucho tiempo. Todavia porque no se piense que ha nascido de las pasiones que ha havido entrel (i.e. Medinaceli) y el Marques de Oriolo, sera necesario aguardar que el marques aya salido de aquel reyno, y con alguna honesta ocasion se entretenga en el de Napoles, mientras esto se pone por obra.' Simancas MS. Secret. Prov. leg. 980.

or would not implicate the baroness, they murdered him. At this stage Colonna intervened; but on the advice of the president of the Great Court the murder was hushed up.[1] Galceran repented of his jealousy but, disliking the routine life of Palermo society, took every opportunity of going abroad with the Sicilian galleys. Eufrosina, left alone for weeks on end, was immediately under suspicion and her name was soon coupled with that of Colonna, the man who had sent her father-in-law to Sciacca as a captain-at-arms. Pressed by his creditors and enraged by rumours of the disgrace which his son's wife was bringing on the family, the old baron returned to Palermo without leave. Having thus lost the protection of his office he was promptly imprisoned for debt. His daughter-in-law again refused to help him and it was rumoured that the viceroy would not allow a settlement with his creditors. Within a few months Miserendino died in prison.[2]

Rid of his father's counsels of suspicion, the young baron returned to his wife. Soon, however, he accepted an invitation from Pompeo Colonna to accompany him to Malta to settle a dispute among the knights of St. John. On the 18th August 1581, Pompeo sent an urgent letter to his brother with the news that on the previous night Galceran Corbera had been murdered. Late at night he had visited a courtesan known to be the mistress of several French adventurers. A few hours later his body was found in the streets of Valetta, covered with dagger wounds. His assailants were never identified.[3]

From then on events moved rapidly to their climax. The death of the old baron now looked more suspicious than ever. Ottavio Bonetta saw a chance of laying hands on the baroness' money and ruining Colonna. He had not forgotten that the viceroy had frustrated his plans once before. In a stormy interview with Eufrosina he accused her of being the direct cause of her husband's death and said that he had papers to prove it.[4] To procure the Corbera inheritance he then arranged with the *capitan* of Palermo to have Galceran's brother, a boy of seven, taken away from the guardianship of the baroness and placed in the charge of other relatives. Eufrosina tried to get the boy back by appealing to the viceroy. Apart from the

[1] Colonna to Philip II, Sept. 14th, 1582; Letters and Papers..., vol. II, B.M. MS. Add. 28 400, fo. 41. I have here followed Colonna's own account which on this incident seems the most plausible. But the evidence for the whole Miserendo case is both incomplete and highly partisan.
[2] Memorial sent by Ottavio Bonetta to the king, Jan. 11th, 1582; Letters and Papers ... Sicily, B.M. MS. Add. 28 396, fo. 140, 326–9.
[3] Ibid. fo. 119–120.
[4] Hieronimo Campo to Colonna, Sept. 20th, 1581. Ibid. fo. 123.

question of inheritance, her consent to his removal would have amounted to a public admission of her guilt.

When Colonna ordered the boy's return to his sister-in-law,[1] Bonetta thought it safer to leave Sicily. It was essential to give the impression of official persecution. Bonetta sailed for Spain at night, leaving behind a number of friends to spread the tale that the viceroy's men were on his heels though, in point of fact, the only charge laid against him was made by the *capitan* of Palermo, and that was for a number of financial frauds.[2]

While the Miserendino affair was openly talked about in the streets of Sicily, Bonetta found powerful friends in Spain who presented his case to Granvelle and the king. Colonna defended himself with dignity and skill. He spoke of his services and told how his enemies, having found no other means of attack, now tried to besmirch his personal honour. He asked whether his word, the word of a caballero, was to be trusted less than that of Bonetta, a man with a proven criminal record who had at one time been condemned to the galleys.[3] He claimed that the baroness of Miserendino was always closely chaperoned by a relative, a woman whose respectability was well known, and added that no other members of the Corbera family had made any complaints. Finally he reminded the king of his promise always to give him a chance to disprove any accusation levelled against him; for this he was willing to submit himself to the sindication of Bravo, in the same way as the most humble of his officials.[4]

It is impossible to say whether Colonna and Eufrosina really were lovers or whether they plotted the death of her father-in-law and her husband. Bonetta's action against the viceroy dragged on for years in the Council of Italy and finally faded into the limbo of forgotten cases. It was inevitable in the face of pressure from the Colonna party and the inertia of Spanish law courts. Of real significance was the fact that Bonetta, an unknown adventurer, had succeeded in bringing about the recall of the hero of Lepanto. 'And believe me, sir, no decent person can suffer it,' the marquis de los

---

[1] Memorial of Bonetta to the king. Ibid. fo. 326–9.
[2] Colonna to Philip II, Sept. 14th, 1582. Letters and Papers . . . , vol. II, B.M. MS. Add. 28 400, fo. 38.
[3] There is no evidence for this accusation, apart from Colonna's assertion. On Sept. 15th, 1584, the Council of Italy wrote to Bravo that a great number of lawsuits both criminal and civil, were being brought against Bonetta in Sicily, but only since he had arrived in Spain. During the 47 years of his life which he had lived in Sicily it had never happened to him. Simancas MS. Estado, leg. 1155.
[4] Letters and Papers . . . , vol. II, B.M. MS. Add. 28 400, fo. 38–42.

Velez had written about the Spanish court. 'For if you do not have the king's favour they all will trample on you, and if you have it they will take your life and your honour.'[1] All the old feuds against the viceroy were canalized in this one issue. Granvelle was so impressed by the volume of opinion against Colonna that he thought Bonetta's charges warranted a thorough inquiry. Such an inquiry could not be carried out as long as Colonna was viceroy of Sicily. The cardinal therefore suggested that he should be transferred to the governorship of Valencia or Milan. If he were acquitted, the prestige of his office and his personal honour would not suffer; the king, moreover, would not be willing to send him back to Sicily 'where the people were such friends of novelty.'[2]

In the spring of 1584 Colonna was recalled, officially with full honours, but with his future career very much in the balance, for the king's will was unknown even to Granvelle. Philip's marked favour to Bonetta was an ominous sign. However, on August 1st 1584 Colonna died on the way to Madrid. He was reported to have suffered concussion in a fall. In a letter to the *sindicatore*, Granvelle appeared to have no doubts that death was due to natural causes.[3] although it was inevitable that there should have been immediate suspicion of poison.

Most contemporaries had no doubts about Colonna's illicit relations with the baroness. Even Granvelle was shocked when the king received a letter from the viceroy's widow stating that she had taken the baroness with her in order to protect her from the wrath of her relatives and to arrange a new marriage for her in Italy.[4] In Rome the baroness married Lelio Massimo, a rich widower. Shortly afterwards she was strangled by her new stepsons who resented the fact that their father had married another man's mistress. They paid with their lives for the crime. Old Lelio Massimo died of a broken heart.[5] Another feud had ended in general disaster. Only

[1] A. Pérez, Relaciones (Paris 1624), p. 13; also quoted by Ranke, Die Osmanen..., p. 151.
[2] Granvelle to Bravo, June 26th, 1584; Simancas MS. Estado, leg. 1154. Granvelle to Chinchón, Jan. 3rd, 1582, Letters and Papers... Sicily, B.M. MS. Add. 28 396, fo. 138. Same to Vázquez, March 31st, Apr. 14th, 1582; ibid. fo. 141–3. Same to same, Jan. 2nd, 1583, Letters and Papers..., vol. II, Add. 28 400, fo. 44–47.
[3] Granvelle to Bravo, Aug. 9th, 1584; Simancas MS. Estado, leg. 1154. There seems to be no good reason for doubting the correctness of his version.
[4] Felice Colonna-Orsini to Philip II, Oct. 5th, 1584; ibid. Granvelle to Bravo, March 27th, 1585: 'No puede ser que no haya dado escandalo la yda de la Baronessa de Miserendino a Roma.' Ibid. leg. 1155.
[5] Di Giovanni, Del Palermo..., Bibl. Lett. e Stor., ser. 2, vol. II, pp. 239 f. Unfortunately I have found no further sources for this last part of the tragedy, but it seems perfectly credible, after what went before. Buonfiglio e Costanzo does not mention the

Bonetta lived to enjoy the king's favour at the court of Madrid.[1]

The career of Marc Antonio Colonna has been related in some detail to show the atmosphere of both Sicilian and Spanish politics. Ranke has pointed out[2] that fundamentally the opposition in Sicily was due to the old conflict between the estates and the crown. But as the result of the viceregal system of government, all passions aroused by such conflicts were focused on the person of the viceroy. The king himself (and with him the basis of Spanish dominion), was as effectively screened from the opposition as a modern consitutional ruler by his Parliamentary government. Violent party contention in sixteenth century Sicily resulted inevitably in the removal of the viceroy; and when his successor had been appointed the struggle began anew.

After the truce with the Turks in 1580,[3] Philip was no longer under the necessity of having military viceroys in the key dominion of the central Mediterranean. His preference for politicians over soldiers, and for Spaniards over Italians, is clear from the last four appointments he made: three of these were Castilian grandees and only one a Sicilian nobleman. The first, Diego Enríquez de Guzmán, count of Alvadeliste, was a man whom the Italians regarded as the typical Spanish grandee, reticent, unapproachable, dignified and without any respect for the rights of others.[4] His governorship saw Sicilian resources stretched to breaking point to supply Spain's imperial ambitions. The nobility was solidly arrayed in support of the Inquisition, with whom the viceroy's relations were more strained than ever before. The viceroy himself was often incapacitated by bad health, and to crown his misfortunes there occurred the terrible famine of 1591, blamed by high and low alike on the government's incompetence. Yet at no time was it more clear how firmly Spanish rule was rooted in Sicily. The opposition remained splintered into sects, each intent only on its own advantage. The *braccio militare* was both mentally and physically unprepared to fight for its demands,

Miserendino case at all, but attributes Colonna's downfall to the finding of certain letters by the *straticò* of Messina, showing that the viceroy had been negotiating with Aluch Ali, captain-general of the Turkish navy (Historia Siciliana, pp. 658 f). The *straticò*, count of Briatico, was Colonna's immediate successor. These negotiations did take place, but (*a*) Philip knew about them at the time, since Colonna informed him (Nov. 26th, 1580, Simancas MS. Estado, leg. 1149), and (*b*) these negotiations implied treason on the part of Aluch Ali, but not on the part of Colonna.

[1] Philip II to Alvadeliste, April 22nd and May 20th, 1585. Ibid. leg. 1648, fo. 24, 27.
[2] Ranks, Die Osmanen . . . , pp. 215 ff.
[3] Merriman, The Rise . . . , vol. IV, p. 154.
[4] e.g. his disregard of Sicilian privileges when he claimed to commence his duties while still in Naples; above, pp. 96 f.; also his treatment of the Inquisition; above, ch. 6 sect. 3.

and the two other estates saw no cause to quarrel with the king for the benefit of the nobles.¹ Once the resistance of the nobility had collapsed, the individual barons were only too anxious to ingratiate themselves with the government. Favara, the professional intriguer who had played a leading part in the 'revolt' of his *braccio*, now busied himself with uncovering popular disaffection. The results of his efforts were meagre enough. He could only send the king a copy of a popular song heard in the streets of Palermo. The verses lamented the famine and the bad government, urged Philip not to forget his poor kingdom and ended with familiar dark hints of another Sicilian Vespers.² No pamphlets against Spanish rule were found, such as became common in the seventeenth century;³ the guilds made no move, and so great was the misery of the poor that there were not even bread-riots, otherwise so common in the sixteenth century. When Alvadeliste left Sicily in 1592⁴ the mob gave vent to its feelings by crowding the quay-side and hurling insults at the viceroy;⁵ but never was Sicily further from the spirit that destroyed the Angevin tyranny.

Philip's last three appointments were more fortunate. Enrique de Guzmán, Count of Olivares and father of the famous *conde-duque* of Velázquez' portraits⁶ was a career diplomat and politician. Coming, as did his predecessor, from one of the most distinguished Castilian families,⁷ he had shown his ability in various court and military offices in Spain and had been ambassador extraordinary both to France and Rome.⁸ Unimaginative, dry and practical⁹ he proved to be one of the most efficient of all Sicilian viceroys. He was, moreover one of the very few whose reputation did not suffer severely by his

¹ Cf. above, ch. 6 sect. 2.
² Favara to Philip II, July 12th, 1591, enclosing a copy of the song (cf. Appendix IV), Simancas MS. Estado, leg. 1157.
³ I have been unable to find in Palermo any popular anti-Spanish literature of the sixteenth century.
⁴ He had asked for his recall on the grounds of ill-health before the outbreak of the famine and the revolt of the *braccio militare*. Alvadeliste to Philip II, Oct. 5th, 1590; Simancas MS. Estado, leg. 1157.
⁵ Paruta e Palmerino, Diario della Città di Palermo; Bibl. Stor. e Lett. ser. 1. vol. I, p. 129. – Buonfiglio, Historia Siciliana, p. 663, says that the crowd forced Alvadeliste to return to his palace and await the arrival of the new viceroy.
⁶ A small engraving in the B.M. Department of Prints and Drawings, Folder: Olivares, shows his aristocratic face with an open and more pleasant expression than the heavy panache of Philip the Fourth's favourite.
⁷ In 'Acta inter Angliam et Hispaniam,' B.M. MS. Cotton, Vesp. C. VI, fo. 51, his family is called Andalusian.
⁸ E. F. de Navarrete, Los Vireyes Lugartenientes ... de Napoles; in Documentos Inéditos ..., XXIII, p.271.
⁹ Cf. his memorandum 'Cosas del Govierno etc.', in Papeles varios tocantes ..., B.M. MS. Add. 14009, fo. 364–97.

tenure of the office, perhaps because he was fortunate enough to be promoted to the viceroyalty of Naples after only three years in Sicily. A man, however, who had used his position in Sicily to increase his, private income from 18,000 to 30,000 scudi a year,[1] was not likely to escape unscathed. After a few years in Naples during which he and his secretaries lived up to their Sicilian reputation[2] the inevitable opposition in Madrid effected his recall.

Renewed danger from the Turks induced the king to maintain in office for three years the president, Giovanni Ventimiglia, marquis of Geraci, who had been responsible for the defence of Messina against Sinam Pasha in 1594.[3] Geraci, like Terranova, had the advantage of an intimate knowledge of Sicilian conditions, yet he, too, did not escape the thorny problem of Sicilian privileges and lost much of his original popularity when he fell foul of the senate of Palermo over the appointment of the *pretore*.[4] This, however, did not prevent his re-appointment in the reign of Philip III.

Philip the Second's last appointment, in 1598, followed the now traditional custom of appointing Spanish grandees. Bernardino de Cardenas, duke of Maqueda, and one of the wealthiest of Castilian nobles, had had previous experience, as viceroy and captain-general of Catalonia.[5] Like his predecessors, he was haughty, reticent and ruthless. He took particularly vigorous action against bandits and Corsairs, and shared with Medinaceli the unusual distinction of managing to avoid a major clash with the Inquisition.[6] Maqueda died in office, in December 1601.[7]

[1] Giralamo Ramusio, Relazioni di Napoli, 1597; Albèri, Relazioni..., Appendix, p. 325.
[2] Ibid. p. 326.
[3] Buonfiglio e Costanzo, Historia Siciliana, pp. 666 ff. Reports of Geraci and Olivares to Philip II, Sept.–Dec. 1594; Simancas MS. Estado, leg. 1158.
[4] Cf. above, p. 110.
[5] Casas Ylustres de España, B.M. MS. Eg. 468, fo. 180.
[6] On Nov. 6th, 1598, Maqueda sent Philip III a relation on the state of Sicily which presented economic conditions in such a favourable light, that one is inclined to suspect it to be the work of some official in the Patrimony trying to ingratiate himself (Simancas MS. Estado, leg. 1158). Viceroys with experience of Sicily were not usually inclined to paint a very optimistic picture of the state of the country. Nor does such a picture correspond to the one presented only 18 months later in a *consulta* of the Council of Italy, May 29th, 1600; ibid.
[7] The traditional story of his end is unusual, even for the Italy of his time. Maqueda's privateers had captured a richly laden Turkish vessel. A box, believed to contain treasure, was opened in his presence and revealed the corpse of a Turk which emitted an odour so deadly that it straightway killed the viceroy and those around him (Di Giovanni, Del Palermo..., Bibl. Lett. e. Stor., ser. 2. vol. II, pp. 257 f., where the story is accepted by the editor, di Marzo). There is however, no reference to this incident in the letter of Maqueda's son. On Dec. 18th, 1601, Jorque de Cardenas informed Philip III that his father had died on the previous day, after an illness lasting 12 days. Simancas MS. Estado, leg. 1159.

The system of viceregal government, as practised in Sicily, proved the graveyard of the reputation of its governors. The viceroys represented no more than one of several centres of authority, all virtually independent of each other, each manoeuvring for the most favourable position, and none strong enough to eliminate its rivals. As Madrid failed to establish complete administrative control over Sicily, the Spanish Monarchy had to rely on the tension between the viceroy and his opponents in Church, Parliament or council to preserve a balance of power in which the king was left with the deciding voice. It was not a preconceived plan. The rival forces themselves prevented the attainment of the higher objective of direct central control, while this objective itself was never consciously worked out in all its logical and political implications. Undoubtedly Spain was greatly helped in her relations with Sicily by the ever present menace of the Turkish fleet, the common enemy of both countries. The Sicilians might well ponder that without Spanish galleys and Spanish troops, their fate would have been similar to that of the Hungarians or the knights of Rhodes. The absence of this common danger, the most powerful force which can link two states together, proved one of the greatest handicaps to Spanish rule in the Netherlands. Yet, in contrast to the Netherlands, in Sicily Spanish statesmanship was able to make Spanish rule fundamentally acceptable to the country. The bitter faction fights, which ruined the careers of many of the king's most faithful ministers, never touched the foundations of Spanish rule. Only in the long run, after centuries of sacrificing its best servants needlessly, did the Spanish Empire feel the full effects of a system which prevented its natural development and which left it helpless before the attacks of more vigorous rivals. But neither Philip II nor any of his contemporaries could see so far ahead.

CHAPTER EIGHT

Conclusion

THE imperial obligations of the Spanish Monarchy imposed a course of action for which neither the king nor his subjects were emotionally nor intellectually prepared. Conservative by tradition and temperament, and bound to the terms of the old conflict between crown and feudal estates, the Spanish government had to evolve an entirely novel system of centralized imperial administration for its vast empire. The necessity for these innovations was only partially understood and met with only partial success. Philip the Second's rule was absolutist only in the sense that ultimate responsibility lay in the person of the king. Administratively the power of the crown was never fully canalized into the royal councils. The king exercised his authority not only through the viceroys and their ministers, but also through the independent agencies of the Inquisition and the visitors. Moreover, large areas of public authority were reserved by the old medieval opponents of the crown, the Church and the feudal estates.

The spheres of influence of these organizations and institutions were not clearly defined. Inevitably they came into conflict with each other. Yet the resulting interaction, the constant movement and balancing of forces, did not increase royal control. The Sicilian Parliament, therefore, was able to preserve the island from the degree of imperial exploitation which had ruined Naples and Milan. It was commonly said that in Sicily the Spaniards nibbled, in Naples they ate, and in Milan they devoured. In the early seventeenth century Sicilians claimed that only two Parliaments still preserved their rights and powers: London and Palermo.[1] Yet it would be misleading to press the analogy. English political history is intelligible in terms of the relations between Parliament and the executive. The same does not hold true for Sicily. The Sicilian Parliament was only one of the bodies which competed for power within the political system of the island; it was not the viceroy's most powerful nor persistent

[1] Relazione sulle cose di Sicilia di Giuseppe Toppoli; quoted in Titone, La Sicilia Spagnuola, p. 41.

rival. Such a role was filled by the Inquisition with its power based on an army of Sicilian familiars, and deriving its authority from the king just as much as the civil government.

Neither Parliament nor Inquisition was able to rise above its sectional interests. Unlike the English Parliament they could therefore never develop either a measure of partnership with, or a system of control over, the executive. In consequence Sicily failed to evolve constitutional government in the English sense. The constant struggle between the political forces in the island and the limitations imposed on the civil government by the existence of autonomous authorities, produced only negative results – a lack of governance, without the compensation of genuine political development.

The positive achievements of the Spanish domination of Sicily were thus confined to two fields: the successful defence of the island against Turkish aggression together with the preservation of internal peace, and the building up of a system of conciliar administration, both in the island itself and at the centre of the empire, in Spain. For the first time since the Roman Empire an attempt was made in western Europe to construct a comprehensive organization for the administration of a number of originally independent states. The degree of success achieved along these lines distinguished the Spanish Empire from its medieval predecessors. It was the contribution of the Spanish monarchy to the political development of modern Europe. But the ultimate political failure of the Spanish European Empire was the result of its inability to turn administrative experiment into constitutional progress.

APPENDIX ONE

Viceroys and Presidents of Sicily in the Sixteenth Century

NOTE—Presidents are given only for the reign of Philip II. Names by which the undermentioned are referred to in the text are shown in small capitals.

1495 – 1506	JUAN LA NUZA
1507 – 1509	RAIMONDO DE CARDONA
1509 – 1516	HUGO DE MONCADA
1517 – 1535	Ettore Pignatelli, duca di MONTELEONE
1535 – 1546	FERRANTE GONZAGA
1547 – 1557	JUAN DE VEGA
1557	*President* Pietro d' Aragona e Tagliavia, cardinal and archbishop of Palermo
1557 – 1565	Juan de la Cerda, duque de MEDINACELI
1558	*President* Niccolò Caraccioli, bishop of Catania
1559	*President* Ferdinando de Silva, marquese de la FAVARA
1565	*President* Bartolomeo Sebastiano, bishop of Patti
1565 – 1568	GARCIA DE TOLEDO
1565	*President* Antonio Doria marchese di Santo Stefano
1566	*President* Bartolomeo Sebastiano, bishop of Patti
1566 – 1568	*President* Carlo d'Aragona e Tagliavia, duca di TERRANOVA, principe di Castelvetrano
1568 – 1571	Francesco Ferdinando Avalos di Aquino, marchese di PESCARA
1571	*President* Giuseppe Francesco LANDRIANO
1571 – 1577	*President* Carlo d'Aragona e Tagliavia, duca di TERRANOVA, principe di Castelvetrano
1577 – 1584	MARC ANTONIO COLONNA, duca di Tagliacozzo
1582	*President* Fabrizio Ruffo, principe di Scilla
1584	*President* Giovanni Alfonso Bisbal, conte di BRIATICO
1585 – 1592	Diego Enríquez de Guzmán, conde de ALVADELISTE
1592 – 1595	Enrico de Guzmán, conde de OLIVARES
1595 – 1598	*President* Giovanni Ventimiglia, marchese di GERACI
1598 – 1601	Bernardino de Cardenas, duque de MAQUEDA.

APPENDIX TWO

Some Sicilian Coins and Measurements

Coins	1 ounce (oncia)	=	30 tari (the ounce was a unit but no coin)
	1 scudo	=	12 tari = about 400 maravedis (Spanish)
	1 florin	=	6 tari
	1 tari	=	20 grana
	1 grano	=	6 danari
Volume	1 salma (liquid)	=	128 quartucci = 21½ gallons (English)
	1 salma grossa	=	20 tumoli (of corn) = 10 bushels (English)
	1 salma generale[1]	=	16 tumoli (of corn) = 8 bushels (English)
		=	2 cantara or quintals (Sicilian)
		=	20 tumoli (of oats and barley)
		=	5 hanegas (Spanish)
	1 tumolo	=	4 mondelli
	1 quintal (Sicilian)	=	c.1⅔ quintals (Spanish)
Weight	1 cantaro	=	100 rotoli = 175 lbs (English)
	1 rotolo	=	33 ounces (Eastern Sicily) = 1¾ lbs (English)
		=	30 ounces (Palermo)
	1 pound (libra)	=	12 ounces
Length	1 canna	=	8 palmi
	3½ palmi	=	1 yard (English)

---

[1] Figures in the text are given in this type of salma.

APPENDIX THREE

Notes on the Political Thought of Scipio di Castro

A COUNTRY with as many political cross-currents as the Sicily of Philip II was likely to be a fertile ground for political thought. The prevalence of legal studies among both the educated middle classes and the educated nobility, coupled with the Sicilian love for litigation turned most political discussion into legal and juristic channels; but there was at least one thinker who treated systematically of politics in a non-legalistic form.

Scipio di Castro was of mixed Spanish and Sicilian parentage. He was born about 1520. From 1549 to 1554 he lived at Ferrante Gonzaga's court at Milan, and later travelled extensively in western and central Europe. He returned to Sicily where he seems to have held some official position at the court of Medinaceli. In 1560 he fell foul of the Inquisition and was banished from Sicily, but returned in 1565. From then on he acted as technical adviser, mainly on hydraulic engineering, to several Sicilian viceroys and, after 1574, to Pope Gregory XIII. Towards the end of his life he suffered $3\frac{1}{2}$ years' imprisonment, probably because of his controversial writings and his knack of making enemies. He died about 1588.[1]

Castro's writings on political matters form two distinct categories. He started by analysing a number of concrete political problems and situations and then, towards the end of his life, he abstracted the experience he had gained into a general analysis of the structure of states. The first group of his works were, in their treatment of contemporary subjects, a combination of the style of the reports of contemporary ambassadors and statesmen, and of Machiavelli's systematic analysis of the problems described in such reports.

The most considerable of Castro's writings of this type was the *avvertimenti* for Marc Antonio Colonna, written in 1577, which

---

[1] C. Giardina, La Vita e l'Opera di Scipione di Castro; Atti... 3rd ser. vol. XVI, pp. 272–330. Despite Giardina's researches many points of Castro's career remain obscure.

described the political situation in Sicily for the benefit of the newly-appointed viceroy.[1] Castro started with the historical fact that the government of Sicily had been fatal to the reputation of nearly all her viceroys for the last 80 years, and then proceeded to discuss the causes and the nature of the appalling difficulties which faced the viceroys. He analysed his points with great subtlety, quoting contemporary examples and deducing from these examples methods and maxims of how to deal with any particular problem. Castro's point of view was that of the professional civil servant. He saw clearly the administrative difficulties arising out of the corruption of Sicilian officials. He recognized, at least by implication, the political weakness of the viceroy's position and appreciated his precarious balance between the opposing forces of the hostile Sicilian estates and the fickle court of Spain. But he failed to see the significance of economic questions and contented himself with a description of some of the hazards involved in the viceroy's control of the corn trade.

Castro's other political writings of this type lacked the grasp of detail which characterized his study of Sicilian politics. Probably because he did not know Milan as well as Sicily, his advice to his old master, the duke of Terranova, on how to govern that duchy, was written in much more general terms than his advice to Colonna. It shows, however, a clear understanding of the nature of the Spanish empire (defined as 'very extended but not ancient, not united, not well armed, not rich, and not provided with a successor capable of ruling such a vast organization') and of the strategic position of Milan.[2] But in his work, as in his advice to ministers and ambassadors of how best to fulfil their duties, Castro's aim was not merely to help individual statesmen to deal with particular problems, but to establish general rules for political action in specific, well-defined circumstances.

This tendency to formulate general rules from particular examples became more marked in Castro's later writing. While his conclusions from Sicilian conditions were not intended to be applied outside Sicily, his description of the relations of the duchy of Milan to its neighbours prompted him to establish a number of general principles of foreign policies for states ruled by governors. He counselled the governor to observe strictly all treaties and never to tolerate the

[1] Castro, Avvertimenti..., Thesoro Politico, vol. II. Also in Letters and Papers ...Sicily, B.M. MS. Add. 28 396, fo. 371–398.
[2] Giardina, p. 373.

slightest infringement of these treaties by his neighbours. The governor was advised to promote reciprocal commerce and to try to become the arbiter in his neighbours' quarrels while at the same time feeding the distrust between them.[1] This was advice given in the same way as Machiavelli gave advice to his prince. In his comments on the archduke Mathias' venture into the Netherlands, Castro argued almost entirely from a priori principles of political experience.[2] His understanding of the problems of the Netherlands was superficial, but he made some shrewd comments on the likelihood of severe restrictions being imposed on the archduke's authority, since a people throwing off one tyranny would not want to subject itself to another, and he quoted the case of Peter of Aragon and the restrictions which the Sicilians imposed on his power. Castro's suggested solution of the whole problem of the Netherlands was also based on what he considered to be a general rule: that 'the multitude is courageous as long as it sees the danger from afar, and that it loses courage in proportion as danger approaches, for no one who can live wants to die.'[3] It was therefore best, Castro argued, to use the utmost severity against those who resisted, and the most exemplary humanity towards those who submitted.

Having arrived at a number of general precepts for the good government of a state by careful analysis of both concrete situations and of historical incidents, Castro proceeded to set down these precepts in a generalized form. His work on 'The Foundations of the State and the Qualities of the Prince'[4] is a classic example of the use of the inductive method in political thinking, a technique in keeping with his own development.

Castro's 'Foundations' was wholly in accord with the secular traditions of the political thought of Machiavelli. Counsel, Force and Reputation were the three pillars on which rested Castro's state.[5] Counsel was the 'Natural reason' of the prince in reigning – a reason which was to be trained by a careful education on the accepted Renaissance-humanist lines. Force was the union of six conditions

[1] Ibid. pp. 373 f.
[2] 'Discorso del Signor D. Scipione di Castro sopra l'andata dell'Arciduca Matthia d'Austria in Fiandra. La Terza Parte del Thesoro Politico' (Turnoni 1605) pp. 128–36.
[3] Ibid. p. 134.
[4] Castro, Delli fondamenti dello Stato et delle parti essentiali che formano il Prencipe. Bodl. MS. Rawl. D.625, fo. 433–69. It was also printed in the Thesoro Politico, vol. II (Milan 1601) pp. 337–64, and there is a MS. translation into English in Bodl. MS. Rawl. C.293, fo. 28. All these versions differ in detail and none of them is complete. Giardina has summarized the missing parts from the only complete copy of the work in the Archivio Boncampagni in Rome.
[5] Castro, Delli fondamenti..., MS. Rawl. D.625, fo. 433–4.

which made the prince powerful; i.e. to have his state loving, great, ancient, united, armed and wealthy.¹ Reputation, finally, meant the prince's fame with other states. The idea of natural right or natural law did not enter into his severely practical conception of the basis of the state any more than it did in Machiavelli's. Castro's only aim was to show what conditions made a state and a prince powerful and by what means this power could be preserved and extended. Thus he advised the prince to appear religious, for when a reputation for piety had been established it would seem that all other virtues must follow as of necessity and the people would feel assured of good government.² Yet he must neither be superstitious nor should he 'wear religion as a mark', for this would make him hated and suspect. Again like Machiavelli, Castro regarded religion as a useful, even vital, part of the life of the state and the prince, but only because of the practical benefits it conferred.

This point becomes still more clear in Castro's treatment of rebellion. There was for him only one justification for rebellion, that of the prince giving up the true religion,³ for any novelty in religion was 'the breeding ground of civil war.'⁴ Otherwise the subjects were to tolerate a prince, however bad. Castro said nothing to justify this obligation, but added that the prince, in his turn, should not forget his duties to his subjects, 'for few subjects attain to such a perfect degree of obedience and all hold the firm belief that the sword, and nothing else, is the true medicine for a bad prince.'⁵

Because Castro never considered the ultimate aims of the state, he failed completely to appreciate the 'political obligation' of the people. The administration of justice,⁶ a warning against excessive taxation⁷ and every other virtue which he advocated, were justified solely on the grounds of expediency. He exhorted the prince to follow prudent rather than astute counsels – a remark probably aimed at Machiavelli – for astuteness would give him a bad reputation and would influence his councillors 'so that within a few days

---

¹ Ibid. According to Castro, most of these conditions were absent in the Spanish empire, cf. above, p. 202.
² Ibid. fo. 444.
³ Ibid. fo. 458.
⁴ Ibid. fo. 457. Giardina, p. 410, regards Castro as the forerunner of Mariana, Suárez, Bellarmin and Molina because he justified rebellion on religious grounds. But this is a misunderstanding of Castro's whole position. Heresy, in his view, was evil because of the evil consequences to the state, not because it was inherently wicked nor because it challenged the authority of the Catholic Church.
⁵ Castro, fo. 458.
⁶ Ibid. fo. 460.
⁷ Ibid. fo. 467.

he will see himself surrounded by advisers who are so many wolves.'[1] In his discussion of *raison d'état*, he mentioned that dishonesty was disliked by God,[2] but his emphasis was on the bad effects it had. If, on the other hand, the prince broke faith only on occasions, this would be excused even by his enemies, 'for all princes have what is practically a law between them, to excuse each other (in such cases).'[3]

Because of his common sense and sound judgment of political situations, Castro nearly always gave advice which tended to fairness and moderation – though to no other end than the power of the prince. There was no place in Castro's thought for Aristotle's 'good life,' nor for Machiavelli's liberation of Italy. He propounded, in fact, no political philosophy at all; and the power of the prince was left with no moral justification. If Castro's political writings did not earn him the evil name which 'The Prince' earned for Machiavelli, this was because he did not combine an attack on accepted ideas of morality with a picture of the political practice of his time. Castro's precepts were acceptable to contemporary moral standards – (the nearly contemporary English translation of 'The Foundations' in the Bodleian Library has written on it 'This Castro is a very excellent man') – yet the implications of his teachings were even more devastating than those of Machiavelli; for with Castro political thought had developed to the point of not only rejecting morality, but of ignoring its very existence.

---

[1] Ibid. fo. 448–50.
[2] Giardina, pp. 422 f. Castro said: '... disfavorita in tal guisa da Iddio' a very mild expression.
[3] Ibid. p. 424.

APPENDIX FOUR

Popular Song, 1591

THESE verses were sung in the streets of Palermo, 'amid a thousand other pasquinades', after the great famine of 1591.[1]

O' Ré Filippo che hai gran doluri
Della Sicilia tua, povera, e mesta,
Mandaci presto a un Governatori
Che sia un' grand' homo e tutta la ricetta[2]
Non vedi ch'è morto il gran Pereturi[3]
D'esto palermo con grande tempesta
Vedi che se tardi con la to' favori
La tua sicilia ritroverai persa.

O' Ré Filippo scrive et manda presto
Alla sicilia tua piena di guai.
Tu la provedi con soccorro presto
Se non la tua sicilia aperderai
Che ne morirá assai per la gran peste[4]
Hora di fame con tormenti, et guai
Se la vedessi, con quanto rispetto
Tu proprio da un' canto piangerai.

---

[1] Sent by the marquis de la Favara to Philip II, July 12th, 1591. Simancas MS. Estado, leg. 1157. In Favara's comment one has to allow for his habitual exaggeration. So far was the attitude of the people from rebellion that Favara had no difficulty in persuading the author of the song to write out a copy for him.
[2] da tutti ben accettato.
[3] Pretore (?)
[4] The great plague of 1575.

O' Ré Filippo ti manda à pregari
Lo to palermo povero e 'nfelice;
Non lo lassare tanto maltrattari
Ch'un giorno perdi li tuoi cari Amici.
Ci hanno levato li spadi, e pugnali
Et non está beni come quasi dici
Che l'ha accatato[1] con Thesoro, e denari,
Ch'é consuma[2] to palermo felice.

Sacra Corona vogli governari
La tua sicilia poverella, e mesta;
Vogliaci presto soccorso mandar(i) –
Se non la perdi come la goletta.
Che é tutta maltrattata come cani,
Et assai peggio che non fu la pesta;
Li poveri non puonno[3] piu campari
Veddi che presto ne senti la festa.

Sacra corona delle volte millia
Non andi[4] il terremote, e la Tempesta
Che patte[5] la scontenta tua Sicilia
Chionca di un braccio, et dolesi la Testa,
Tutta stracciata, et non tene retilia[6]
Di mali est inforata la sua vesta –
Non vedi ch'è Venuto la Vigilia
Non stare tanto che vegna la festa.[7]

---

[1] Barattato.
[2] ha consumato.
[3] possono.
[4] venga.
[5] patisce.
[6] Probably Sicilian ritagghia = a piece of cloth, a rag.
[7] i.e. We are on the eve of a Sicilian Vespers.

BIBLIOGRAPHY

1. Manuscripts

Bodleian Manuscripts

Cartas Reales y de Ministros del Reyno di Sicilia. Mendham 28.

Castro, Scipio di:
 Delli Fondamenti dello Stato et delle parti essentiali che formano il Prencipe. MS. Rawlinson, D.625. Also MS. translation in vol. Political Tracts of Don Scipio di Castro. MS. Rawl. c.293.
 General Remembrances for the Ministers of Princes etc. in Political Tracts of Don Scipio di Castro. Translation, Rawl. c.293.

Communications between the Kingdom of Sicily ... and the Popes on ecclesiastical affairs etc. Collection by F. Peria, probably Palermo 1610–11, Cherry 5.

The King of Spayne his Revenuew 1610. Anonymous French, Tanner 93.

Papeles Curiosos Españoles Manuscritos. Transcripts from Spanish State Papers 1457–1647. Rawlinson. D.582.

A Punctuall Relation of all the Chiefe Counsels and Supreme Tribunals which Ordinarily are Resident in the Courte of Spaine etc. (no date; possibly late 16th or early 17th cent.), Tanner 99.

Ragazzoni, Placido. Relatione di Sicilia. Rawl. D.616.

British Museum Manuscripts

Acta inter Angliam et Hispaniam. Cotton Vesp. C.VI.

Capitoli dell'Illustrissima Academia della Stella creata l'anno 1595 in Messina. Additional 25 685.

Cardinal Burgos, Discorso del Cardinal Burgos al Ré Filippo sopra le cose d'Italia, Egerton 534 (fo. 84–99).

Casas Ylustres de España, Egerton 468.

Celestre, P., Idea del Govierno del Reyno di Sicilia, 1611. Add. 24 130.

Correspondence relating to Naples.
 I, 1574–77. Add. 28 397.
 II, 1583–1609. Add. 28 398.

Correspondence relating to Naples and Sicily.
  I, 1577–82. Add. 28 394.
  II, 1583. Add. 28 395.
Correspondence with the Ambassador at Rome.
  vol. II. Add. 28 404.
Curia Española.
  Harleian 3569.
Drafts of letters of Philip II.
  I, 1557–81. Add. 28 357.
Instructions of Philip II to Governors of Provinces etc.
  1546–98. Add. 28 701.
Letters of Don Juan de Zúñiga, Ambassador at Rome.
  I, Jan.–May 1570, Add. 28 405.
  III, Oct.–Dec. 1570, Add. 28 407.
Letters from Italy, 1567–72.
  Add. 28 401.
Letters and Papers relating to Italy.
  I, 1568–79. Add. 28 399.
  II, 1580–84, Add. 28 400.
Letters and Papers relating to Sicily.
  1572–1603. Add. 28 396.
Official Papers etc. Spanish, II.
  1578–88. Add. 28 360.
Papeles del Consejo de la General Inquisicion.
  I, Egerton 1506.
  II, Egerton 1507.
Papeles Tocantes a la Historia de España 1522–1696.
  Egerton 367.
Papeles varios.
  Add. 21 960.
Papeles varios Tocantes a Napoles, Sicilia, Milan.
  Add. 14 009.
Papers relating to ceremonial 1579–1588.
  Add. 28 361.
Papers relating to Italian States.
  I, Add. 28 465.
  II, Add. 28 466.
Papers relating to military affairs, 1565–1583.
  Add. 28 366.
Peramo, L. A.
  De Monarchia Sicula. 1605. Add. 19 319.

Spanish State Papers, Home Correspondence.
Vol. VIII Add. 28 341.
Vol. XI Add. 28 344.

Stado de España.
Cod. Soc. XVI. Harleian 3315.

Tratados Varios.
II, Egerton 2078.

Varie Notizie di alcune cose notabile successe in ... Palermo ... all'anno 1568 ... all'anno 1606 ... dal nobile Francesco Perino.
Add. 19 325.

Madrid, Biblioteca Nacional, Manuscripts

Bilancio de Patrimonio Regio de Sicilia ... dell'Anno 1580 infin'Al ... 1581.
MS. 7633.

Blasones de Castilla.
MS. 1325.

Notas concernientes Estado y Guerra en el Reyno de Sicilia.
Anonymous, about 1582. MS. 1761.

Papeles Varios.
MS. 11 004.

Riol, S. A. :
Creacion de todos los Tribunales. MS. 10 558.

Un-named Manuscripts.
MSS. 956, 989, 2842, 9372, 10 300, 11 055, 18 674.

Varias Cartas.
MS. 1429.

Varios escritos tocantes a la Monarchia de Sicilia.
Vol. II, MS. 2665.

Madrid, Real Academia de la Historia, Manuscripts

Castro, S. de:
Reflexiones sobre el Govierno de Sicilia. 17th cent. translation. Estante 21 gr. l.a. No. 3.

Matute, F. de:
Descripcion de las Cosas del Govierno, Justicia, Hazienda Real, Milicia de Mar y Terra del Reyno de Sicilia. 17th cent. Estante 21 gr. l.a. No. 3.

Olivares:
Relacion sobre el Govierno de Sicilia, with notes by the Conde de Castro. MS. of 1685. Estante 21 gr. l.a. No. 3.

Simancas, Archivo General, Manuscripts
Sección Estado.
    Legajos 1119–1159.
Sección Secreterías Provinciales.
    Legajos 890, 892, 980–987, 1514, 1597–1600, 1648.

Genoa, Archivio di Stato, Manuscripts
Lettere Consoli
    Messina, No. 2634, Mazzo 1.
    Palermo, No. 2647, Mazzo 14.
    Trapani, No. 2651, Mazzo 18.

Naples, Biblioteca Nazionale, Manuscripts
Trattato di Sicilia.
    Anonymous. MS. of 1593. X.D. 46.

Palermo, Archivio di Stato, Manuscripts
Conservatoria di Registri.
    (Conti). Anno 1560. Nos. 898–910.
Relazioni de Estrazioni infra e fuori Regno, 1582–1585.
    Tesoreria Generale, MS. 1193.
    Tesoreria Generale, Giornale di Tavola, 1571/2, MS. 513.

Palermo, Biblioteca Communale, Manuscripts
Corvaia, T. :
    Discorsi a intorno la desrittione et regimento del regno di Sicilia etc. No date. Dedicated to Philip III. Qq. C. 52.
Lettere e Istruzioni Reali dal Anno.
    1422–1626. 3. Qq. C. 33.
    1556–1563. 3. Qq. C. 35.
Lettere Reali ai Vicerè di Sicilia, 1560– 1590.
    All letters addressed to the viceroys of Naples. 3 Qq. E. 34.
Lettere Regie de' Secoli XVI e XVII.
    3 Qq. E. 33.
Relazione del Governo di Sicilia.
    Anonymous in this copy. Author: P. Celestre, MS. of 17th cent. Qq. f. 29.

Venice, Archivio di Stato, Manuscripts
Relazione di Placido Ragazzoni (not published in Albèri)
    Senato III (Secreta), F. 24. Folder: Sicilia.

2. Printed Documents and Contemporary Sources

Albèri, E. Relazioni degli Ambasciatori Veneti al Senato durante el secolo decimosesto (Firenze 1858 etc.):
    Relazioni del Regno di Sicilia, Series 2, vol. 5.
    Relazioni del Regno di Spagna, Series 1, vols. 3, 5, 6, Appendix.
    Relazioni di Napoli 1597, Series 1, Appendix.

Biblioteca Storica e Letteraria di Sicilia, ed. G. di Marzo.
    Anonymous, Notitie di Successi varii nella Città di Palermo. From various papers, Series 1, vol. 1.
    Giovanni, Vincenzo di. Del Palermo Restaurato, Series 2, vol. 2.
    Palmerino, N. and Paruta, F. Diario della Città di Palermo, Series 1, vol. 1 (Palermo 1869).
    Villabianca. De giuochi bellici cavallereschi usati in Sicilia. (Quoted in a note in Series 1, vol. 1, pp. 240 ff).

Buonfiglio e Costanzo, G.
    Historia Siciliana (Venice 1604).
    Messina Citta Nobilissima (Venice 1606).

Cabrera de Córdoba, L. Filipe Segundo Rey de España. 4 vols. (Madrid 1876).

Calendar of State Papers (Venetian) vol. 7 (London 1890), vol. 9 (London 1897).

Capitoli et Ordinationi. Fatti delli ... Signori Marc Antonio Colonna et Altri Vicerè ... raccolti de D. Ido Lercaro (Palermo 1694).

Castro, Scipio di.
    Avvertimenti al Sig. Marc Antonio Colonna, quando andò Vicerè in Sicilia. In Thesoro Politico, vol. 2 (Milan 1601).
    Discorso sopra l'andata dell'arciduca Matthia d'Austria in Fiandra. In Thesoro Politico, vol. 3 (Turnoni 1605).

Collección de Documentos Inéditos para la Historia de España. Por Marques de Pidal, Miguel Salva and others:
    Don John of Austria. Letter to Philip II, Naples 12.12.1575, vol. 28 (Madrid 1856).
    Escobedo. Letter to Philip II, Naples 1.12.1575, vol. 28.
    Medinaceli. Advertencias que el duque de M. dejó á D. García de Toledo sobre el gobierno del reino de Sicilia, vol. 28.
    Moncada, H. de. Correspondence, vol. 24 (Madrid 1854).
    Ortiz de Rio, Pedro. Relación de los soldados y gente de servicio que hay en la Goleta, vol. 29.

Toledo, García de. Correspondence, vol. 29 (Madrid 1856) and vol. 30 (Madrid 1857).

Zúñiga, Juan de. Correspondence, vol. 97 (Madrid 1890) and Letter to king from Rome, 11.8.1574, vol. 28 (Madrid 1856).

Colonna, M. A. Constitutione Prammaticali sopra l'officio di corriero maggiore di Sicilia (Palermo 1584). (In volume of miscellaneous Sicilian 16th century publications BM. catalogue: 5359 aa.18)

Davila, Gil Gonzalez.
Teatro de las Grandezas de Madrid (Madrid 1623).

Documenti per Servire alla Storia di Sicilia; Società Siciliana per la Storia Patria:

Aragona, Carlo d'. Corrispondenza particolare con Filippo II: June 1574–May 1575 ed. S. V. Bozzo; July 1575–May 1577 ed. G. S. Cozzo, Series 1, vol. 2 (Palermo 1879).

Bernardino di Bologna, Baldassare di. Ceremoniale dell'Illustrissimo Senato Palermitano etc., Series 4, vol. 3 (Palermo 1895–99).

Colla, F. la. Statuti inediti delle Maestranze della Città di Salemi, Series 2, vol. 3, fasc. 1 (Palermo 1883).

Genuardi, L. Terre Comuni ed Usi Civici in Sicilia. Studi e Documenti, Series 2, vol. 7.

Giuffredi, A. Avvertimenti Cristiani, ed. L. Natoli, Series 4, vol. 4 (Palermo 1896).

Gonzaga, D. Ferrando, Relazione delle cose di Sicilia fatta all'Imperatore Carlo V. 1546, ed. F. C. Carreri, Series 4, vol. 4 (Palermo 1896).

Lionti, F. Statuti inediti delle Maestranze della città di Palermo, Series 2, vol. 3, fasc. 2 (Palermo 1883).

Galán, D. Cautiverio y travajos, 1589–1600 (Madrid 1913).

Giardina, C. Capitoli e Privilegi di Messina (Palermo 1937).

Granvelle, Cardinal de. Correspondence, ed. Ch, Piot, vols. 4, 5, 9, 11 (Bruxelles 1884, 86, 92, 94).

Papiers d'Etat, ed. Ch. Weiss, vol. 5. In Collection de Documents Inédits sur l'Histoire de France (Paris 1844).

Herrera y Tordesillas, A. de. Historia General del Mundo... del Tiempo del Rey Felipe II, 3 vols. (Madrid 1606–12).

Ingrassia, G. F. Informatione del Pestifero et Contagioso Morbo... nell'Anno 1575 et 1576 data allo Re Filippo II (Palermo 1576).

Mongitore, A. Parlamenti Generali del Regno di Sicilia dall' anno 1446 sino al 1748... ristampati colle addizioni, e note di Francesco Serio e Mongitore, 2 vols. (Palermo 1749).

Moryson, F. Itinerary Shakespeare's Europe ed. C. Hughes (London 1903).

Ordinazioni e Regolamenti della Deputazione del Regno di Sicilia raccolti e publicati per ordine di Ferdinando III (Palermo 1782).

Pérez, A. Relaciones (Paris 1624).

Pragmaticarum Regni Siciliae Novissima Collectio, 3 vols. (Palermo 1636–1700).

Regni Siciliae Pragmaticarum Sanctionum, 2 vols, ed. R. Raymundettus (Venice 1574).

Riba, C. El Consejo Supremo de Aragón en el Reinado de Felipe II (Valencia 1914).

Sandys, G. A Relation of a Journey begun An. Dom. 1610 (London 1627).

Testa, F. Capitula Regni Siciliae quae ad hodiernum diem lata sunt, edita cura eiusdem regni Deputatorum, 2 vols. (Palermo 1743).

Villalón, C. de. Viaje de Turquía, 2 vols. (Madrid-Barcelona 1919).

3. Later Works

Amari, M. History of the War of the Sicilian Vespers; transl. Earl of Ellesmere; 2 vols. (London 1850).

Archivio Storico per la Sicilia
  Giardina, C. Le fonti della legislazione Siciliana, vol. I, 1935; and Sul Governo centrale spagnuolo e sull'anno di fondazione del supremo consiglio d'Italia; vol. 4–5, p. 521 ff. (Palermo 1938–39).

Archivio Storico per la Sicilia Orientale:
  Pardi, G. Carlo V a la communità di Mineo, anno 2 (Catania 1905) (Prints documents).
  Verdirame, G. Le istituzioni sociali e politiche di alcuni municipi della Sicilia Orientale nei secoli XVI, XVII, XVIII, Anno. 1, 2 (Catania 1904–05).

Archivio Storico per le Provincie Napoletane:
  Faraglia, N. Bilancio del Reame di Napoli degli anni 1591, e 1592 (Napoli 1876), p. 211 ff. (Prints documents).

Archivio Storico Siciliano, Nuova Serie:
  Arenaprimo, G. Il retorno e la dimora a Messina di don Giovanni d'Austria etc., vol. 28 (Palermo 1903) (Prints documents).
  Avolio, C. La Schiavitù in Sicilia nel Sec. XVI, vol. 10 (Palermo 1885) (Prints documents).
  Capasso, G. Il Governo di Don Ferrante Gonzaga in Sicilia del 1535 al 1543, vols. 30 and 31 (Palermo 1905–06) (Prints documents).
  Crocchiolo, M. Sul viceregno di Marco Antonio Colonna in Sicilia, vol. 37 (Palermo 1912) (Prints documents).
  Franchina, A. Un censimento di Schiavi nel 1565, vol. 32 (Palermo 1907–08).
  Garufi, C. A. Contributo alla storia dell'Inquisizione in Sicilia nei secoli XVI e XVII. Documenti dagli Archivi di Spagna, vol. 38–43 (Palermo 1913 etc.) (Prints documents).
  Genuardi, L. La formazione delle Consuetudini di Palermo, vol. 31 (Palermo 1906).
  Giardina, C. L'istituto del Vicerè di Sicilia (1415–1798), vol. 51 (Palermo 1931) (Prints documents).
  Giuffrè, L. L'epidemia d'influenza del 1557 in Palermo etc., vol. 15 (Palermo 1890).
  Manceri, A. Editor: 'I capitoli del consolato dell'arte di seta a Messina,' vol. 52 (Palermo 1932) (Prints documents).
  Pardi, G. Un commune della Sicilia e le sue relazioni con i dominatori dell' Isola etc., vol. 26 (Palermo 1901).

Pitrè, G. Pasquinati, Cartelli, Motti, e Canzoni in Sicilia, vol. 31 (Palermo 1906); and Notizie delle Sacre Rappresentazioni in Sicilia, vol. I (Palermo 1876).

Pontieri, E. Il Tramonto del Baronaggio Siciliano, vol. 51 (Palermo 1931).

Rocca, P. M. Due contratti di pace tra privati nel sec. XVI, vol. 18 (Palermo 1893).

Ruffo, V. La regia Zecca di Messina, da documenti inediti. (Continuation from previous vols. of A.S.S.N.S.), vol. 41 (Palermo 1916) (Prints documents).

Salomone-Marino, S. Alcune note al Libro 'La Sicilia nella Battaglia di Lepanto,' vol. 18 (Palermo 1893).

De famosi uomini d'arme Siciliani fioriti nel sec. XVI vol. 4 (Palermo 1879) (Prints documents).

Starrabba, R. Suppliche e capitoli dell'Università di Monreale (an. 1516) An. 12 (Palermo 1887) (Prints documents).

Capitoli della terra di San Michele 1534, vol. 4 (Palermo 1879) (Prints documents); and Contratto di appalto per la spazzatura e per l'inaffiamento della strade di Palermo dell'anno 1600, vol. 2 (Palermo 1877) (Prints documents).

Travali, G. Un contratto di pace tra privati nel secolo XVI, vol. 13 (Palermo 1888) (Prints documents).

Villanueva, L. S. Di una pretesa abolizione della milizia urbana in Sicilia. vol. 23 (Palermo 1898).

Vitale, V. Trapani nelle Guerre di Carlo V in Africa e contro i Turchi, vol. 29 (Palermo 1904) (Prints documents).

Archivio Storico Siciliano, Terza Serie:
Garufi, C. A. Patti Agrari e Comuni Feudali di nuova Fondazione in Sicilia, dallo scorcio del secolo XI agli albori del Settecento Part 1, vol. 1 (Palermo 1946).

Atti della Regia Accademia di Scienze, Lettere e Belle Arti di Palermo:
Giardina, C. La vita e l'Opera Politica di Scipione di Castro, Series 3, vol. 16 (Palermo 1931),pp. 267–441.
Sul donativo straordinario del Parlamento di Sicilia al Marchese di Vigliena, Series 3, vol. 18 (Palermo 1934).
Il Supremo Consiglio d'Italia, Series 3, vol. 19 (Palermo 1936).

Auria, V. Historia cronologica delli Signori Vicerè di Sicilia, 1409–1697 (Palermo 1697).

Ballesteros y Beretta, A. Historia de España y su Influencia en la Historia Universal, IV, pt. 2 (Barcelona 1927).

Bianchini, L. Della storia economico – civile di Sicilia, 2 vols. (Napoli 1841).

Blasi e Gamba-Corta, G. E. di. Storia Cronologica de Vicerè, vol. 2 (Palermo 1790).

Brydone, P. A Tour through Sicily and Malta, 2 vols. (London 1773).

Burckhardt, J. The Civilization of the Renaissance in Italy; transl. S. G. C. Middlemore (Vienna and London, Phaidon, no date).

Calisse, C. Storia del Parlamento in Sicilia (Torino 1887).

Carini, J. Gli Archivi e le Biblioteche di Spagna, 1 (Palermo 1884).

Caruso, G. B. Memorie Istoriche di quanto e accaduto in Sicilia, part 3, vol. 1 (Palermo 1744) Discorso istorico-apologetico della Monarchia di Sicilia; ed. G. M. Mira (Palermo 1863) (Prints documents).

Colla, F. la. Delle antiche maestranze della città di Palermo. Introduction to documents in Documenti per servire alla storia di Sicilia. Soc. Sic. per la Storia Patria, Series 2, vol. 3. fasc. 1 (Palermo 1883) (Prints documents).

Colonna, P. I Colonna dalle origini all'inizio del secolo XIX (Rome 1927).

Corbett, J. S. Papers relating to the Navy during the Spanish war 1585–87 (Navy Records Society 1898).

Croce, B. La Spagna nella vita Italiana durante la rinascenza (Bari 1917). Storia del Regno di Napoli (Bari 1925).

Cusumano, V. Storia dei Banchi della Sicilia. Part I, I Banchi Privati; part II, I Banchi Pubblici (Rome 1887, 1892).

Doren, A. Italienische Wirtschaftsgeschichte, vol. 1 (Jena 1934).

Dryden (Jnr.), J. A voyage to Sicily and Malta (London 1776).

Emmanuele e Gaetani, F. M. Della Sicilia Nobile, 2 vols. (Palermo 1754–7).

Enciclopedia Italiana, vol. 10 (Milan, Rome 1931).

Enciclopedia Universal Ilustrada, vol. 62 (Bilbao, Madrid, Barcelona, 1928).

Essen, L. van der. Alexandre Farnèse, 5 vols. (Brussels 1937).

Ferrara, A. F. Storia generale della Sicilia, 9 vols. (Palermo 1830–8).

Ferrari, J. Histoire de la Raison d'Etat (Paris 1860).

Fisher, L. E. Viceregal administration in the Spanish-American colonies (Berkeley, California, 1926).

Formentini, A. La dominazione Spagnola in Lombardia (Milan 1881) (Prints documents).

Genuardi, L. Parlamento Siciliano, vol. 1.
   Atti delle Assemblee Costituzionali Italiane (Bologna 1924).

Gothein, E. Die Kulturentwicklung Süd-Italiens (Breslau 1886).

Gounon-Loubens, M. J. Essais sur l'administration de la Castille au XVI siècle (Paris 1860).

Gregorio, R. Introduzione allo studio del dritto publico Siciliano (Palermo 1794).
Opere Scelte (Palermo 1853).

Hakluyt, R. The principall navigations, voiages, traffiques and discoveries of the English nation, vol. 6 (Glasgow 1904).

Hartwig, O. Die mittelalterlichen Stadtrechte Siziliens (Cassel und Göttingen 1867) (Prints documents).

Historische Zeitschrift, Philippson, M. Philip II v. Spanien und das Papsttum, vol. 39 (München 1878).

Laloy, E. La révolte de Messine, l'expédition de Sicile et la politique Française en Italie (1674–78),vol. I (Paris 1929).

Lavisse, E. and Rambaud, A. Histoire Générale, vol. 5 (Paris 1895).

Lea, H. C. A History of the Inquisition of Spain, 4 vols. (New York 1906). The Inquisition in the Spanish Dependencies (New York 1908).

Loncao, E. Il Lavoro e le classi rurali in Sicilia durante e dopo il Feudalismo (Palermo 1900).

Lumia, J. La. Storia Siciliana, 4 vols. (Palermo 1882) (Prints documents).

Madariaga, S. de. The Rise of the Spanish American Empire (London 1947).
The Fall of the Spanish American Empire (London 1947).

Maggiore-Perni, F. Palermo e le sue Epidemie (Palermo 1894).
La populazione di Sicilia e di Palermo dal X al XVIII secolo (Palermo 1892) (Prints documents).

Mantia, F. G. La. I parlamenti del regno di Sicilia e gli atti inediti (1542 e 1594) (Torino 1886) (Prints documents).

Mantia, V. La. Storia della legislazione civile e criminale di Sicilia, 2 vols. (Palermo 1874).

Merriman, R. B. The Rise of the Spanish Empire, vol. 3 (New York 1925),vol. 4 (New York 1934).
Suleiman the Magnificent, 1520–66 (Cambridge Mass. 1944).

Natoli, L. Storia di Sicilia (Palermo 1935).

Navarrete, E. F. de. Notes to José Ranco, Los Vireyes Lugartenientes ... de Napoles, 1634 in Colección de Documentos Inéditos para la Historia de España, vol. 23.

Nuova Rivista Storica:
Pardi, G. Storia demografica della città di Palermo (Milan 1919-1920, and Storia demografica della città di Messina (Milan 1920–21).

Orlando, D. Il Feudalismo in Sicilia (Palermo 1847).

Palmieri, N. Saggio Storico e Politico sulla Costituzione del Regno di Sicilia infino al 1816 (Losanna 1847).

Pastor, L. von. Geschichte der Päpste, etc.,vols. 8, 9 (Freiburg i. Br. 1921 etc.)

Ranke, L. von. Die Osmanen und die Spanische Monarchie, in Sämtliche Werke, Bd. 35/36 (Leipzig 1877).

Révue Hispanique:
  Giannini, A. Impressioni italiane di viaggiatori spagnuoli nei secoli XVI e XVII, vol. 55 (New York and Paris 1922).

Rivista di Storia del Diritto Italiano:
  Genuardi, L. Diritto publico Spagnuolo in Sicilia, Anno. 6, pp. 39-99 (Bologna 1933).
  Perez, J. Beneyto. Il Diritto Catalano in Italia, Anno 6.
  Viora, M. Sui Vicerè di Sicilia e di Sardegna, Anno 3 (Bologna 1930).

Rodocanachi, E. La Réforme en Italie, vol. 2 (Paris 1921).

Saltillo, Marques del. Juan de Vega, Embajador de Carlos V en Roma (1543-47) (Madrid 1946).

Sentis, F. I. Die Monarchia Sicula (Freiburg i. Br. 1896) (Prints documents).

Stefano, F. de. Storia della Sicilia dal Secolo XI al XIX (Bari 1948).

Titone, V. Economia e Politica nella Sicilia del Sette e Ottocento (Palermo 1947).
  La Sicilia Spagnuola. Saggi Storici (Palermo 1948).

Tocco, V. di. Ideali d'Indipendenza in Italia durante la Preponderanza Spagnuola (Messina 1926).

Toynbee, A. J. A Study of History, 6 vols. (London, New York, Toronto 1945-46).

Usher, R. G. The Rise and Fall of the High Commission (Oxford 1913).

Welz, G. de. Saggio su i Mezzi da moltiplicare prontamente le Richezze della Sicilia (Paris 1822).

Zanichelli, N. Ed. Gli Archivi di Stato Italiani (Bologna 1944).

4. Additional Bibliography

Annali del Mezzogiorno:
　Verlinden, C. Schiavitù ed economia nel Mezzogiorno agli inizi dell' età moderna, vol. III (Catania 1963).

Archivio Storico per la Sicilia Orientale, Ser. 4:
　Scichilone, G. Origine e Ordinamento della Deputazione del Regno di Sicilia, anno III, 1950 (Catania 1951) (Prints documents).
　Torrisi, N. Aspetti della crisi granaria siciliana nel sec. XVI, anno X (Catania 1957) (Prints documents).

Bataillon, M. Érasme et l'Espagne (Paris 1937).

Braudel, F. La Méditerranée et le Monde méditerranéen, 2nd ed., 2 vols. (Paris 1966).

Caracciolo, F. Il Regno di Napoli nei Secoli XVI e XVII, vol. I, Economia e Società (Rome 1966).

Catalano, G. Controversie giurisdizionali tra Chiesa e Stato nell'età di Gregorio XIII e Filippo II (Palermo 1955) (Prints documents).

Comandé, G. B. Ricerche di Storia Siciliana (secoli XV–XIX) (Palermo 1956).

Coniglio, G. Il Regno di Napoli al tempo di Carlo V (Naples 1951).
　Il Viceregno di Napoli nel Sec. XVII (Rome 1955).

Elliott, J. H. Imperial Spain, 1469–1716 (London 1963).
　The Revolt of the Catalans (Cambridge 1963).

Garrad, K. The Causes of the Second Rebellion of the Alpujarras (1568–1571) (to be published).

Giunta, F. Sicilia Spagnuola (Vicenza 1962).

Griffiths, G. Representative Government in Western Europe in the Sixteenth Century. Commentary and Documents for the Study of Comparative Constitutional History (Oxford 1968).

Hartung, F. Quelques problèmes concernant la Monarchie absolue, X International Congress of Historical Sciences, Relazioni, Storia Moderna, IV (Rome 1957).

Koenigsberger, H. G. The Parliament of Piedmont during the Renaissance, 1460–1560, IX International Congress of Historical Sciences. Studies presented to the International Commission for the History of Representative and Parliamentary Institutions, vol. XI (Louvain 1952).
　The Parliament of Sicily and the Spanish Empire. Mélanges Antonio Marongiu (Palermo 1967).

Lynch, J. Spain under the Habsburgs, vol. I (Oxford 1964).

Mack Smith, D. A History of Sicily: Medieval Sicily 800–1713 (London 1968).

Magdaleno, R. Catalago XIX del Archivo de Simancas, Papeles de Estado, Sicilia, Virreinato español (Valladolid 1951).

Marongiu, A. L'Istituto Parlamentare in Italia (Rome 1949).
Il Parlamento in Italia nel Medio Evo e nell'Etá Moderna. Studies presented to the International Commission for the History of Representative and Parliamentary Institutions, vol. XXV (Milan 1962); Medieval Parliaments, translated and adapted by S. J. Woolf (London 1968).
I Parlamenti di Sardegna nella storia e nel diritto pubblico comparato (Rome 1932).

Moscati, R. Per una storia della Sicilia nell'età dei Martini (Messina 1954) (Prints documents).

Mousnier, R. Quelques problèmes concernant la monarchie absolue, X International Congress of Historical Sciences, Relazioni, Storia Moderna, IV (Rome 1957).

Pepe, G. Il Mezzogiorno d'Italia sotto gli Spagnoli (Florence 1952).

Petino, A. I prezzi del grano . . . a Catania dal 1512 al 1630. Studi in onore di Gino Luzzatto, vol. II (Milan 1950).

Saitta, A., ed. Avvertimenti di Don Scipio di Castro a Marco Antonio Colonna quando andò Vicerè di Sicilia (Rome 1950).

Schäfer, E. El Consejo Real y Supremo de las Indias, 2 vols. (Seville 1935–1947).

Titone, V. Cultura e vita morale (Palmero-Milano 1943).
La Politica dell' Età Barocca (Caltanissetta 1950).
Politica e civiltà (Palermo 1951).
Riveli e platee del regno di Sicilia (Milan 1961) (Prints documents).
La Sicilia dalla Dominazione Spagnola all'Unità d'Italia (Bologna 1955).
Storia e sociologia (Florence 1964).
Storia Mafia e costume in Sicilia (Milan 1964).

Tricoli, G. La Deputazione degli Stati e la Crisi del Baronaggio Siciliano (Palermo 1966) (Prints documents).

Vicens Vives, J. Estructura administrativa estatal en los siglos XVI y XVII, XI International Congress of Historical Sciences, Rapports IV, Histoire Moderne (Göteborg-Stockholm-Uppsala 1960).

Villari, R. La rivolta antispagnola a Napoli. Le origini (1585–1647) (Bari 1967).

INDEX

Abarbanel, Isaac, 27
Abjuration, Act of, 172 n.2
Acuña, Juan de, 12, 28
Adrian IV, 18
Agnello, Vincenzo, 117
Agrarian organization, 75-80
Aguaglia, d', family of, 88
Alagona, family of, 74
Albamonte, Guglielmo, 88
Albanian peasants, 77
Albert and Isabel, archdukes, 24
Alcalá de Henares, university of, 30
Alcalá, duke of, 171 n.2, 172
Alderete, Diego Gracián de, 14
Alexandria, 112
Alfonso V of Aragon, 21, 45, 96, 108
Ali, Aluch, 190 n.5
Ali Pasha, 53
Alva, duke of, 13, 23, 48, 180, 182 n.1, 184
Alvadeliste, marquis of, 55, 81, 96, 97, 102, 107, 109, 113, 114, 121, 133, 138, 156, 157, 171 n.2, 176; relations with Inquisition, 167-69; career, 192-93
Alvarez, Fernando, 27
America, Spanish colonies in, 11, 28, 31, 43, 44, 45; treasure, 50, 140; Indians, 51, 53
Amodei, Francesco, 88
Andalucia, 45
Anjou, House of, 52, 83, 172 n.2, 193
Antonello da Messina, 75, 90
Apulia, corn trade of, 142
Aquinas, St. Thomas, 123 n.4
Arabs, 164 n.7
Aragon, 10, 11, 17, 18, 20, 21, 60
Aragon, House of, 172 2n.
Aragona, family of, 160
Aranda, Pedro de, 27
Aristotle, 205
Asaro, family of, 88
Asturias, 30
Avila, Alfonso de, 27

Badajoz, *concordia* of, 166, 167 n.1
Balearic Islands, 25, 59
Bandits, 73, 116, 117-21, 174,·194; extradition of, 69, 117

Banks, 81
Barajas, count of, 68
Barberi, Luca, 145
Barbosa, Pedro, 23
Barcelona, 45; merchants, 59
Barletta, contest of, 88
Bayarte, Juan, 183
Beccaria, Cesare, marquis of, 123 n.4
Bellarmin, Robert, Cardinal, 204 n.4
Bezerra, Inquisitor, 165
Bicocca. battle of, 88
Bivona, duke of, 100, 179
Bonavia, regent, 27
Bonetta, Ottavio, 188-92
Bosco, del, family of, 88, 160
Bosco, Ottavio del, 65
Bravo de Sotomayor, Gregorio, 187, 188, 190
Briatico, count of, 191-2 n.5
Brussels, 180; assembly of 1555, 11
Budgets, 124, 128 n.2, 133
Burgos, Alonso de, 27
Burgos, Cardinal, 51
Burgundy, 10

Cabinet, the English, 104
Cabrera de Córdoba, 120 n.5, 171, 180
Cabrero, Dr., 29
Calderón, Rodrigo, 15
Caltagirone, 106, 109
Camarate, count of, 156
Canales, official, 177
Captains-at-arms, 80, 114, 115, 117, 122
Cardenas, Jorque de, 194 n.7
Cardona, Pietro de, 88
Cardona y Fernández de Córdoba, Antonio Folch de, 28
Carillo, Alfonso, 18
Cartagena, Padro de, 27
Carvajal, Galíndez de, 24, 29
Carvajal, regent, 100
Casa de Contratación, 31
Casale, 76
Castellammare, 169
Castelmoncayo, marquis of, 34
Castile, 10, 11, 17, 18, 30, 34, 46, 73, 105; money from, 54, 55, 57; officials and ministers from, 60, 96, 192-94

223

Castilla, Alonso de, 29
Castro, count of, 121 n.3, 139
Castro, Scipio di, 37, 98, 100, 120 n.5, 123, 163 n.4, 171, 201-5
Catalonia, 11, 20-22, 26, 28, 59, 60, 194; merchants, 82, 143
Catania, 108; university of, 90, 91
Catholic Kings *see* Ferdinand II, Isabella
Cavalleria, Alfonso de, 26
Celdran, treasurer-general, 27
Celestre, family of, 88
Charles of Anjou, 52
Charles V, emperor, 10, 12-15, 17, 21, 32, 33, 44, 45, 47, 51, 59, 85, 86, 106, 137, 178; abdications, 11; Inquisition, 162
Charles II of Spain, 34
Chiaramonte, family of, 74
Chinchón, count of, 13, 61, 65, 67, 71, 177
Church *see* Clergy, Papacy
Cifuentes de Heredia, Luca, 92, 183, 189
Cisneros, Pedro de, 73
Clergy of Sicily, 49, 138, 144, 147, 149, 161, 174, 195, 196; benefices of, 49, 62, 64, 127; *braccio ecclesiastico*, 150-58 *passim*
Cobos, Francisco de los, 13, 15, 25
Colonial Office, the British, 63
Colonna, family of, 56 n.3
Colonna, Marc Antonio, 49, 55, 73, 79, 90, 91, 97-103, 108, 111, 115, 118, 120 n.2, 121, 131, 132, 135 n.5, 136, 147, 149, 155, 159, 171, 173 n.4, 175 n.2, 176, 178, 201, 202; views on empire, 56-58; re-organization of Patrimony, 93-95; relations with Inquisition, 165-67, 169; career, 184-92
Colonna, Pompeo, 115, 188, 189
Columbus, 24
Communes *see* Towns
Conca d'Oro, 73
Constantinople, 44, 47, 94
Conversos, 26, 27, 29
Corbera, family of, 188
Corbera, Galceran, 188, 189
Córdova, family of, 185
Córdova, Geronimo de, 185
Córdova, Gonzalez de, 45
Corn trade, 50, 69, 79-81, 112, 113, 126 n.4, 130, 131, 141, 142, 202
Corsairs, 45, 47, 55, 75, 124, 174, 176, 194
Cortes of Aragon, 150

Cortes of Castile, 27
Cortes of Portugal, 23
Cortés, Hernán, 24
Corts of Catalonia, 22
Councils of
  Aragon, 16, 20-22, 25, 26, 29, 60-62, 65, 67; loses control over Italy, 22, 59
  Castile, 16, 19-21, 24-26, 28, 29, 32, 68
  Cruzada, the, 16
  Finance, 29, 33
  Flanders, 16, 24, 25, 34
  Hermandad, the, 16
  Indies, 16, 24, 26-29, 31-34, 69
  Inquisition, 16, 17, 19, 28, 70, 161-70 *passim*; *Junta* with Council of Italy, 71, 166-69
  Italy, 16, 24, 25, 34, 39, 40, 49-58; *passim*, 60-72 *passim*, 73, 83, 84, 86, 93, 95, 98, 99, 100, 109, 120 n.2, 126, 133, 135, 136, 137, 155, 156 n.9, 170, 173, 176, 178, 179 n.7, 183, 186, 190; established 21, 22, 60; *Junta* with Council of the Inquisition, 71, 166-69.
  Mesta, the, 16
  Military Orders, the, 16, 32
  Portugal, 16, 23, 24, 25
  State, 16, 17, 26, 28, 31, 63, 64, 70, 103; secretaries of, 66
  War, 16, 17, 32-34
Counter-Reformation, 45
Curia *see* Papacy
Currency rates, 124 n.1
Cutinario, regent, 66, 135 n.5

Dantisco, Antonio Gracián, 14
Davila, Pedro Arias, 27
Debts, Government, 134-5, 153
Deputation, 150, 152, 159, 160
Deza, Diego de, 17
Dominicans, 164
Donato, Leonardo, 50, 52, 58 n.1
Doria, family of, 56 n.3
Doria, Gian Andrea, 132
Doria, Giannettino, 149
Dragut, 53
Duplessis-Mornay, 172 n.2

East Indies, 45
Empire,
  Aragonese, 45, 59, 60
  Medieval Roman, 44

INDEX

Empire,
  Ottoman, 77, 94, 129, 130, 166, 192; threat to Sicily, 40, 43, 44, 45, 51, 54, 55, 107, 125, 132, 150, 197; League against, 69, 129, 131, 182
  Roman, 9, 58, 72, 197
  Spanish, 9, 22, 33, 34, 40, 43-46, 47-58 *passim*, 60, 69, 83, 96, 104, 105, 124, 139, 144, 161, 195-97; in Italy 37, 59; economic policy of, 142, 143
England, 71; ships, 44; merchants, 68 n.4; parliament, 153, 160, 196, 197; absence of Inquisition, 165
Enguera, Joan de, 18
Enríquez, Diego, 185
Erasmus, 14
Eraso, Francisco de, 15, 181
Espinola, Pedro de, 136
Etna, 81 n.9

Famines, 113, 114, 139, 192
Fardella, family of, 88
Favara, Ferdinando de Silva, marquis de la, 154, 180
Favara, Lorenzo Téllez de Silva, marquis de la, 103, 118, 183, 186, 193, 206 n.1
Ferdinand I of Aragon, 96
Ferdinand II of Aragon, the Catholic, 10, 11, 17, 19, 20, 21, 25, 26, 29, 31, 32, 33, 46, 49, 59, 60, 96, 125, 137, 153
Feria, duke of, 170
Figueroa, president of Royal Council, 145
Flanders, 49, 55
Florence, 106, 117
Fonseca, Juan Rodríguez de, 24, 25
Fortunato, Francesco, 39, 47, 97, 98; views on judicial procedure, 122-23
Francavilla, duke of, 60, 70
France, 44, 45, 193; absence of Inquisition, 165, 166
Franche Comté, 11
Franchis, *solicitatore fiscale*, 94, 188 n.3
Franco, Gonzalo, 27
Franquesa, secretary, 15
Frederic II of Aragon, 149
Frederic II, emperor, 43
Funes Muñoz, G., 34

Gaitan, secretary, 64 n.5, 65, 66, 67, 183
Galán, Diego, 94
Gallipoli, 143
Gante, Martin de, 23, 67

Ganzaria, baron of, 77
Garibaldi, Giuseppe, 43
Gasco, Inquisitor, 165
Gassol, Gerónimo, 14
Gattinara, marquis of, 10, 12, 21, 25
Genoa, 45, 133; bankers, 81, 143, 156 n.3; merchants, 82, 143
Geraci, marquis of, 48 n.5, 110, 127 n.5; career, 194; relations with Inquisition, 169
Gerba, defeat of, 125 n.3, 148 n.7
Germany, 10, 44; absence of Inquisition, 165
Gioeni, family of, 76
Giovanni, Mariano di, 88
Giovanni, Vincenzo di, 88
Giuffredi, Argisto, 122
Giuliana, marquis of, 186
Giuliana, marchesa of, 186
Goletta, 40, 53, 54, 55, 128, 183
Gómez de Silva, Ruy, 13, 60, 103 n.4, 179; party of, 180, 182
Gonzaga, Ferrante, 99, 135, 148, 178 n.6, 201
Gorronero, Inquisitor, 165 n.3, 167
Granada, 11, 27, 32, 45
Granvelle, Antoine Perrenot, Cardinal, 39, 60, 63, 67, 70, 98; friendship with Medinaceli, 179; relations with Colonna, 184, 187, 188 n.2, 190, 191
Granvelle, Nicolas Perrenot, 13, 21
Great Court, 84-87, 91-95, 98, 99, 106, 118, 122, 136, 147, 155, 160; relations with Inquisition, 166-69
Greek peasants, 77
Gregory XIII, 201
Guevara, Dr., 29
Guipúzcoa, 30

Haedo, Diego, 165, 167-69
Hapsburg Monarchy *see* Empire, Spanish
Heresies, 44
High Commission, court of, 147
Holy Conscience, court of, 47, 91, 95, 99, 147; established, 87
Holy Council, 84, 98, 104, 155, 157
Huguenots, The, 164 n.7
Hungary, 44, 195

Idiáques, family of, 15
Idiáques, Francisco de, 22, 23, 65, 66, 67
Idiáques, Juan de, 13, 28
Idiáques, Miguel, 101

Illánes, Inquisitor, 169
Indies, see America
Inquisition of
  Castile, 45; familiars, 31
  Sicily, 38, 40, 71, 123, 144, 149, 161-70, 185, 186, 192, 194, 196-97; familiars, 156, 162-70, 197
Inquisition, Council of, see Council of the Inquisition
Isabella of Castile, 10, 17, 18, 19, 24, 25, 27, 29, 32, 46, 60, 96
Islam, 44, 45
Italy, 44, 46, 47

James I of England, 54
Jean le Sauvage, 12
John II of Aragon, 20, 26, 27, 96
John of Austria, Don, 55, 97, 107, 129, 177, 182, 184
Junta de Guerra de Indias, 33, 34, 35
Junta de Hacienda de Indias, 33
Jurisdiction, disputes over, 70, 95, 149; between Inquisition and viceroys, 162-69

Laguna, marquis de la, 35
Lando, Alvise, 56 n.3
Landriano, Giuseppe Francesco, 130 n.3
Las Casas, Bartolomé de, 51
La Valette, Jean de, 181
Law, Canon, 147, 148
Law, Roman, 30
Law, Sicilian, procedures, 85, 87, 109, 110, 118-23, 147, 156, 163, 164
Lemos, count of, 173 n.3
León, 11, 30
León, Pedro de, 71, 94, 100, 183
Lepanto, 54, 88, 107, 129, 131
Lerma, duke of, 15, 33
Licata, 88
Lievana, Francisco Hernández de, 66, 70
Light cavalry, 176, 177
Lisbon, 23, 45
Loaysa, García de, 13, 18, 25
Locadello, *maestro razionale*, 94
Lombardi, Andreotto, 88
López, Ruy, 27
Los Vélez, marquis de, 65, 190, 191
Low Countries, see Netherlands
Loyola, St. Ignacio, 45
Luna, Sigismondo de, 75

Machiavelli, Niccolò, 51, 201, 203-5
Madrid, 23, 83, 108, 153, 155, 166, 168; court of, 50, 55, 61, 63, 71, 72, 87, 97, 112, 124, 128, 130, 145, 157, 161, 164, 170; relations with viceroys, 171-95 *passim*, 202
Mafia, The, 99
Mai, regent, 27
Majorca, 11, 26
Malta, 40, 44, 53, 54, 57, 88, 129, 176, 181, 189
Maluenda, Juan de, 27
Maqueda, duke of, 94, 111, 137, 173 n.4; career, 194; relations with Inquisition, 169
Margaret of Austria, 10
Mariana, Juan, 204 n.4
Martin I of Aragon, 52, 104, 149
Mary, B.V. 154
Mary of England, 11, 22
Massa, bishop of, 155
Massimo, Lelio, 191
Mathias, archduke, 203
Matos de Noronha, Rui de, 23
Matute, Fernando de, 39, 98, 99 n.1; views on torture, 123 n.4
Medinaceli, duke of, 69, 86, 112, 120, 125, 129, 134, 136, 145, 148, 153, 159, 171, 173 n.4, 176, 183, 188 n.4, 201; career, 179-80; relations with Inquisition, 164, 194
Medina de Riosecco, duke of, 185
Meli, Giovanni, 90
Mendoza, Juan de, 181
Messina, 40, 43, 55, 74, 75, 96, 107-109, 113, 126, 128, 140, 176; mint of, 127; privileges of, 106, 154-56; revolt of, 139 n.6; siege of, 194; silk trade, 81 82, 126
Messina, Straits of, 47
Milan, 10, 11, 22, 23, 46, 48, 52, 59, 60, 72, 161, 196, 202; duke of, 45; contributions to defence, 57; seal of, 65; governors of, 69, 201; laws of inheritance of, 76 n.1; Inquisition, 164 n.7
Militia, 126 n.1, 185
Minafria, family of, 88
Mineo, 106
Miranda, count of, 67
Miserendino, baron of, 188-89
Miserendino, Eufrosina Zaragossa, baroness of, 188-91
Modica, county of, 185
Molina, Luis de, 204 n.4

INDEX

Monarchia Sicula, 38, 40, 144-49, 154, 161, 162, 182; clash with Inquisition, 167, 168
Moncada, Ugo de, 88, 153, 156, 158 n.4, 162, 163
Mondéjar, marquis of, 177 n.4
Monrreal, Estévan de, 94, 101, 178 n.2, 186
Montalvo, marquis of, 34
Monte di San Giuliano, 109
Monteleone, duke of, 156, 178 n.6
Montesclaros, marquis of, 187 n.1
Moors, 45, 162
Moriscos, 162
Morosini, Francesco, 142
Moryson, Fines, 77
Moura, Christóvão de, 13, 23
Mussomele, count of, 167-69

Naples, 10, 11, 21, 22, 23, 28, 46, 49, 52, 53, 59, 60, 72, 86, 97, 133, 142, 160, 161, 192 n.5, 196; loyalty of, 58 n.1; seal of, 65; viceroys of, 68, 97 n.7, 174, 181; laws of inheritance of, 76 n.1; Collateral Council of, 103; Inquisition, 164 n.7
Navarre, 11, 28
Netherlands, 10, 11, 14, 43, 46, 60, 71, 88, 133, 171, 172 n.2, 195, 203; Estates General, 24; Inquisition, 164 n.7, 165, 166; Medinaceli in, 180
Nicosia, 109
Nobility, Aragonese and Catalan, 70
Nobility, Sicilian, 70, 111, 112, 115, 116, 144, 150, 182, 201; *braccio militare*, 151-58 *passim*, revolt of, 192, 193; right of jurisdiction, 70 n.1, 135, 137-39; legal immunity, 118; feuds, 74, 75, 88, 99, 100, 116, 117, 171, 188-92; loss of political influence, 84, 85, 87-90; Colonna's policy towards, 185; relations with Inquisition, 163-70 *passim*, 192
Norman rulers of Sicily, 74, 75
Nuza, Juan la, 171

Offices, sale of, 127, 135-37, 139
Olivares, count-duke of, 13, 15, 33, 34, 193
Olivares, count of, 95, 97, 105 n.1, 111, 113, 114, 118, 135, 138, 139; career, 193-94; views on *ex abrupto*, 121, 123; relations with Inquisition, 169
Order of St. John, 54, 189, 195
Oriolo, marquis of, 188 n.4

Oropeso, Dr., 29
Osuña, duke of, 33, 99 n.1
Otranto, 143

Padilla, Antonio, 65, 67, 70 n.3
Palacios Rubios, Dr. Juan López, 29
Palanzuela, Alonso de, 27
Palermo, 40, 43, 73, 74, 75, 81, 96, 97, 107, 108, 113, 116, 117, 126, 134-5, 140, 143, 149, 153, 162, 176, 189, 193; court of, 63; population of, 74 n.2, 78; exports, 82; fair, 83; interdict, 168; popular song, 206-7; quarrel with president, 110, 194
Palizzi, family of, 74
Panormita, 75
Papacy, 12, 19, 98, 144, 145-49, 150, 151, 154, 161, 173 n.4
Páramo, Lodovico, 156, 169
Parco, abbey of, 50 n.3, 64, 185
Parliament of Sicily, 37, 40, 48, 50, 84-87, 89, 98, 121, 144, 149-61, 176, 177 n.1, 195-97; donatives, 53, 54, 124-43 *passim*, 162; donatives to viceroys, 97, 98
Parma, Alexander Farnese, duke of, 71, 88, 178 n.3
Paternò, princes of, 76
Patrimony, court of, 55, 78, 84, 85, 87, 101, 102, 105 n.2, 114, 119, 178; reorganization, 92-95
Patti, bishops of, 87 n.1, 110 n.6, 164
Paul III, 179
Paul IV, 48
Peirera, Solórzano, 12
Peña, Inquisitor, 167, 169
Pérez, Antonio, 14, 64 n.5, 65, 66, 102
Pérez, Gonzalo, 14, 60, 64 n.5
Perollo, Giacomo, 75
Peru, silver from, 45, 55
Pescara, family of, 56 n.3
Pescara, marquis of, 93, 102, 130 n.1, 145, 171, 173 n.4; career, 182; reform of tribunals, 86; visits prisons, 121; relations with Inquisition, 164
Pescara, marchesa di, 97
Peter III of Aragon, 52, 149, 203
Peter IV of Aragon, 20
Philip III of Spain, 19, 28, 33, 67, 138, 169, 177 n.1
Philip IV of Spain, 19, 23, 33, 34, 35
Philip V of Spain, 25
Piazza, 88
Pirates, *see* Corsairs
Pius V, 130, 131

INDEX

Pius IX, 149
Plagues, 131, 133, 139, 206
Ponce de Valencia, 18
Ponte, Juan Francisco de, 63 n.1
Population, 74, 78, 79, 125, 140
Portugal, 24, 44; Spanish invasion of, 55, 70
Prado, *fiscal*, 29
Prices, 113, 140-42
Priuli, Lorenzo, 69, 70
Privy Council of England, 63, 104
Procida, John of, 52
Promotorio, Antonio, 81 n.4
Protestantism, 44
Provence, 112

Quiroga, Gaspar de, Cardinal, 60, 65, 71, 156 n.9, 166, 168, 177, 183

Racalmutto, count of, 167-69
Ragazzoni, Placido, 37, 39, 73, 129, 130, 131
Ram, regent, 27
Ramondetta, Ramondo, 50 n.1
Rao, Gian Francesco, 94, 169, 188 n.3
Requesens, Luis de, 13, 23, 24, 181
Rhodes, Knights of, *see* Order of St. John
Riots, 88, 89, 175 n.2
Rivarola, Agostino, 81
Rocroi, battle of, 45
Roger, count of Sicily, 52, 145
Rojas, Antonio de, 29
Rojas, Juan de, 165
Rome, 191, 193
Ruiz, de Medina, Dr. Juan, 17
Ruyz, Alfonso, 181

Salamanca, university of, 30, 32
Salazar, Juan de, 31
Salomone, Francesco, 88
Sánchez, Luis, 27
Sanclemente, family of, 88
Sapunara, Rizzo di, 117
Sardinia, 10, 11, 21, 25, 59
Savoyard fleet, 132
Sciacca, 75, 189
Secretaries of the
  king, 14, 15, 61
  Council of Italy, 22, 23, 60, 64-67, 177
  Council of State, 66
  viceroy, 101, 102
Senior, Abraham, 27
Sepúlveda, Juan Ginés, de, 51
Sessa, duke of, 177 n.4, 182 n.1, 185

Seville, 32, 45
Sicilian estates, *see* Parliament
Sicilian fleet, 55, 124, 128-30, 189
Sicilians, character of, 87, 120-23, 174-75
Silk trade, 50, 79, 81, 126
Sinam Pasha, 194
Sixtus IV, 17
Society of Jesus, 45, 164, 165
Soto, Juan de, 177
Spanish fleet, 54, 112, 129, 181, 195; the Armada, 55, 113, 132
Spanish trade with Indies, 44, 140
Spanish troops, *see* Tercio
Stizzia, Nicola, 147
Suárez, Francisco, 204 n.4
Suleiman the Magnificent, 53
Suprema, *see* Council of Inquisition

Taboada, *consultore*, 101, 186, 187 n.3
Taxation, 124-43 *passim*, 160, 204; gabelles of Messina, 107, 154-56
Tello, Dr., 29
Tercio in Sicily, 55, 124, 128, 133 n.4, 173 n.4, 185, 195
Terranova, duke of, 38, 54, 88, 93, 101, 102, 103, 129, 130, 134-40, 155, 158 n.2, 159, 177, 178 n.2, 185 n.1, 186, 194, 202; career, 182-84; estates of, 75; pro-noble policy, 111, 115, 135, 137-38; relations with Inquisition, 165
Terranova, marquis of, 163
Toledo, García de, 15n, 39, 60, 86, 101, 108, 129, 151, 155, 176, 177; career, 180-81; defence of Malta, 44, 53, 180-81; action against bandits, 116-17; relations with Inquisition, 164
Toledo, Pedro Diaz de, 27
Toledo y Zúñiga, Pedro de, 28
Torquemada, Tomás de, 17, 18, 27, 45, 161
Tournaments, 89
Towns, 82, 105-10, 144; rights of jurisdiction, 109, 138; rivalries, 74, 154; *braccio demaniale*, 151-58 *passim*
Trapani, 82, 88, 107, 175 n.2
Trent, Council of, 145
'Trial, The', 61 n.2
Trimarchi, Ramondo, 108
Tripoli, expedition to, 125
Tunis, 54, 55, 128
Turkish fleet, 53, 125, 155, 195

Urban II, 145, 146
Utrecht, Treaty of, 58

INDEX

Val de Demone, 81
Valdés, Alfonso de, 14
Val di Noto, 106
Valencia, 11, 20, 21, 26, 28, 59
Valetta, 189
Valladolid, Alfonso de, 27
Valladolid, university of, 30, 32
Vargas, Diego de, 60, 64 n.5, 65, 66
Vargas, Leonardo, 29
Vázquez de Arce, Rodrigo, 28
Vázquez de Lecca, Mateo, 13, 14, 48, 50 n.3, 64, 67, 102, 185
Vega, House of, 148
Vega, Juan de, 39, 62 n.1, 80, 86, 95, 96, 99, 102, 113, 114, 120, 121, 122 n.5 126 n.1, 129, 134-36, 164, 176, 187; career, 178-79; relations with Inquisition, 165; views on duties of viceroy, 174-75
Velázquez, Pedro, 48 n.3, 100, 101, 116, 159, 172 n.2, 182, 183
Velázquez de Cuellar, Sancho, 18
Venice, 54, 106, 131, 143; merchants, 82; Spanish relations with, 63, 69; Turkish attack on, 130
Ventimiglia, family of, 76, 160
Vespers, the Sicilian, 53, 183, 193, 207; wars of, 43, 52, 83
Viceroy, office of, 38, 84, 87, 95-104, 144, 170, 171-78 *passim*, 195
Villalón, Cristóbal de, 47
Villeinage, 76
Villena, marquis, of, 97, 98, 160
Voltaire, 123 n.4

Ximénez de Cisneros, Francisco, Cardinal, 18, 24
Ximénez, de Urrea, Lope, 96

Zafra, Fernando de, 27
Zapala, Luis, 24
Zárate, Juan López de, 23, 67
Zayas, Gabriel de, 22, 66, 67
Zúñiga, Baltasar de, 28
Zúñiga, Juan de, 130
Zurbano, Martin de, 18
Zurita, Gerónimo, de, 14